American literature and Irish culture, 1910–55

Manchester University Press

American literature and Irish culture, 1910–55

The politics of enchantment

Tara Stubbs

Manchester University Press

Copyright © Tara Stubbs 2013

The right of Tara Stubbs to be identified as the author of this work has been asserted by her in accordance with the Copyright, Designs and Patents Act 1988.

Published by Manchester University Press
Altrincham Street, Manchester M1 7JA
www.manchesteruniversitypress.co.uk

British Library Cataloguing-in-Publication Data
A catalogue record for this book is available from the British Library

ISBN 978 1 5261 1676 5 paperback

This edition first published 2017

The publisher has no responsibility for the persistence or accuracy of URLs for any external or third-party internet websites referred to in this book, and does not guarantee that any content on such websites is, or will remain, accurate or appropriate.

Typeset
by 4word Ltd, Bristol
Printed in Great Britain
by TJ International Ltd, Padstow

Contents

Preface	*The politics of enchantment*	*page* vii
Acknowledgements		xvii
Introduction	'Why do we like being Irish?'	1
1	Cultural and racial (dis)affiliations	17
2	American modernists and the Celtic Revival	64
3	Rural Ireland, mythmaking and transatlantic translation	102
4	Enchantment and disenchantment in political poetry	135
5	The legacy of Yeats's poetic conviction	164
Conclusion	Cultural credibility in America's Ireland – and Ireland's America	211
Select bibliography		218
Index		231

Preface
The politics of enchantment

Marianne Moore had been Editor of the New York-based periodical *The Dial* for over two years when, in a 'Comment' of March 1928, she discussed the visit to the city of the Irish spiritualist, critic and poet Æ (George Russell). Æ had come to the USA to raise money for his journal *The Irish Statesman*, and Moore had attended the first of his public lectures. She describes his visit in detail:

> Æ is here, and having held out a welcome to him for many years, it is not likely that, as the newspapers suggest, we shall confuse his identity with that of George W. Erskine Russell, or Bertrand Russell, or of another. At first not quite hearing him since our fellow-townsmen are, under excitement, spectators rather than audience, but entirely believing him, we can accept his implication that poetry is invariably at the core of reanimation in Ireland.[1]

Although Moore's public voice is broadly accepting of Æ's fame and authority, underlying reservations emerge from her implicit criticism of the 'excitement' of the 'spectators' and her overemphatic admission of 'entirely believing him', which hints at her own private misgivings. Moore, as a staunch Presbyterian, mistrusted the secular spiritualism that Æ espoused, having described it as 'cheap brainless fakirism [sic]' in a letter to her brother John Warner Moore in 1915.[2] Yet despite her reservations, Moore acquiesces to Æ's contention concerning the reanimating powers of poetry in Ireland.

Later in the same 'Comment', Moore discloses her particular susceptibility to Irish writing – a susceptibility shared by readers of the magazine, as her editorial 'we' implies. As she puts it: 'Susceptible to Irish magic in its various strengths, we cannot say we are not enchanted with disenchantment in *The Plough and the Stars*; that we are indifferent to certain of James Joyce's lyrics "carved from the air and coloured with the air" as Mr Russell denotes them; or to George Moore's "novel", *Hail and Farewell* (p. 270). Moore's use of double, or even triple, negatives suggests that she is attracted to the kind of 'Irish magic' Æ describes, despite her concerns about what such 'magic' might connote. Meanwhile the assumption of a shared susceptibility to such 'magic', though an editorial commonplace, underlines Moore's expectation that the readers of *The Dial*, who are unlikely to confuse the identity of Æ with other famous Russells, will also be aware of recent developments in Irish literature. Indeed, Gilbert Seldes had reviewed *The Plough and the Stars* for *The Dial* in the previous month's issue, in an edition that also included the Irish critic John Eglinton's review of the Irish-born poet Pádraic Colum's *New Poems*, which had opened with a similarly enchanted description of an Irish literary Parnassus: 'Commend me to Mr Colum among the Irish poets!'[3]

Moore's responses to Ireland and its culture – as an editor, critic and poet – seem suffused with the lexicon of enchantment. Most famously, in her 1941 poem 'Spenser's Ireland', Moore urges Ireland to overcome its troubles by 'reinstating / the enchantment' of its literature and traditions.[4] In private, her reading notebooks reveal a susceptibility to 'Irish magic' that echoes her 'Comment' in *The Dial*, as she notes that on page 50 of Harry Levin's *James Joyce: A Critical Introduction*, he writes 'This is the state of mind that confers upon language a magical potency'.[5] Publically she expresses a similar sentiment in a 1919 review of Robert Lynd's *Old and New Masters in Literature* for the *New York Times Books Review*, where she describes the effects of 'Yeats's magic' upon the author.[6]

This association between Irish literature and 'magic' reveals Moore's enchantment with Ireland's writing and its writers, inspired by the kind of self-belief that Æ embodies through 'his implication', as Moore puts it, 'that poetry is invariably at the core of reanimation in Ireland'.[7] The potency of Æ's conviction is undeniable even to those, like Moore, who are sceptical of his spiritual practices; indeed, we only have to look to the pages of 'Spenser's Ireland' to see how Moore rehearses Æ's exhortations about the reanimating power of Irish writing in her poetry. Beyond this, moreover, is the implication that Irish poetry can provide some sort of cure for what Moore terms later in the same 'Comment' the 'restiveness' of American cultural life:

> The Venerable Bede finds that 'when some persons have been bitten by serpents, the scrapings of leaves of books that were brought out of Ireland, being put into the water, and given them to drink, have immediately expelled the spreading poison, and assuaged the swelling'. And we are grateful that there should have been administered to our restiveness, the poems and thoughts which Mr Russell has brought us.[8]

Just as poetry can encourage 'reanimation' in Ireland through its power to enchant – emphasised further by Bede's tales of the magical powers of Ireland's literature – so too, Moore implies, might it do the same in America.

But as her underlying misgivings concerning the rabble-rousing power of Æ's oratory suggest, Moore's enchantment with Irish writing is not something she is willing to accept without question. Other American writers during this period were similarly questioning of their enchantment with Irish culture. F. Scott Fitzgerald, for example, came to resent the lure that his maternal Irish background held for him – and to attempt to shake off the Celtic and Catholic overtones of his first novel, *This Side of Paradise* (1920); while John Steinbeck, who lovingly recreated his Northern Irish grandfather in his 1952 novel *East of Eden*, feared visiting Ireland in case it failed to live up to the promise of the stories told to him in his youth. Other writers came to Ireland late in life in search of solace; Wallace Stevens, for example, sought comfort in the spiritual, natural Ireland that was presented to him in letters from his zealous Irish correspondent Thomas McGreevy, despite the fact that he realised that his view of Ireland was probably an illusion. Some became enchanted with Ireland through reading writings by Irish writers, or books on Ireland itself: Moore assembled 'Spenser's Ireland' from fragments of materials by writers as diverse as Edmund Spenser, Donn Byrne, Maria Edgeworth and Pádraic Colum; Babette Deutsch became an avid reader and critic of Irish poetry; and Wallace Stevens subscribed to Elizabeth Yeats's Cuala Press. Some saw in Ireland's political fervour resonances with their own political ideologies. Moore celebrated the Easter Rising of 1916 in her poem 'Sojourn in the Whale' (1917), establishing parallels with her own experience as a young woman poet trying to succeed in New York; and the socialist poet Lola Ridge proclaimed her desire to join the insurgents on Sackville Street in her response to the Rising, 'Tidings (Easter, 1916)'.

The excitement of an Ireland that was going through political, cultural and national turbulence and upheaval, a desire for new mythologies, and a growing anglophobia within American culture created a turn towards Ireland within American modernist literature: one that has received little critical scrutiny beyond ethnic or racial frameworks. Thus this study takes as its impetus the moment(s) at which American modernist writers chose actively to engage with Ireland thanks to an attraction towards its culture, its landscape or its politics. Eamonn Wall has noted how, as 'Irish culture has become so widely disseminated and influential in the US, and travel has become so easy', contemporary American poets have begun to 'bypass Irish America and come straight to Ireland';[9] but we can trace this tendency back to the modernist period. By describing and contextualising these moments of engagement with Ireland, we are able to scrutinise each writer's attitudes towards this engagement, and the problems or questions that their engagement raises.

All of the writers covered by this study – Moore, Stevens, Fitzgerald, Ridge, Steinbeck and Deutsch among them – were enchanted by aspects of the Irish experience, be they political, cultural or spiritual. Some became enchanted early in their career, and later came to question or abandon this attachment; some grew enchanted with Ireland late in life; and some were suspicious of the authenticity of their enchantment with Ireland. Others, meanwhile, maintained an attraction to Ireland, which was stimulated and sustained by political or literary affiliations. By highlighting instances of American modernist writers' engagement with Irish culture, I aim neither to be exhaustive nor inclusive, but instead to sound the Irish note in American modernist writing. And by scrutinising the politics of enchantment within these writers' turns towards Ireland, I am able to unravel some of the complex issues of credulity and authenticity that preoccupy writers and critics of these two countries whenever the subject of transatlantic interaction is raised.

★

The past twenty-five years have seen a growth in critical volumes concerning Irish American writing, preoccupied largely with questions of ethnicity and immigrant identity. In his seminal study *The Irish*

Voice in America (1990), for example, Charles Fanning focuses his critical interest on 'American writers of Irish birth or background' who 'have been exploring what it means to be an immigrant or ethnic in America'.[10] Fanning's *Exiles of Erin* (1987) and his more recent edited collection *New Perspectives on the Irish Diaspora* (2000) have celebrated a marginalised immigrant voice that has received insufficient critical attention in Ireland in particular. This latter concern is at the forefront, too, of Daniel Tobin's recent collection *Awake in America: On Irish American Poetry* (2011), which 'aims to affirm a creative and critical awareness of the presence and extent of Irish American poetry within the American literary tradition and also within the tradition of Irish poetry, more broadly considered and conceived'.[11] To this list ought also to be added Ron Ebest's study *Private Histories: The Writing of Irish Americans, 1900–1935* (2005), which might serve as a counterpoint to Fanning's assertion that there was a 'hiatus' in Irish-American literary activity between the turn of the century and the early 1930s.[12]

In *The Irish Voice in America*, Fanning states his decision to exclude from his study two types of writers: those 'of Irish background who have chosen *not* to consider Irish ethnic themes', and 'American writers not themselves of Irish background' who nevertheless create 'the history and images of the Irish'.[13] Tobin, meanwhile, prescribes an Irish American identity to poets, like Wallace Stevens and the contemporary American poet Ben Howard, who have no family connection with Ireland, in order to support his critical paradigm, which focuses on 'the double life of Irish and Irish American inheritance'.[14] What the present study aims towards, in comparison, is an extension of the study of Irish cultural influence within American writing beyond ethnic lines – using as its timeframe (1910–55) a period when Irish cultural and political events coincided with the search of American modernists for new experiences and inspirations. Thus my approach has more in common with that of Paul Giles in his 1990 study *American Catholic Arts and Fictions*, where Giles identifies Roman Catholicism as 'a residual cultural determinant and one aspect of the social context within which various American artists of this century have been working'. On the pressure to map the influence of Catholicism onto trends within Irish or Italian immigration to the USA, Giles notes: 'Anyone can recite immigration statistics, but to apprehend those silent areas where religion flies free of rigid conceptual pigeonholes and begins exerting pressure in a more intangible fashion seems a more interesting and valuable task'.[15]

If we see Irish culture within American modernist literature as, to use Giles's wording, a 'residual cultural determinant', and if we analyse this cultural presence in a way that exceeds the constraints of genealogical ('Irish') or hybridised ('Irish-American') readings, we might also embark on a task that is itself 'interesting and valuable'. This might then allow us to think about American literature more generally in terms of the processes by which American writers gather their cultural influences. This aligns my investigations with Wai Chee Dimock's recent work, which extends the study of American writing beyond geographical, spatial and historical limitations. In *Through Other Continents: American Literature Across Deep Time* (2006), Dimock contends that 'Rather than being a discrete entity', American literature should be seen as 'a crisscrossing set of pathways, open-ended and ever multiplying, weaving in and out of other geographies, other languages, and cultures'. These pathways, Dimock adds, 'are input channels, kinship networks, routes of transit, and forms of attachment – connective tissues binding America to the rest of the world', which thread 'the long durations of those cultures into the short chronology of the United States'.[16] For Dimock, then, a genealogical inheritance – one formed by 'kinship networks' – is just one of the pathways by which American literature receives and channels its influences: just as important are the influences we absorb through travel, through reading, or through the personal (and sometimes idiosyncratic) attachments we form to other cultures. The Irish-American poet and critic John Montague discussed this issue in relation to his hybrid identity in a 1977 interview, where he described the 'ideal method for poetry' as 'on the one hand continually to dig deeper in your own garden patch, in whatever garden patches you have been given or you have claimed, and on the other hand, to try to discover anything across the world which can become accessible to you'.[17] This metaphor of 'digging deeper' suits, curiously, Dimock's notion of 'deep time' as revealing layers of influences that extend far beyond the short chronology of America's history.

For critics of American literature, then, the challenge is to unearth the substrata of influences that lie beneath the superficial facts of genealogy or ethnicity: to use Giles's phrase, what might be a 'useful and valuable' exercise might be identifying those instances of cultural cross-pollination that don't quite add up. In the case of this study, this might mean scrutinising American writers of Irish background who are only interested in certain aspects of their inheritance – or who might have an ambiguous, or even problematic, relationship with this inheritance; or it might mean analysing why, and how, American writers with no family connections to Ireland use (and misuse) images of Ireland within their work. By focusing on these variant strains of cross-pollination we can in turn gain a wider sense of the influence of Irish culture on American literature, allowing Irish culture to function as an influence in its own right, flying free of 'rigid conceptual pigeonholes', as Giles puts it.

But this, also, is where the politics of enchantment come into consideration – that moment at which upon engaging with what Tobin terms 'the powerful attraction to Ireland as a nexus of identity', writers risk coming under the spell of idealisation, or romance, or illusion. Again we hear echoes of Moore's guarded acquiescence to the kind of 'Irish magic' that Æ promotes. Tobin, a poet himself, claims that 'The authentic urge must find an authentic voice'. A secondary aim of this study, then, is to analyse instances of cultural attraction to Ireland within the work of American modernists alongside a consideration of the authenticity of this attraction, in order to determine whether an inauthentic urge really can inhibit the search for an authentic voice. Discussing the notion of poetic influence within Irish-American poetry, Tobin claims that negotiating one's Irish influences 'requires more of the poet than a simple return to a homeland whose very idea has been founded – in part at least – on a self-generating industry of idealizations and simulacra; it requires also an effort at authenticity'.[18] But what hope do American writers have if their stimulus in Ireland is itself no more than smoke and mirrors? And is it not the case that once one makes an effort to achieve authenticity, anything approaching authenticity is inevitably lost?

This study offers an alternative route. In a 1995 essay on Seamus Heaney, Michael Allen discusses Heaney's claim, made in 1987, that his experience of America as another location for his poetry enabled him to achieve 'a certain distance from [his] first self'.[19] In the same way, American writers have been able to look to Ireland as a way of creating distance between their 'first selves' and the other selves that they project onto Ireland; and like Heaney, the writers covered in this study know that this opening up of the self is a poetic process – and therefore possibly an inauthentic one. But what modernism allowed writers – or in fact made apparent to them in sometimes painful ways – was the acceptance of the inauthentic nature of the poetic process itself: an acknowledgement of poetry as what Marianne Moore calls 'fiddle';[20] or of the painful process of writing by which the 'state of personal existence' afforded by artistic sincerity 'is not to be attained without the most arduous effort', as Lionel Trilling argues in his lectures on *Sincerity and Authenticity*;[21] or of the 'technical excellence' that T. S. Eliot deems as essential to generate the ideal of aesthetic 'impersonality' within the poetic work.[22] Thus it is interesting and valuable to scrutinise the ways in which American modernists, aware of the inauthentic nature of artistic selection and creation, channelled their enchantment (and disenchantment) with Irish culture into their own work. And by taking examples from a range of writers, and a range of texts, we can begin to see whether Tobin's thesis really rings true: does the authentic urge need to find an authentic voice, or can an authentic voice be discovered through an 'inauthentic' process of cultural assimilation – by digging others' garden patches, to borrow Montague's metaphor? In her poem 'Poetry', Moore memorably describes poems as 'imaginary gardens with real toads in them'. It is up to us to decide if these 'toads' are princes or frogs.[23]

Notes

1 Marianne Moore, 'Comment', *The Dial* 84.3 (March 1928), 269–70 (270).
2 Moore to John Warner Moore, 10 October 1915, in *The Selected Letters of Marianne Moore*, ed. Bonnie Costello, Celeste Goodridge and Cristanne Miller. London: Faber, 1998, pp. 101–3 (101).
3 John Eglinton (W. K. Magee), 'New Poems by Padraic [sic] Colum', *The Dial* 84.2 (February 1928), 124–6 (124).
4 Moore, 'Spenser's Ireland' (1941), in *Complete Poems*, ed. Clive Driver. London: Faber, 1984, pp. 112–14, ll. 19–20.
5 Marianne Moore Archive, Rosenbach Museum and Library, Philadelphia, USA ['RML'] VII:02:03, Reading notebook 1250/7 AMS: 1938-1942, page headed 'November'.

6 Moore, 'Old and new masters in literature', review of a new book by Robert Lynd, *New York Times Book Review*, 12 October 1919, p. 536, reprinted in *Complete Prose*, ed. Patricia Willis. London: Faber, 1987, pp. 41–3 (42).
7 Moore, 'Comment', *The Dial*, 84.3 (March 1928), 270.
8 Ibid., p. 270. Moore quotes from the well-known opening of Bede's 'Geographical Prologue' to *The Ecclesiastical History of the English People* (c. 730), where he compares the geographical qualities of Britain and Ireland.
9 Eamonn Wall, *From the Sin-é Café to the Black Hills: Notes on the New Irish*. Madison, Wisconsin and London: University of Wisconsin Press, 1999, p. 57.
10 Charles Fanning, *The Irish Voice in America: Irish-American Fiction from the 1760s to the 1980s*. Lexington, Kentucky: University Press of Kentucky, 1990. p. 1.
11 Daniel Tobin, *Awake in America: On Irish American Poetry*. Notre Dame, Indiana: University of Notre Dame Press, 2011, p. ix.
12 Fanning, *The Irish Voice in America*, p. 3. Chapter 7 of the book, entitled 'A Generation Lost', outlines Fanning's reasons for identifying 'this new literary generation's wholesale movement away from considerations of Irishness' (p. 238). Ebest's study necessarily counters this assertion.
13 Fanning, *The Irish Voice in America*, p. 4.
14 Tobin, *Awake in America*, p. 216.
15 Paul Giles, *American Catholic Arts and Fictions: Culture, Ideology, Aesthetics*. Cambridge: Cambridge University Press, 1992, pp. 1, 26.
16 Wai Chee Dimock, *Through Other Continents: American Literature Across Deep Time*. Princeton and Oxford: Princeton University Press, 2006, p. 3.
17 'Global regionalism: interview with John Montague', *Literary Review*, 22.2 (Winter 1979), 153–74 (156); interview recorded in 1977.
18 Tobin, *Awake in America*, pp. 331, 332, 340.
19 Michael Allen, 'The parish and the dream: Heaney and America, 1969–1987', *The Southern Review*, 31.3 (Summer 1995), 726–38.
20 See Moore, 'Poetry', longer version, *Complete Poems*, pp. 266–7, l. 1.
21 See Lionel Trilling, *Sincerity and Authenticity*. London: Oxford University Press, 1972, p. 6.
22 See T. S. Eliot, 'Tradition and the Individual Talent' (1919), *The Sacred Wood: Essays on Poetry and Criticism*. London: Faber, 1997, pp. 42–53 (49).
23 See Moore, 'Poetry' (longer version), l. 24.

Acknowledgements

This book would not have been completed without the support of family and friends, and particularly the following people: Alex Knights, Will May and Andrew Blades. I want also to thank my friends and colleagues at Oxford, and especially Abigail Williams and Francis Leneghan, for their advice and ideas. I have had many helpful discussions along the way with colleagues at Trinity College Dublin and University College Cork – most notably, Philip Coleman and Lee Jenkins – and with my excellent DPhil student Frank Hutton-Williams. Other colleagues working in American and Irish studies have been instrumental in helping me to formulate and discuss my thoughts: so additional thanks go to Nick Selby, Fiona Green, Bernard O'Donoghue, Susan Schreibman and Rebecca Beasley. Working for John Kelly on the Yeats letters was also crucial to this project.

Thanks to Mum, who inspired in me a love of Irish literature and a fascination with its politics; to Dad, for (necessarily) tempering that passion; and to Tristan, for facilitating many of those debates, and guiding me through the particularities of American history. My gratitude also extends to the staff of the following research libraries, for their efficiency and professionalism: the Rosenbach Museum and Library, Philadelphia; the New York Public Library; the Beinecke Rare Book and Manuscript Library, Yale; the Huntington Library, San Marino, CA; the library of Washington University in St. Louis; and the library of Trinity College Dublin. Several of these trips would not have been possible without the help of the English Faculty, University of Oxford, and more recently the Department for Continuing Education, University of Oxford; while a Visiting Fellowship at the Long Room Hub at Trinity College Dublin was central to the research for this project. Thanks, also, to Kim Walker and Matthew Frost of Manchester University Press for bringing the book to its quietus.

Quotations from Louis MacNeice's *Autumn Journal* are reproduced here with the permission of David Higham. W. B. Yeats's 'On Being Asked for a War Poem' is reprinted in full with the permission of A.P. Watt. Lines from Wallace Stevens's 'Our Stars Come from Ireland', 'The Irish Cliffs of Moher', 'Of Modern Poetry' and 'The American Sublime' are reproduced with the permission of Faber and Faber; and lines from Marianne Moore's 'Spenser's Ireland', 'Sojourn in the Whale', 'To a Prize Bird' and 'To William Butler Yeats on Tagore' are reproduced with the permission of Faber and Faber. Unpublished materials from Marianne Moore are reprinted here with the permission of the Moore Estate. Unpublished materials from Thomas McGreevy are reprinted here with the permission of the McGreevy Estate. Unpublished letters from McGreevy to Babette Deutsch are cited with the permission of Washington University Library, St. Louis, Missouri.

This book is dedicated to Alex Knights, with thanks for 12 years of love, support and friendship.

Introduction
'Why do we like being Irish?'

> Why do we like being Irish? Partly because
>   It gives us a hold on the sentimental English
> As members of a world that never was,
>   Baptised with fairy water;
> And partly because Ireland is small enough
>   To be still thought of with a family feeling,
> And because the waves are rough
>   That split her from a more commercial culture;
> And because one feels that here at least one can
>   Do local work which is not at the world's mercy
> And on this tiny stage with luck a man
>   Might see the end of one particular action.
> It is self-deception of course;
>   There is no immunity on this island either[1]

Louis MacNeice's epic poem *Autumn Journal*, composed between August and December 1938, was written in reaction to the turbulent events in Europe and to Ireland's growing isolationism as a nation. In this section of the poem, MacNeice's intended audience appears to be Irish: his sardonic attack is aimed at the Irish – and, one assumes, at its government, led by Éamon de Valera, in particular – who deceive themselves into thinking that Ireland's culture and traditions can protect it from the political turbulence of the outside world. MacNeice's summative comment on Ireland's 'self-deception' points beyond those Irish who are complicit in the packaging of Irish culture as an historical, even mythological, artefact, to those outside Ireland who choose to collude in the myth of Ireland's separation from the rest of the world. In *An Age of Innocence* (1998), Brian Fallon questions the one-sidedness of such negative views of Ireland during this period; however, he still notes that: 'The newborn Ireland was grappling, sometimes hesitantly, and sometimes ineptly, with its role or place in the modern world'.[2] Yet Irish culture – as an export – had arguably never been more popular.

The cultural consequences of the Celtic Revival, instigated by W. B. Yeats, Lady Gregory, J. M. Synge and Douglas Hyde around the turn of the twentieth century, coupled with the growth of Irish nationalism and the establishment of Home Rule in the Irish Free State in 1922, had led to a surge of interest in Ireland throughout Europe and America. American writers and thinkers had been particularly inspired by Ireland's self-determination, which recalled the parallel struggles for independence of the two nations; as Fiona Green puts it: 'In the early twentieth century, as in the eighteenth, the Irish nationalist cause was compatible with the American revolutionary spirit'.[3] But MacNeice's warnings, which might also be extended to those Americans who derived inspiration from Ireland during this period, note the political consequences of Irish nationalism while addressing the cultural ramifications of Ireland's self-determination, as 'Irishness' risks becoming a commodity.

The reasons that MacNeice puts forward for why 'we like being Irish' might be extended to the American modernist writers discussed in this book, as each turned towards Irish culture at various stages during their careers. During the first half of the twentieth century, and into the second, American culture was suffering from a crisis of faith. In his essay 'The literary life', published in Howard E. Stearn's *Civilisation in the United States* in 1922, the contentious but influential critic Van Wyck Brooks denounced 'the singular impotence' of the 'creative spirit' of American writing, and expressed his concern for 'the chronic state of our literature'.[4] Likewise, two of the writers discussed in this book, John Steinbeck and Marianne Moore, questioned the dissatisfaction that they identified at the core of American culture. As mentioned in the Preface, in an editorial 'Comment' in *The Dial* in March 1928, Moore described the 'restiveness' of the American spirit as akin to a disease that had to be cured;[5] similarly, in an essay, 'Paradox and dream', in his *America and Americans* collection (1966), Steinbeck noted that 'we are a restless, a dissatisfied, a searching people'.[6]

Meanwhile, American writers had begun to question the usefulness of English culture to their own work. Paul Giles elaborates on this issue, arguing that one of the 'most common impulses' of American modernism 'involved rejecting the legacy of English culture as an inappropriate model for the representation of a brazenly new American world'.[7] T. S. Eliot displayed a dismissive attitude towards English literature in his essay 'The three provincialities', its subject the interrelation between English, American and Irish literatures. In one famous passage Eliot claimed that there had been a 'complete collapse of literary effort in England'.[8] As late as 1949, Wallace Stevens was still disparaging British culture: 'A good many of us are at the moment very much bored with Ireland's neighbor. ... The truth is that the British flatter themselves at the expense of the world, always have and always will'.[9] In *Yeats and American Poetry* Terence Diggory notes a similar trend, where he argues that 'Once the Americans had determined not to make use of English tradition, they found themselves without any tradition, because America had no past of its own'. Although the latter clause can clearly be confuted, what Diggory's arguments make clear is that American writers actively sought a tradition to 'make use' of – and one that allowed them, as Diggory puts it, to declare 'aesthetic independence' from England.[10]

Ireland, on the other hand, could provide a new and exciting locus of inspiration at exactly the time when American and British cultures were falling out of favour. Of the three literatures discussed by Eliot in 'The three provincialities' (American, British and Irish), he presents Irish literature as the most self-assured. Although Eliot is dismissive of the nationalising tendencies of Irish writers, he does credit them with a sense of purpose at a time when other literatures appear to be falling apart. Referring to authors like James Stephens, who advocated a return to the Irish language in their writing, Eliot comments that 'The Irish radicals are commendable in so far as they mark a necessity for a choice' between the traditions of a universal language and the traditions of a nation or race.[11] Although Eliot views this 'choice' as ultimately self-destructive, since universality should be the only aim of literature, he cannot help but admire the Irish writers' self-belief.

★

Returning to MacNeice's lines from *Autumn Journal*, we are given possible reasons for why one might 'like being Irish' that are pertinent to the example of American modernist writers – and which in turn help inform the critical framework of this study. MacNeice theorises that the 'small' size of Ireland can evoke 'a family feeling' (l.66), thus extending a consideration of inheritance beyond genealogical lines and towards the significance of familiarity in shaping one's self-identity. Harold Bloom argues in *The Anxiety of Influence* that 'American poets labor' to '"complete" their fathers',[12] while in *Haunted English* Laura O'Connor discusses 'The role occupied by family as an intermediary zone' between the 'individual and inherited discourses of race'.[13] In each case, the 'family' and the 'fathers' are mediators who function literally and metaphorically: generating an idea of family that is racially and culturally nuanced. This reading of 'a family feeling' is the preoccupation of Chapter 1, which discusses the complexities of affiliation and disaffiliation within the responses to Ireland of American modernists Fitzgerald, Steinbeck, Moore and O'Neill – all of whom had some sort of family connection to that country. For example, F. Scott Fitzgerald and John Steinbeck espoused their maternal Irish backgrounds as a means of giving them a 'discourse', which might mediate between their individual voices and their inherited influences as they were embarking on their literary careers. In Steinbeck's early work *To a God Unknown* (1935) the desire to complete the work of the fictional father saturates every page – but more telling is the starring role of Steinbeck's Irish grandfather in *East of Eden* (1952). Conversely, Fitzgerald's semi-autobiographical novel *This Side of Paradise* (1920) is weighed down by the constant absence of a father, manifested in the protagonist's attempts to replace his father with the religious figure Monsignor Darcy. This father/'Father' contrast reveals a sense of loss and a desire for recovery related to Fitzgerald's Irish Catholic background.

Reading further down the passage from MacNeice, we move from a consideration of family to a description of the natural imagery traditionally associated with Irish culture. The lines 'And because the waves are rough / That split her from a more commercial culture' (67–8) suggest sardonically that Ireland's natural characteristics provide a barrier of cultural self-protection from the outside world. Particularly telling is the association between the natural world and a pure, unsullied 'culture' that has nothing to do with commerciality (although we suspect that MacNeice's concerns for the commodification of Irish culture are pointing that way). This emphasis on nature recalls the arguments of the Celtic Revivalists, which drew on Ernst Renan's 'La poésie des races Celtiques' (1859), and on Matthew Arnold's essays *On the Study of Celtic Literature* (1867), to advocate an intermingling of the natural and the magical within Celtic culture. Consider, for example, Yeats's essay 'On the Celtic element in literature', in which he cites Renan: 'The Celtic race had "a realistic naturalism", "a love of nature for herself, a vivid feeling for her magic"'.[14] The Celtic Revivalists had even set a precedent for actively drawing inspiration from a tradition that was not, strictly speaking, their own: the Anglo-Irish Protestant playwright J. M. Synge had, after all, travelled to the west coast of Ireland to find 'authentic' material for his plays.[15] Even the cynical Ezra Pound admitted to having been 'drunk with "Celticism"' in the early 1900s.[16]

The fact that the Revivalists' idealised Ireland of myth and legend – 'Baptised with fairy water' (l.64) – is, according to MacNeice, 'a world that never was' (l.63), does not necessarily hinder American writers' attraction towards it: indeed its unreality allows them to construct Ireland as their imagination dictates. The modernist period in America coincided with a surge of interest in the Celtic Revival, thanks to the publishing efforts of Elizabeth Yeats's Cuala Press; to the Abbey Theatre tours in the USA in the 1910s; to the dissemination of writings by and on the 'Celtic' in American periodicals; and to the efforts of revivalists such as W. B. Yeats and Æ (George Russell), who made tours of America in the 1920s and 1930s to celebrate what Moore termed, in a 1928 review of the first of Æ's talks in New York, the place of poetry at 'the core of reanimation in Ireland'.[17] Chapter 2 therefore takes as its focus the impact of the Celtic Revival on American modernism, and considers also the mythmaking that was involved in this transmission of 'Celtic' ideals to the USA.

This idea of mythmaking is also extended to Chapter 3, which concentrates on one of the products of the Celtic Revival – a return to the land and an idealisation of rural communities. In the USA, meanwhile, the vogue for travelogues and travel writing, which Nicola J. Watson traces back to the mid-nineteenth century – and to the (largely) American writers who instigated this 'transatlantic sub-genre' – was only increasing. Accompanying this relatively new trend was the tendency for American writers to view idealised landscapes, taken from their reading experiences, as more inspiring than the real thing: as Watson points out, literary locations can be seen as a 'fictive landscape awaiting imaginative (re)possession and (re)discovery'.[18]

Marianne Moore acknowledges the paradox of irony and imaginative potential in this attitude in her 1941 poem 'Spenser's Ireland'. By describing Ireland, a place she has only read about, as 'the greenest place I've never seen',[19] the poet/speaker derives poetic inspiration from her geographical distance from a country that exists mainly in her imagination. Meanwhile in 'I go back to Ireland', his account of a trip to Ireland made in 1952, Steinbeck acknowledges his initial 'powerful reluctance' to see 'the home place', as if he knows it will not live up to his idealised view of his Irish ancestors' home town.[20] Another writer who makes use of the Irish landscape is Wallace Stevens, whose late poems 'Our Stars Come From Ireland' and 'The Irish Cliffs of Moher' rely on a transatlantic translation of the idea of rural Ireland across the Atlantic. What these writers' responses to Ireland's landscape reveal is a process of mythmaking that is generated as much by the stories told by Irish writers as by the deliberate processes of self-enchantment that their American counterparts enact in order to remain attached to the 'green' idyll of the Emerald Isle.

Behind MacNeice's lines, with their emphasis on the 'natural' within Irish culture, lies a more savage reading of Ireland's desire for cultural self-protection. Linked to the potential dangers that MacNeice perceives in the packaging – and commodification – of Celticism is a concern about the growing culture of mistrust that is apparent within Ireland itself. MacNeice's description of Ireland's separation from a 'more commercial culture' (l.68) brings to mind the Irish government's increasingly xenophobic attitude towards external cultural influences, which had developed in the years following the passing of the Censorship of Publications Act in 1929. Donal Ó Drisceoil views the passing of the Act as 'part of a general process of "Catholicization" that became the primary element in the forging of a separate identity';[21] as a Protestant Northern Irish writer, MacNeice would have felt deeply this drive for separation. The Boards appointed between 1930 and 1947, who decided which books could be published in Ireland, consisted of prominent Catholic figures, with one 'hostage Protestant' included as a 'decoy', as banned writer Francis Hackett put it in 1936.[22] Ó Drisceoil notes that 'most of the leading writers of modern fiction from Britain, America, and Continental Europe' were banned, 'leading cynics to dub the *Register of Prohibited Publications* an "Everyman's guide to the modern classics"'. But in fact the Board was crueller still to Irish writers; as Ó Drisceoil puts it, 'the list of banned authors in the 1930s and 1940s reads like a "Who's Who" of Irish literature', and includes Joyce, Beckett, O'Casey, Liam O'Flaherty, Austin Clarke, Frank O'Connor and George Moore.[23]

The concluding lines of the passage from MacNeice, 'It is self-deception of course; / There is no immunity on this island either' (73–4), note the willed 'self-deception' of the Irish in thinking that their culture will somehow provide them with 'immunity' from the harsh reality of an encroaching international situation – the latter line echoing John Donne's famous maxim 'No man is an island' (from *Meditation XVII*). However, whereas MacNeice's Irish seem able to endorse their continued separation from the rest of the world – a fact that would manifest itself in their majority support of de Valera's policy of neutrality during World War Two – American writers with Irish sympathies or interests would not have been able to continue so easily with this apparent 'self-deception'. John F. Callahan questions the tendency of modern American writers to 'seek mythologies of fraudulent innocence':[24] although this is strongly put, we might see how for MacNeice, Irish culture as it stood in 1938–39 might have offered such a mythology. Nevertheless, those Americans who had been attracted previously to the apparent innocence of Irish culture and Celtic mythology would have had to reassess their attitudes once America entered the Second World War in 1941.

Chapter 4, therefore, deals with the knotty issue of politics in relation to individual poets' patterns of enchantment and disenchantment regarding Ireland. Although W. B. Yeats wrote famously in 1915 in 'On Being Asked for a War Poem' that 'I think it better that in times like these / A poet's mouth be silent',[25] following the events of Easter 1916 he felt compelled to respond to political events in Ireland – troubled by a desire simultaneously to condemn the violent direction that nationalism had taken and to inscribe himself into the mythology of events. Facing similar questions concerning public responsibility and also experiencing a desire for poetic self-assertion, Marianne Moore displayed in her two political poems about Ireland – 'Sojourn in the Whale' (1917) and 'Spenser's Ireland' (1941) – a shift from a metaphorical, romanticised celebration of 'Irishness' to a troubled, complex response to the global situation of World War Two and Ireland's continued policy of neutrality. Another New-York based poet, Lola

Ridge, wrote her 1916 poem 'Tidings' in response to the Easter Rising in terms of her own socialist ideologies, imagining herself in Sackville Street, Dublin with the rebels.[26] Each poem displays a nuanced response to the political events in Ireland that tells us as much about the poets' self-identities as Americans (and as women) as about the parlous political situation that their writings aim to record and report.

But even when dealing with political issues, the same American writers remain enchanted by the promise of Ireland: in 'Spenser's Ireland', for example, where Moore's poet/speaker asserts a sense of being 'troubled' by her Irish affiliations, she still seeks solace in the 'enchantment' of Ireland's culture and traditions.[27] In his oft-quoted Preface to *The Playboy of the Western World* (1907), J. M. Synge famously asserted his confidence in the cultural promise of Ireland, connecting it to the inspirational nature of 'local life': 'In Ireland, for a few years more, we have a popular imagination that is fiery and magnificent, and tender; so that those of us who wish to write start with a chance that is not given to writers in places where the springtime of the local life has been forgotten, and the harvest is a memory only, and the straw has been turned into bricks.'[28] The more cynical Irish critic John Eglinton noted in one of his regular 'Dublin letters' for *The Dial* in 1923 that 'our [Irish] authors are fond of making the special claim for Ireland, that almost alone of European nationalities it has remained affiliated to antiquity'.[29] Yet in an earlier letter he had expressed a grudging pride in Irish literature, for its 'proud consciousness of belonging to a secret order, with incommunicable beliefs and traditions'. Moreover, as if in answer to the opening statement of his 'letter' – 'I sometimes think that it is very nice of American readers to be interested in Irish literature' – he had noted that as Irish authors were for the most part 'true and disinterested interpreters of Irish nationality', 'what would the poets and artists of other lands not give to belong to a country in which literature and art are the instrument of national expression?'[30] The importance placed on literature and art within Ireland still holds considerable currency, as acknowledged by the American poet and critic Ben Howard in an essay of 1986. Howard noted that despite having 'no Irish heritage', he still felt 'drawn' to Irish poetry, persuaded as he was by the 'natural eloquence of Irish writers', their 'gift of fluency', and 'the historical capaciousness of Irish poetry, its power to contain and transform its melancholy past'.[31] Who wouldn't want to 'draw' on a culture that promised so much?

During the modernist period, much of this poetic promise was contained within the figure of W. B. Yeats – the subject of Chapter 5. As a main instigator of the Celtic Revival, as a visitor to the USA with the Abbey and on solo trips as a lecturer,[32] and as a poet who saw American sales of his poetry increase from the early 1910s onwards, Yeats provides a cultural epicentre for many of the writers with whom this study is concerned. In a 1934 review of Yeats's *Collected Poems* for *The New Yorker*, the poet and critic Louise Bogan made great claims for Yeats's writings, noting that 'His native gifts – the extraordinary ear underlining his technical brilliance, his heritage of blood in which run wit, bitter intelligence, and a fund of beautiful common speech – always stood him in good stead'.[33] Bogan's view of Yeats as a writer whose 'gifts' are derived from his 'native' identity and 'his heritage of blood' finds parallels with the opinions of the Jewish-American writer Babette Deutsch, an avid reader and critic of Yeats, who claimed in a letter to the Irish poet and critic Thomas McGreevy that Yeats's 'wisdom' was learned from his father, 'that grand old man, John Butler Yeats'.[34] But Bogan's comments also tap into a persuasive view of Yeats within American literary circles as the 'ageing' poet of brilliance – the one to beat. Thus the last chapter – to borrow Philip Coleman's phrase concerning John Berryman's relationship with Yeats[35] – deals with 'the politics of praise' surrounding the nuanced ways in which American modernists responded to Yeats within their criticism and poetry, considering also his lasting legacy as a continued source of influence in American culture.

As discussed in the Preface, a main aim of the book is to consider why American modernist writers might have become enchanted by Irish culture, or disenchanted at other times, and to describe how they responded to these moments of (dis)enchantment. But beyond this, we need to ask what it is about American literature that allows it to absorb and reshape cultural influence to its own ends, according to the affiliations (and disaffiliations) of individual writers. Other studies have discussed this topic in relation to other sources of influence; Paul Giles, for example, has treated this subject in *Virtual Americas: Transnational Fictions and the Transatlantic Imaginary* (2002). In the introduction he outlines his 'main concern' for his project as 'looking at ways in which American writers from Herman Melville to Thomas Pynchon have compulsively appropriated and reinvented aspects of English culture to advance their own aesthetic designs'.[36] Why this 'cultural appropriation' and reinvention? What is it in American culture that allows American writers to carry out such acts of imitation – or plunder – for the pursuit of personal literary aims?

We might contend that American writers are more open to the idea of transnational cultural appropriation, because the relative lack of history in America, when coupled with the complex ethnic and cultural make-up of the country itself, renders traditional notions of nationhood both irrelevant and inaccurate. In its earliest use, 'nation' is defined by the *Oxford English Dictionary* as 'A large aggregate of communities and individuals united by factors such as common descent, language, culture, history, or occupation of the same territory, so as to form a distinct people'; from its very outset, then, America could not have claimed to have many of these common 'factors'. In *American Crucible*, Gary Gerstle makes a deconstructionist claim for the idea of a nation, with the American nation particularly in mind: 'That nations are invented and variable underscores how much they are socio-political creations and, as such, historically contingent. Their origins may be purposive or accidental. They can gain or lose strength, expand their territory or lose it, fortify their myths of origins and belonging or see them undermined or altered, celebrate aspects of their literary history or repress them'.[37] If a nation is 'invented and variable', a 'socio-political creation' contingent on historical change, then there is no reason why a writer might not borrow ideas from another nation's culture, as no nations are stable, and all are in constant flux. Looking back across the twentieth century, Paul Jay has noted that although 'the old narrative' perpetuated by such critics as F. O. Matthiessen 'has a coherence', this coherence 'is derived from an idealized myth of national origins and identity'. In *American Renaissance: Art and Expression in the Age of Emerson and Whitman* (1941), Matthiessen celebrates the flowering of a national American literature in the mid-nineteenth century. Instead Jay proposes the view, as first propounded by the Mexican philosopher Edmundo O'Gorman in *The Invention of America* (1958), that 'we cannot separate the history of the Americas from the history of modernity':[38] helping to explain, perhaps,

American modernists' open-minded and sometimes iconoclastic views of national literature and cultural influence.

Gerstle's claim that nations can 'celebrate aspects of their literary history or repress them' is particularly useful for this study, which assesses the degrees to which American writers engaged and disengaged with Irish culture at various stages in their literary careers. Again this reading is appropriate to American modernist writers in particular, as we are reminded of the culture of experimentalism encouraged by Pound's dictum to 'make it new': in these writers' often fickle literary experiments with Irish culture we perceive both the modernity of the American experience and its uneasy relationship with history and tradition. Of course, the irony is that for some of these writers, the very qualities that they were seeking in Irish culture – permanence, coherence, continuity – were the same qualities that they were prepared to break with in their understanding of nations and national literatures. However, what I am careful to stress here, additionally, is the idea that some of these 'breakages' found their models in the activities of the Irish writers themselves – through the mythmaking, and cultural constructions, that informed the activities of the proponents of the Celtic Revival.

A counterpoint to Gerstle's and Giles's more deconstructionist approach can be found in Ron Ebest's introduction to his *Private Histories: The Writing of Irish Americans, 1900–1935*, in which he asserts the importance of 'ancestry' to an Irish-American identification, despite the question of 'desire':

> It is also a question of self-identification: to be Irish American, in other words, is to some degree a matter of choice. That does not mean that Irish-American ethnicity is arbitrary or fictional; not anyone, after all, can be Irish; ancestry, no matter how elastic intermarriage may make the definition, remains the crucial element. What it does mean is that to some degree, for those descendants of Irish Protestants of the eighteenth century, or of Irish Catholics of the famine generation, ethnicity is an expression neither of nationality nor of religion nor of class nor of race. It is an expression of desire.[39]

Adding complexity to Ebest's arguments, this book emphasises the importance of 'desire' in American writers' use of Irish cultural models while exploring instances of cultural appropriation and interaction that exceed the boundaries of an Irish-American paradigmatic framework. Whereas Ebest contends that 'to be Irish American' is 'to some degree a matter of choice', we might complicate this statement by adding two further categories of Americans: those whose background leads to a desire for identification or affiliation with Ireland, and those who simply express an interest in Ireland at certain times, and for certain reasons. For neither of these categories would the label 'Irish American' be accurate.

What an avoidance of terms such as 'Irish American' allows is the acknowledgement that for certain American writers, although their connection with Ireland might have provided inspiration at certain times, it always came second to their self-identification as American. As William Vincent Shannon puts it in *The American Irish*, 'To describe one group of Americans in terms of their ancestry and background is not to say that they are any less American for what they did and are'.[40] Fiona Green comments on this issue when discussing the peculiar case of Marianne Moore, who despite claiming to be 'Irish by descent, possibly Scotch also, but purely Celtic' in an oft-quoted letter to Ezra Pound in 1919, was actually a mixture of English, Anglo-Irish, and Ulster/Scots-Irish Presbyterian.[41] Describing Moore's 'flexible approach' to Ireland, Green notes that Moore's 'own generational ties prompt her at certain times to call herself Irish, but to call that identity into question if it compromises what she regards as her proper position as an American'.[42] Of course, it is not the same thing to describe oneself as 'Irish' as to term oneself 'Irish American'. Moore's 'desire' to describe herself as 'Irish' is related less to ancestry, and more to 'a matter of choice' within her self-framing as 'American'. Although Ebest argues that 'not everyone, after all, can be Irish', it seems that certain American writers thought they could be, if they so chose.

F. Scott Fitzgerald, another subject of this study, might fit more comfortably into the 'Irish American' bracket, thanks to his maternal Irish immigrant background. Nevertheless, the change 'from Irish zeal to abandonment of the idea' that his early letters and his semi-autobiographical novel *This Side of Paradise* (1920) display marks Fitzgerald as a compulsive appropriator of Irishness, rather than a dedicated Irish American. Ebest comments that Fitzgerald 'reconceptualised Irishness as a collection of abstract personality traits', therefore 'divest[ing] the term (and its traits) of any historical, cultural or geographical punctuation'.[43] While Ebest's claim is perhaps reductive as an overall assessment of Fitzgerald's responses to Ireland, it does show how by making 'Irishness' appropriate to his literary endeavours, Fitzgerald was able mould it into his individual American expression.

Most significantly for this study, the avoidance of racial or cultural labels allows in turn for an avoidance of their associated assumptions. By expanding traditional investigative parameters beyond ethnic or racial lines to consider individual instances of cross-cultural pollination, I am able to discuss instances that might have little to do with genealogical 'desire', and additionally to incorporate the one-way traffic of cultural appropriation. This is why I do not cover the same ground as Ron Ebest's *Private Histories*, or Charles Fanning's studies on Irish-American fiction and the literature of the Irish diaspora, or Daniel Tobin's recent studies on Irish-American poetry.[44] There will be some overlaps, however. Although the present study discusses some of the same writers as Ebest's study – such as Fitzgerald and O'Neill – the critical perspective shifts to their interests in Irish and American culture and the relations between them, rather than focusing just on their responses to Irish America: an important distinction. Similarly, by discussing Stevens's interests in Ireland, I cover similar ground to Daniel Tobin in his recent work on Stevens; however, my focus is on Stevens's use of Ireland, from which he is necessarily *separate*, as a model of enchantment for his modernist American expression. I am less convinced by a reading of Stevens's late poems on Ireland as preoccupied with the routes of emigration and return, through what Tobin perceives as Stevens's response to 'the Irish experience of historical disinheritance, emigration [and] diaspora', as what I emphasise throughout is the imaginative potential that Stevens derives from his distance from, and lack of real experience of, Ireland itself.[45]

Edna Longley has discussed the need for a new focus, which extends the study of Irish and America beyond narratives of exile, immigration and return, and focuses instead on Ireland as a cultural resource for American writing. In her essay 'Irish bards and American audiences' (2000), Longley notes that questions of 'American-Irish literary interaction' have remained 'largely untouched' by critics on both sides of the Atlantic.[46] Some critical work has been carried out in this area; for example, John Harrington has written on Irish drama and the New York stage, Joseph Kelly on the reception of Joyce in America, and Terence Diggory on Yeats and American poetry.[47] This book will open out these (and other) areas of study by describing and contextualising instances of American-Irish cultural interaction and appropriation taken from a broad range of American modernist writing.

Rachel Buxton points out in her introduction to *Robert Frost and Northern Irish Poetry* that 'the reception of literature can depend upon who is reading it, the community to which they belong, and the contemporary political and cultural situation'.[48] Meanwhile Patrick Ward links the 'migratory' and 'modernist' experiences, where in both cases the experience might be as much imagined as real: he describes 'the migratory artists of modernism; migratory in the literal and the metaphoric modes in a loose, transnational association of highly self-conscious artists, imposing their narrative order on culture and experience'.[49] This book will consider both of these contentions, describing how American modernist writers appropriated Irish culture in relation to their contemporary political and cultural situation – and illustrating how the 'migratory' aspects of American modernism (literal, yes, but most often metaphorical) are peculiarly suited to this act of appropriation.

Notes

1. Louis MacNeice, *Autumn Journal*, XVI, ll. 61–74, in *Collected Poems*, ed. E. R. Dodds. London: Faber, 1966, pp. 101–53 (131–4).
2. Brian Fallon, *An Age of Innocence: Irish Culture 1930–1960*. Dublin: Gill and Macmillan, 1998, pp. 1–2.
3. Fiona Green, '"Your trouble is their trouble": Marianne Moore, Maria Edgeworth and Ireland', *Symbiosis: A Journal of Anglo-American Literary Relations*, 1.2 (October 1997), 173–85 (174).
4. Van Wyck Brooks, 'The literary life', in *Civilisation in the United States: An Enquiry by Thirty Americans*, ed. Howard E. Stearns. London: Jonathan Cape, 1922, pp. 179–98 (179, 180).
5. Moore, 'Comment', *The Dial*, 84.3 (March 1928), 269–70 (269).
6. Steinbeck, 'Paradox and dream', in *America and the Americans*, reprinted in *Of Men and Their Making: The Selected Non-fiction of John Steinbeck*, ed. Susan Shillingshaw and Jackson J. Benson. London: Allen Lane, 2002, pp. 330–8 (330).
7. Paul Giles, 'From decadent aesthetics to political fetishism: The "oracle effect" of Robert Frost's poetry', *American Literary History*, 12.4 (Winter 2000), 713–44 (720).
8. T. S. Eliot, 'The three provincialities' (first published 1922), reprinted in *Essays in Criticism*, 1.1 (January 1951), 38–41 (39).

9   Wallace Stevens to Thomas McGreevy, 9 September 1949, in *Letters of Wallace Stevens*, ed. Holly Stevens. Berkeley and Los Angeles: University of California Press, 1996, pp. 646–7 (646).
10 Terence Diggory, *Yeats and American Poetry: The Tradition of the Self*. Princeton: Princeton University Press, 1983, pp. 4, 8.
11 Eliot, 'The three provincialities', p. 39.
12 Harold Bloom, *The Anxiety of Influence: A Theory of Poetry*. New York and Oxford: Oxford University Press, 1997, p. 68.
13 Laura O'Connor, *Haunted English – The Celtic Fringe, The British Empire, and De-Anglicization*. Baltimore: Johns Hopkins University Press, 2006, pp. 160–1.
14 W. B. Yeats, 'The Celtic element in literature' (1897), collected in *Ideas of Good and Evil*. Dublin: Maunsel & Co., 1905, pp. 270–95 (270).
15 See J. M. Synge, *Travelling Ireland Essays, 1898–1908*, ed. Nicholas Grene. Dublin: Lilliputt Press, 2009.
16 Ezra Pound, *Literary Essays of Ezra Pound*, ed. with an introduction by T. S. Eliot. London: Faber and Faber, 1954, p. 287.
17 Marianne Moore, 'Comment', *The Dial*, 84.3 (March 1928), 269–70 (270). See also further discussions on this in the Preface.
18 Nicola J. Watson, *The Literary Tourist: Readers and Places in Romantic and Victorian Britain*. Basingstoke: Palgrave Macmillan, 2006, pp. 10, 4.
19 Moore, 'Spenser's Ireland', *Complete Poems*, ed. Clive Driver. London: Faber, 1987, pp. 112–14, l. 4 (counting title as first line, as was Moore's practice).
20 Steinbeck, 'I go back to Ireland', first published in *Collier's*, 31 January 1953, reprinted in *Of Men and their Making*, pp. 262–9 (263).
21 Donal Ó Drisceoil, '"The best banned in the land": censorship and Irish writing since 1950', *The Yearbook of English Studies*, 35 (2005), 146–60 (146).
22 Francis Hackett, 'A muzzle made in Ireland', *Dublin Magazine* (October to December 1936), 8–17 (15).
23 Ó Drisceoil, '"The best banned in the land"', pp. 147, 148.
24 John F. Callahan, *The Illusions of a Nation: Myth and History in the Novels of F. Scott Fitzgerald*. London and Chicago: University of Illinois Press, 1972, p. 3.
25 W. B. Yeats, 'On being asked for a war poem' (initially entitled 'A reason for keeping silent'), *The Variorum Edition of the Poems of W. B. Yeats*, ed. Peter Allt and Russell K. Alspach. New York: Macmillan, 1966, p. 359, ll. 1–2.
26 Lola Ridge, 'Tidings (Easter, 1916)', *The Ghetto and Other Poems*. New York: B. W. Huebsch, 1918, p. 101; see ll. 11–12.
27 See Moore, 'Spenser's Ireland', ll. 67, 20.
28 Synge, 'Preface', *The Playboy of the Western World*, in *Collected Works, Volume IV: Plays, Book 2*, ed. Ann Saddlemyer. Gerrards Cross: Colin Smythe, 1982, p. 54.
29 John Eglinton (W. K. Magee), 'Dublin letter', *The Dial*, 76.1 (January 1924; letter dated December 1923), 53–7 (54).
30 Eglinton, 'Dublin letter', *The Dial*, 75.2 (August 1923; letter dated July 1923), 179–83 (179).
31 Ben Howard, 'The pressed melodeon' (1986), *The Pressed Melodeon: Essays on Modern Irish Writing*. Brownsville, Oregon: Story Line Press, 1996, pp. 3–27 (3–4).

32 For example, Roy Foster discusses in some detail Yeats's tour of the United States in January to May 1920, during which he gave lectures and readings in New York, Washington, Yale, Chicago, California and Oregon; addressed two Mormon universities in Utah; and by April was 'introducing the poets of the 1890s to Waco, Texas'. See Foster, *W. B. Yeats: A Life. Volume II: The Arch-Poet*. Oxford: Oxford University Press, 2003, pp. 163–6.

33 Louise Bogan, review of Yeats's *Collected Poems*, *The New Yorker*, 7 April 1934; collected in *A Poet's Prose: Selected Writings of Louise Bogan*, ed. Mary Kinzie. Athens, Ohio: Swallow Press / Ohio University Press, 2005, pp. 200–1 (200).

34 Babette Deutsch to Thomas McGreevy, 17 February 1948, Trinity College Dublin ['TCD'] MS 8120.

35 See Philip Coleman, '"The politics of praise": John Berryman's engagement with W. B. Yeats', *Études Irlandaises*, 28.2 (Automne 2003), 11–27.

36 Giles, *Virtual Americas: Transnational Fictions and the Transatlantic Imaginary*. Durham: Duke University Press, 2002, p. 1.

37 Gary Gerstle, *American Crucible: Race and Nation in the Twentieth Century*. Princeton and Oxford: Princeton University Press, 2001, pp. 11–12.

38 Paul Jay, 'The myth of "America" and the politics of location: modernity, border studies, and the literature of the Americas', *Arizona Quarterly*, 54.2 (Summer 1998), 165–92 (166, 177).

39 Ebest, *Private Histories: The Writing of Irish Americans, 1900–1935*. Notre Dame, Indiana: University of Notre Dame Press, p. 7.

40 Willam Vincent Shannon, *The American Irish: A Political and Social Portrait*. New York: Macmillan, 1966, p. xiii.

41 Moore to Pound, 9 January 1919, in *The Selected Letters of Marianne Moore*, ed. Bonnie Costello, Celeste Goodridge and Cristanne Miller. London: Faber, 1998, pp. 122–5 (122).

42 Green, '"Your trouble is their trouble"', p. 181.

43 Ebest, *Private Histories*, pp. 98, 101.

44 See Preface for further discussion of these texts.

45 See Daniel Tobin, 'The westwardness of everything: Irishness in the poetry of Wallace Stevens', in *Awake in America: On Irish American Poetry*. Notre Dame, Indiana: University of Notre Dame Press, 2011, pp. 87–112 (104).

46 Edna Longley, 'Irish bards and American audiences', *Poetry and Posterity*. Newcastle upon Tyne: Bloodaxe, 2000, pp. 235–58 (248).

47 See John P. Harrington, *The Irish Play on the New York Stage, 1874–1966*. Lexington, Kentucky: University Press of Kentucky, 1997; Joseph Kelly, *Our Joyce: From Outcast to Icon*. Austin, Texas: University of Texas Press, 1998; and Diggory as referenced above.

48 Rachel Buxton, *Robert Frost and Northern Irish Poetry*. Oxford: Oxford University Press, 2004, p. 5.

49 Patrick Ward, *Exile, Emigration and Irish Writing*. Dublin/ Portland, Oregon: Irish Academic Press, 2002, pp. 234–5.

Chapter 1
Cultural and racial (dis)affiliations

> And partly because Ireland is small enough
> To be still thought of with a family feeling[1]

A study of American modernism and Irish culture must necessarily begin with a consideration of family. The affiliations and disaffiliations to Ireland experienced by the American writers discussed in this chapter reveal a reading of 'family' as literal and metaphorical, building on the kind of familial intimacy implied by the 'family feeling' that MacNeice places, in the above lines, at the centre of the 'small' domestic sphere of Irish life. This 'smallness' might also have appealed to American modernists thanks to what Paul Giles, quoting Fitzgerald in *This Side of Paradise*, attributes to 'nearly all of the major writers of the time': that is, 'The widespread feeling after the First World War that the world was now "too huge and complex" for "individualism"'.[2] Thus the writers included in this discussion, all searching in different ways for an individual voice that might somehow connect with their American literary expression, have nuanced and often troubling relationships with Ireland – thanks to family connections that are sometimes enhanced, and at other times played down, according to complex channels of racial and cultural influence and interference.

F. Scott Fitzgerald, for example, keenly emphasised the Irish, maternal side of his heritage during his early career, making most use of it in his first novel *This Side of Paradise* (1920). John Steinbeck, meanwhile, appeared to be preoccupied with his Northern Irish maternal heritage throughout his working life: referencing Irish themes in early works such as *Cup of Gold* (1929), displaying the influence of the Celtic Revivalist playwright J. M. Synge in his 'play-novelette' *Burning Bright* (1950), and giving the Northern Irish, Hamilton side of his family the contrapuntal saga to the Trasks in *East of Eden* (1952). Marianne

Moore claimed in a letter to Ezra Pound in January 1919 that she was 'Irish by descent, possibly Scotch also, but purely Celtic', despite only having loose family connections to Ireland through a maternal Anglo-Irish/Scots-Irish heritage.[3] Finally, Eugene O'Neill described himself as 'the last of this pure Irish branch of the O'Neills', dismissing his unfortunate children as 'a weird mixture, racially speaking'.[4]

What all of these writers have in common is the fact that their Irish heritage was exaggerated or romanticised in order to give their writing an intimacy and cultural depth. Ron Ebest points out that 'ethnicity is itself to some extent an act of personal and social imagination; as the Great Famine recedes into history, maintenance of Irish-American identity requires more and more of both'.[5] Although this book is concerned with a broader labelling of identity which discusses American writers with a variety of inherited links to Ireland, Ebest's description is telling: as each of the writers discussed here applies something of their 'personal and social imagination' to their interpretation – and misinterpretation – of their family relations to Ireland. In several of these examples, too, such relations are accompanied by racial assertions: Fitzgerald, for example, described himself in a letter to John O'Hara as 'half black Irish and half old American stock with the usual exaggerated ancestral pretensions',[6] while Steinbeck was concerned to stress his 'pure Ulster' heritage and his distaste for the 'dirty rednecks' of the southern Irish Free State.[7]

Such comments coincide with a growing interest in racial heritage during the period, which was marked by the publication of Edward A. Ross's *The Old World in the New: The Significance of Past and Present Immigration to the American People* (1914) and Madison Grant's *The Passing of the Great Race* (1916), the latter running to several editions and reaching its peak popularity in the early 1920s. A declared eugenicist text, *The Rising Tide of Color Against White-World Supremacy* (1920), by Lothrop Stoddard, is even referred to inaccurately by the bigoted Tom Buchanan in Fitzgerald's novel *The Great Gatsby* (1925).[8] Concurrent with, and thanks in part to, the dissemination of such publications, 1924 saw the passing of a new Immigration Act. Matthew Frye Jacobson notes that the 'provisions' of the Act 'ensured that those new arrivals who were still allowed entry, in the self-congratulatory words of the immigration commission, once more "looked exactly like Americans"'. However, Jacobson traces the start of 'such views of race and immigration' to an earlier point in history, arguing that they 'had become fixed in the lexicon of the state as early as 1911'.[9]

Though it is important that we do not overstate the significance of eugenicist texts by writers like Grant, Ross and Stoddard, Fitzgerald's deliberately inaccurate reference to Stoddard's text in his 1925 novel, written at the height of the immigration debates, is telling:

> 'Civilization's going to pieces', broke out Tom violently. 'I've gotten to be a terrible pessimist about things. Have you read *The Rise of the Coloured* [sic] *Empires* by this man Goddard?'
> 'Why, no,' I answered, rather surprised by his tone.
> 'Well, it's a fine book, and everybody ought to read it. The idea is if we don't look out the white race will be – will be utterly submerged. It's all scientific stuff; it's been proved.'[10]

The narrator, Nick Carraway, expresses 'surprise' at Tom Buchanan's vitriolic 'tone', a surprise that enables Fitzgerald to offer a critique – through the inaccuracy of the reference to Stoddard's text, and through Buchanan's sweeping summary – of the ways in which eugenicist texts have assumed a generalised authority within white upper-class American circles. Later in the same discussion, Buchanan offers the thesis that: 'This idea is that we're Nordics. I am, and you are, and you are … And we've produced all the things that go to make civilization – oh, science and art, and all that. Do you see?'. This association between the 'Nordics' and 'civilization' allows Tom Buchanan, a 'sturdy straw-haired man of thirty', with a 'cruel', hulking body, to contrast with the outsider Jay Gatsby, an 'elegant young rough-neck', with 'tanned skin', whom Buchanan suggests might hail from 'Oxford, New Mexico' rather than Oxford University;[11] thus Buchanan insults Gatsby with an entwined dismissal of his dark appearance and his claims to a 'civilized' education.

A brief consideration of the eugenicist texts published in the first half of the twentieth century is, therefore, valuable for considering the extremes of class-based and racial views disseminated within American society. For the purposes of this study, an analysis of the ways in which such texts treated the indigenous Irish is also helpful. In *The Passing of the Great Race* Grant associates nationalism and patriotism with the desire of 'inferior' races to rise against the 'master race': 'The resurgence of inferior races and classes throughout not merely Europe but the world, is evident in every despatch from Egypt, Ireland, Poland, Rumania, India and Mexico. It is called nationalism, patriotism, freedom and other high-sounding names, but it is everywhere the phenomenon of the long-suppressed, conquered servile colonies rising against the master race'. Grant goes on to worry about 'the hyphenated aliens in our midst upon whom we have carelessly urged citizenship'.[12] Edward A. Ross expands upon the ethnic make-up of American immigrant groups, distinguishing between the 'Scotch-Irish' whom he claims 'molded our national character' 'more than any other stock', and the 'Celtic Irish' to whom he is less kind: 'During its earlier period, Irish immigration brought in a desirable class, which assimilated readily. Later, the enormous assisted immigration that followed the famine of 1846–48 brought in many of an inferior type, who huddled helplessly in the poorer quarters of our cities and became men of the spade and the hod'.[13]

In a later text, *The Social Systems of American Ethnic Groups* (1945), this distinction between the 'inferior type' of the 'Celtic Irish' and the lionised Scotch-Irish group is emphasised still further. The text's authors, W. Lloyd Warner and Leo Strole, drew up tables of 'Cultural and Racial types' based on the following criteria: degree of subordination, strength of ethnic and racial subsystems, time for assimilation, and form of American rank. In this table, the 'Racial Type I – Light Caucasoid', which is placed at the top of the hierarchy, is sub-divided into 'Cultural Types'. 'Cultural Type 1', in which the degree of subordination is 'very slight' and the time for assimilation 'very short', includes 'English-speaking Protestants', with the test cases consisting of 'English, Scotch, North Irish, Australians, Canadians'. For the 'south Irish', we have to wait for 'Cultural Type 3', in which the degree of subordination is 'slight' and the time for assimilation 'short to moderate'. 'Cultural Type 2' consists of Protestants who do not speak English, including 'Scandinavians, Germans, Dutch, French'.[14] In *The Passing of the Great Race* Madison Grant strengthens such arguments with a table entitled 'CLASSIFICATION OF THE RACES OF EUROPE, THEIR CHARACTERS AND DISTRIBUTION'. In this table Grant classes the English, Scotch and most Irish as 'Nordic' (the superior race), but notes that there are 'doubtful traces among West Irish and among the old black breed of Scotland and Wales' of the lowest European race, the '*Middle Paleolithic*', which has a 'broad nose', and is 'short and powerful', with 'probably very dark' hair and eyes; he is also 'probably non-Aryan'.[15]

In the context of such pervasive ethnic and class-based stereotyping, it is perhaps unsurprising that American writers during the period seemed compelled to describe or even define their connections to Ireland. However each writer discussed in this chapter displays rather inconsistent attitudes towards these issues. For example, Fitzgerald's pejorative description of his 'black Irish' heritage – referring to Irish of Mediterranean appearance but also associated with the term 'wild Irish', which describes 'the less civilised Irish'[16] – seems at odds both with his portrayal of the red-haired 'Irish' sophisticate Dick Diver in *Tender is the Night* (1934) and with his declared attraction to Celticism as a young writer starting out. In one memorable letter to Edmund Wilson Fitzgerald, he declared his desire to 'prove myself a Celt', and signed off another 'Gaelically yours'.[17] Marianne Moore was similarly disingenuous in her attitude towards her apparently 'purely Celtic' background. While Moore's family inheritance was not 'purely Celtic' – being derived from an English/Anglo-Irish/Scots-Irish, Dublin/Ulster background – in her poem 'Spenser's Ireland' (1941) she uses an imagined conversation to remark sarcastically upon a dismissal of a potential suitor on grounds of race:

> 'Although your suitor
> be perfection, one objection
> is enough; he is
> not Irish.'[18]

Meanwhile Moore's mother Mary Warner Moore famously dismissed a potential bride for her son on similar grounds.[19] Moreover, and perhaps even more surprisingly, in an early short story, 'Pym', Moore has her eponymous character describing how he stood 'like the idiot Celt, head back, mouth open, eyes gleaming';[20] although written in 1908, this small extract shows how even the apparently 'purely Celtic' Moore was influenced by the racial stereotyping of the Irish that saturated contemporary American society. This example also confirms how each writer seems to stress – or even invent – certain aspects of their heritage, and play down others, if and when it is convenient for them to do so.

An important counter-movement to the work of eugenicists such as Grant and Ross theorised that national or ethnic groups might be viewed in cultural rather than racial terms. For example Ruth Benedict, in *Patterns of Culture* (1934), offered an alternative approach to questions of community: 'The racial purist is the victim of a mythology. For what is "racial inheritance"? We know roughly what heredity is from father to son. Within a family line the importance of heredity is tremendous. But heredity is an affair of family lines. Beyond that it is mythology ...What really binds men together is their culture – the ideas and the standards they have in common'. Benedict is particularly shocked that 'we have come to the point where we entertain racial prejudice against our blood brothers the Irish'.[21]

Benedict's idea of 'culture' as 'what really binds men together' certainly offers an alternative to the heredity arguments offered by 'racial purists' – but although she describes racial theorists as pursuing a mythology, she is offering a kind of cultural mythology of her own. Her arguments also reflect a larger shift in American political thinking following the 1924 Immigration Act, and the horrendous consequences of eugenicist thinking in the 1920s and 1930s. This shift was to have an effect on the ways in which Americans viewed the question of Irish ethnicity. As Frye Jacobson points out, 'The notion that Irishness, like other "ethnic" whitenesses, was a cultural trait rather than a visual racial clue became deeply embedded in the nation's political culture between the 1920s and the 1960s'.[22] For the writers discussed here, the shifting patterns of racial, ethnic and cultural views of inheritance and identity within American society manifest themselves in their complex relationship with Ireland. Each writer's relationship displays both a concern with 'family feeling' – a romantic affiliation to an 'affair of family lines' – and a personally defined sense of cultural inheritance that is peculiar to their interests in, and affiliations to, Ireland.

F. Scott Fitzgerald (1896–1940)

F. Scott Fitzgerald was a writer for whom a maternal Irish background provided inherited cultural references at a time when he was struggling to find his literary identity. Many of his early associations with Ireland are bound up with a cultural mythology of Irishness – specifically

Celticism and Catholicism – and particularly with what this mythology might offer an individual in relation to society. It was noted in the Introduction how John F. Callahan remarks that modern American writers tend to 'seek mythologies of fraudulent innocence';[23] and indeed Madison Grant appears to view the Irish cultural renaissance in similar terms: 'the Irish National movement centers chiefly around religion reinforced by myths of ancient grandeur'.[24] But surely the appeal of myth to writers such as Fitzgerald – at least early in their career – was its ability to inspire ideas of innocence or grandeur in a world that contained neither of these things? As Callahan goes on to argue, in relation to Fitzgerald, 'Myth as lie, as stereotype in the reductive mode, restricts possibility, freezes experience, denies freedom; whereas myth as truth, as archetype, with its modes of connotation and implication, suggests new arrangements of human essentials confirmed by past experience'.[25] Thus it might be simplistic to merely dismiss an indulgence in myth as a preference for un-truths. Moreover, as the American poet and critic Ben Howard has pointed out, Irish writers have inspired their American counterparts by modelling a search for authenticity shaped, and complicated, by illusions of their own making: 'Irish writers have endeavored to discover the "real Ireland" behind the sentimental stereotypes, the warring ideologies, the outworn pieties and outright shams. That the veils of illusion have been partially the creation of Irish writers only complicates the project'.[26]

While drafting early versions of his first novel *This Side of Paradise*, and engaging in close correspondence with the Anglo-Irish Catholic writer Shane Leslie and the Catholic-American Bishop Monsignor Fay, Fitzgerald appeared determined to view Celtic and Catholic myths as truths that might suggest new modes of literary expression confirmed by the 'past experience' both of his Irish Catholic family and of his literary mentors. Andrew Turnbull describes Shane Leslie (1885–1971) as 'a young Irish author visiting America who took Fitzgerald under his wing while he was groping his way toward *This Side of Paradise*'.[27] Indeed Fitzgerald told in the *New York Tribune* in May 1922 how Leslie 'first came into my life as the most romantic figure I had ever known', and acknowledged Leslie as a dedicatee of his second novel *The Beautiful and Damned* (1922).[28] We also know from Princeton University Library's list of books owned by Fitzgerald that in May 1917 Leslie had sent him a copy of a collection of poetry by the nineteenth-century Irish Catholic writer Blanche Mary Kelly entitled *The Valley of Vision* (1916), and that Fitzgerald owned a copy of Leslie's 1917 work *The Celt and the World*.[29] However, Fitzgerald was not as enthralled by Leslie as he would have him believe. This is evident in the contradiction between a letter he wrote to Leslie in February 1918 to ask, 'Did you ever notice that remarkable coincidence? Bernard Shaw is 61 years old, H. G. Wells is 51, G. K. Chesterton 41, you're 31, and I'm 21 – all the great authors in the world in arithmetical progression', and the letter he had sent to Edmund Wilson in autumn 1917 making use of the same 'arithmetical' list: 'Too bad I haven't a better man for 31'.[30] At the same time, though, Fitzgerald had been reliant on Leslie's patronage: it was Leslie, after all, who had sent the first version of *This Side of Paradise*, entitled 'The Romantic Egotist', to his own publisher, Scribner's, for consideration in May 1916.

Father Sigourney Fay, whom Fitzgerald had first met at school in Minnesota, arguably asserted a more profound effect on Fitzgerald's early development: he was the model for Monsignor Darcy in *This Side of Paradise*, and sections of his letters to the young author were replicated almost exactly in the novel. The most notable example of this is Fay's letter to Fitzgerald dated 10 December 1917, with which he enclosed a 'keen', or Irish funeral song; the 'keen' was replicated in its entirety, under the title 'A lament for a foster son, and he going to the War against the King of foreign', in *This Side of Paradise*.[31] James L. West III notes that 'Fitzgerald actually lifted the page from one of Monsignor Fay's letters and put it right into the manuscript [of *The Romantic Egotist*]', adding that his use of Fay's poem 'is not an adaptation; it is a direct steal'.[32]

But what is particularly useful to this study is not what Fitzgerald 'stole' from Fay's letter, but what he added to it. West's comparison of the letter as it appears in the manuscript (and subsequently in the final version of the novel) with the original correspondence remarks upon Fay's focus on bloodlines and ancestry. In the letter, Fay claims that he and Fitzgerald are 'the same person being repeated, over and over', continuing: 'The explanation of our case is that we are all a repetition of some common ancestor. The only blood we have in common is that of the O'Donohue's [sic]'.[33] In the letter in the eventual novel – which represents a letter apparently sent from Darcy to the novel's protagonist, Amory Blaine, in January 1918 – this passage becomes:

'Sometimes I think that the explanation of our deep resemblance is some common ancestor, and I find that the only blood that the Darcys and the O'Haras have in common is that of the O'Donahues [sic]'. Again we can see a concern with family connections and cultural inheritance. Yet the section that precedes this sentence in the novel is more telling for its absence in the original letter from Fay to Fitzgerald. This section sees Darcy despairing at Amory's imminent departure to fight in World War One – hence the concluding 'keen' – while urging him to take refuge in his origins: 'And afterward an out-and-out materialistic world – and the Catholic Church. I wonder where you'll fit in. One thing I'm sure – Celtic you'll live and Celtic you'll die; so if you don't use heaven as a continual referendum for your ideas you'll find earth a continual recall to your ambitions'.[34]

What is ironic here is that Fitzgerald renounced his Catholicism, and with it some of his Celtic leanings, soon after he failed to die in the war (as both Leslie and Fay had expected him to), instead returning to oversee the publication of his first novel in 1920. Following Fay's death in 1918, Leslie was Fitzgerald's only remaining Catholic mentor, but by 1920 Leslie's pronouncements were appearing to fall on deaf ears. In a letter to Fitzgerald sent in September of that year, remarking on the negative criticism *This Side of Paradise* had received in some sections of the Catholic press, Leslie chided: 'You must not mind Catholic criticism for I think it is a Catholic minded book at heart and that you like Fay and myself can never be anything but Catholics however much we write and pose to make the bourgeois stare'.[35] Fitzgerald's reply did little to reassure his mentor of his loyalty to the faith:

> My ideas now are in such wild riot that I would flatter myself did I claim even the clarity of agnosticism. If you knew the absolute dirth [sic] of Catholic intelligentsia in this country! One Catholic magazine, *America*, has only one prim comment on my book – 'a fair example of our non-Catholic college's output'. My Lord! Compared to the average Georgetown alumnus Amory is an uncanonized saint.[36]

In the context of this letter, and particularly in considering the religious metaphors associated with Amory, it comes as little surprise that critics have tended to make comparisons between *This Side of Paradise* and James Joyce's *A Portrait of the Artist as a Young Man* (1916), particularly since it is referenced in the novel, where the narrator notes of Amory: 'He read enormously. He was puzzled and depressed by *A Portrait of the Artist as a Young Man*'.³⁷ Jack Hendriksen notes several parallels between the two novels, including points of convergence in plot and matters of scale, the treatment of Catholicism and women, and moments of 'epiphany': indeed he concludes by wondering 'if there is something about the Catholic Church which produces *bildungsroman* heroes'.³⁸

Semi-autobiographical resonances are present in both novels; as Patrick O'Donnell puts it in his introduction to *This Side of Paradise*, using a description that might be applied equally to *A Portrait of the Artist*, the text is a product of 'the stitching of autobiographical fragments and youthful writing into the design of a novel'.³⁹ Meanwhile Callahan notes that in Fitzgerald's personal copy of *Dubliners*, he had scribbled: 'I am interested in the individual only in his relation to society. We have wandered in an imaginary loneliness through imaginary woods for a hundred years – too long'.⁴⁰ This expressed tension between a desire for collective self-assertion and ennui for the current condition of man, scribbled in the pages of *Dubliners*, tells us that Fitzgerald identifies a similar condition in Joyce's work. Indeed O'Donnell points out that the closing paragraphs of *This Side of Paradise*, in which Amory 'looks upon the spires of Princeton in a moment of self-discovery', resonate with Stephen Dedalus's epiphany at the end of *A Portrait of the Artist*.⁴¹

The closing paragraphs to *This Side of Paradise* are revealing of the parallels and contrasts between Fitzgerald's 'American' text and the 'Irish' novel that it responds to. Amory notes the limits of his self-knowledge, casting off the dreams of his generation along with the 'romantic' ideals that he and Fitzgerald have associated with Catholicism:

> As an endless dream it went on; the spirit of the past brooding over a new generation, the chosen youth from the muddled, unchastened world, still fed romantically on the mistakes and half-forgotten dreams of dead statesmen and poets. Here was a new generation, shouting the old cries, learning the old creeds, through a reverie of long days and nights; destined finally to go out into that dirty gray turmoil to follow love and pride; a new generation dedicated more than the last to the fear of poverty and the worship of success; grown up to find all Gods dead, all wars fought, all faiths in man shaken.⁴²

Though a similar sense of weariness and inevitability reigns over the closing passages of *A Portrait of the Artist*, Joyce arguably leaves more room for hope in the defeated but not defeatist character of Stephen Dedalus than Fitzgerald provides in the ennui of Amory Blaine, where Dedalus famously exclaims: 'Welcome, O Life! I go to encounter for the millionth time the reality of experience and to forge in the smithy of my soul the uncreated conscience of my race'.[43] As O'Donnell points out, despite the obvious similarities between these passages – in addition to the fact that Amory 'confesses to having read *Portrait*', and that in the earliest versions of the novel 'the protagonist is variously named "Stephen Palms" or "Stephen Dalius"' – 'Stephen Dedalus, much more than Amory Blaine, processes experience into vision'.[44] This contrast is clear in the above passages, where Amory takes several flamboyant clauses to conclude, ultimately, that '"I know myself, ... but that is all"',[45] whereas Stephen views himself in almost metonymical terms, planning to manipulate his life experiences so that they represent, and ultimately take responsibility for, 'the uncreated conscience of my race'. We might recall, here, Paul Giles's claim, through Amory, that the majority of modernist writers expressed 'The widespread feeling after the First World War that the world was now "too huge and complex" for "individualism"';[46] but what Stephen offers in contrast is an assertion of the place of the 'individual' in 'relation to his society', recalling Fitzgerald's self-declared 'interest' as scribbled in his copy of *Dubliners*.[47] Though in the conclusion to *A Portrait of the Artist* Joyce mocks the extent of Stephen's belief, and his ego, Stephen clearly remains an inspiration to Amory – and, beyond this, to Fitzgerald, too – in an example of intra-fictional (and extra-fictional) influence.

As O'Donnell notes, Amory's linguistic detachment from his experience – where 'the fit between experience and articulation has not yet been joined' – might be a 'peculiarly "American"' response to the same sorts of challenges Stephen faces: so that rather than forging a racial or national conscience, Amory is content merely to 'frame identity as provisional and nomadic'.[48] Indeed the variety and flexibility of the American experience – in contrast with the relative confines of the Irish Catholic experience – make a metonymical connection between the individual and his society unlikely: in *This Side of Paradise* not even a metaphorical 'fit between experience and articulation' can be forged. It is at this stage in Fitzgerald's novel, and indeed in his work as a whole, that Catholicism ceases to offer any kind of solace – not only are 'all Gods dead', but the strictures and structures of Catholicism are counter to Amory's immersion into the 'dirty gray turmoil' of a 'provisional and nomadic' experience which, as O'Donnell notes, is 'peculiarly "American"'.

★

Critics remain divided about Fitzgerald's use, and under-use, of Irish and Catholic references in his work after *This Side of Paradise*; Charles Fanning, for example, argues that in order to achieve commercial success 'Fitzgerald found his way in part by largely ignoring the possibilities for fiction of the ethnic dimension',[49] while Giles claims that the 'cultural tensions' surrounding Fitzgerald's engagement with Catholicism 'substantially affect the implicit direction of his novels'.[50] Callahan, meanwhile, puts it succinctly that 'Fitzgerald's heritage gave him no crutches. He broke with Catholicism'.[51] However, one might argue that the Irish side of Fitzgerald's heritage, both subtler and more deeply ingrained than his Catholicism, took longer to shake off – as it provided a store of material gathered from his early personal and literary encounters. But it also carried with it cultural and racial baggage.

Following his self-declared abandonment of Catholic and Celtic zeal after the publication, and mixed reception, of *This Side of Paradise*, Fitzgerald displays in his correspondence an increasingly complex attitude towards his Irish background, which reveals a combination of pride and embarrassment about his Irish connections and their connotations. Two letters – one sent to Edmund Wilson in 1922, and another to John O'Hara in 1933 – are worth quoting at length. In the earlier letter Fitzgerald discusses Wilson's essay 'F. Scott Fitzgerald', which he would publish in *The Bookman* in March 1922, and which describes the influences Wilson identifies within Fitzgerald's work. Fitzgerald's comments on reading the essay were sent to Wilson prior to publication in January 1922:

> Now your three influences, St Paul [Minnesota], Irish (incidentally, though it doesn't matter, I'm not Irish on Father's side – that's where Francis Scott Key comes in) and liquor are all important I grant. But I feel less hesitancy asking you to remove the liquor because your

catalogue is not complete anyhow … Don't change the Irish thing – it's much better as it is – besides the quotation hints at the whiskey motif.[52]

Fitzgerald backtracks intriguingly here, moving from downplaying his Irish influences and the drinking with which they are potentially associated, to approving these for the sake of entertainment and coherence: the 'Irish thing' is described as being 'much better as it is' despite not being wholly accurate, while the 'whiskey motif' holds the whole thing together. The 'quotation' to which Fitzgerald refers is Wilson's quotation of Bernard Shaw on the Irish; and in the finished piece, entitled 'F. Scott Fitzgerald', this comes as part of an extended description of the Irish influence at play in Fitzgerald's work:

The second thing one should know about him is that Fitzgerald is partly Irish and that he brings both to life and to fiction certain qualities that are not Anglo-Saxon. … He is vain, a little malicious, of quick intelligence and wit, and has an Irish gift for turning language into something iridescent and surprising. He often reminds one, in fact, of the description that a great Irishman, Bernard Shaw, has written of the Irish: 'An Irishman's imagination never lets him alone, never convinces him, never satisfies him; but it makes him that he can't face reality nor deal with it nor handle it nor conquer it: he can only sneer at them that do … and imagination's such a torture that you can't bear it without whisky [sic].'[53]

It is notable that here Wilson identifies, within Fitzgerald's work and life, 'qualities that are not Anglo-Saxon', as if identifying a cultural and racial difference between 'Irish' and 'Anglo-Saxon' features in a text – such as 'an Irish gift for turning language into something iridescent and surprising'. But the view of the Irish as malicious and witty, with a sneer, smacks of cliché. In citing Shaw, Wilson risks reverting to generalities – particularly in terms of the Irishman's dependence on whisky as a kind of cure for the imagination – yet Fitzgerald is keen to leave it as is, as if he is proud to represent something of Shaw's stage Irishman.

A similar combination of reticence and self-consciousness about his 'part Irish' heritage appears in Fitzgerald's July 1933 letter to the Irish-American novelist John O'Hara, where he waxes lyrical about his Irish family connections:

I am half black Irish and half old American stock with the usual exaggerated ancestral pretensions. The black Irish half of the family had the money and looked down upon the Maryland side of the family ... so being born in that atmosphere of crack, wisecrack and countercrack I developed a two-cylinder inferiority complex. ... I suppose this is just a confession of being a Gael though I have known many Irish who have not been inflicted by this intense social self-consciousness. ... The only excuse for that burst of egotism is that you asked for it.[54]

Fitzgerald's mother, Mary McQuillan, was the eldest of the four children of Philip McQuillan, an Irish immigrant; indeed Arthur Mizener notes Mary McQuillan's pride in the family's lowly origins: 'The McQuillans ... were, as Fitzgerald later put it with revealing intensity, "straight 1850 potato-famine Irish", a fact that his mother seemed determined to advertise by her persistent eccentricity'.[55] Similarly in this passage, we can detect a 'persistent eccentricity' in the way Fitzgerald describes and attempts to define his experience 'of being a Gael': veering between 'inferiority' and 'egotism', between 'social self-consciousness' and wisecracking. What Fitzgerald appears to share with his mother is an exaggeration of Irish identity that associates a lowly background – the potato famine, a culture of whisky drinking – with romantic ideas of Irish eccentricity and 'character'.

The double-edged incisions of Fitzgerald's Irish background bleed into the fabric of Fitzgerald's novels after *This Side of Paradise*, as if picking up from where we left Amory at the end of the novel, poised between knowing himself and knowing nothing at all. In *The Beautiful and Damned* (1922), for example, a combination of sentimentality and ennui can be perceived in the sections dealing with Irish characters – reflecting the romantic lassitude of the story as a whole. In a peculiar episode, the novel's disaffected protagonist, Anthony, tells the girl he is seeing, Geraldine Burke, the story of the 'Deplorable End of the Chevalier O'Keefe', an apparent moral tale:

> He was an Irishman, Geraldine, a semi-fictional Irishman – the wild sort with a genteel brogue and 'reddish hair'. He was exiled from Erin in the late days of chivalry and, of course, crossed over to France. Now the Chevalier O'Keefe, Geraldine, had, like me, one weakness. He was enormously susceptible to all sorts and conditions of women. Besides

being a sentimentalist he was a romantic, a vain fellow, a man of wild
passions, a little blind in one eye and almost stone-blind in the other.[56]

Anthony's self-identification with this womanising 'romantic' Irishman,
flawed by vanity and passion, hints at his attraction to the stereotype
of the 'wild' Irish man with 'a genteel brogue and "reddish hair"'; but
it also points to his awareness of the stereotyping and fictionalising
that he is colluding in: the Irishman is 'semi-fictional', the description of his red hair is enclosed by inverted commas as if to emphasise
the stereotype, and 'exiled from Erin' has all the pomposity of cliché.
It is as if Fitzgerald is keen to shake off the nostalgic burden of the
Irish-American tradition, which has already found something of a
voice in the 'keens' of *This Side of Paradise*.[57] This apparent mockery of
Irish-American tradition reveals what Fanning describes as Fitzgerald's
'discomfort about identity and status';[58] yet Anthony, who at no other
stage in the novel is described as Irish, adopts easily the label 'Irish' by
implicit association with the Chevalier O'Keefe. Is it possible, then,
that Fitzgerald might be at once attracted to the 'romantic', heroic side
of the Irish character, and scornful of the sentimentality that places this
view of Irishness at the centre of Irish-American thought?

Later in the novel, during the breakdown of Anthony and Gloria's
marriage, 'Irish' takes on different connotations, becoming associated
with the Patches' financial decline and increasing disreputability. The
Patches are forced to adopt a more modest lifestyle, which includes the
replacement of their English butler, Bounds, with an Irish maid:

> They rented a small apartment on 57th Street at 150 a month. It included
> bedroom, living-room, kitchenette, and bath, in a thin, white-stone
> apartment-house, and though the rooms were too small to display
> Anthony's best furniture, they were clean, new, and, in a blonde and
> sanitary way, not unattractive. Bounds had gone abroad to enlist in the
> British army, and in his place they tolerated rather than enjoyed the
> services of a gaunt, big-boned Irishwoman, who Gloria loathed because
> she discussed the glories of Sinn Fein as she served breakfast.[59]

This description of the Irish maid is telling in its contrast with
Anthony's depiction of the 'romantic' Chevalier O'Keefe. While
O'Keefe is 'semi-fictional' and therefore can be idealised and kept

separate from the realities of everyday life, the maid is an ever-present, living embodiment of the Patches' financial decline, the poverty of Irish immigrants, and potentially uncomfortable contemporary issues such as Irish nationalism and Home Rule. Indeed this 'loathing' of the discussion of political matters recalls Amory's 'tiring of the Irish question' in *This Side of Paradise*.[60] The attraction of the 'Irish' character seems, for the protagonists of *The Beautiful and Damned* and *This Side of Paradise*, to be rooted in an idealisation of a romantic past rather than in the encroaching realities of the present.

By the time Fitzgerald comes to write *Tender is the Night* (1934), the more uncomfortable aspects of Irish identity that have been touched on in *The Beautiful and Damned* fail to make an appearance – while 'Irish' seems to move ever further away from 'Irish American'. Hence we find several, inconsistent, references to 'Irish' qualities in the characters of both Dick Diver and his one-time lover Rosemary Hoyt: the latter despite the fact that Hoyt is British. In a passage early in the novel, Rosemary regards Dick in the moment that she falls for him:

> Silently she admired him. His complexion was reddish and weather-burned, so was his short hair – a light growth of it rolled down his arms and hands. His eyes were of a bright, hard blue. [...] His voice, with some faint Irish melody running through it, wooed the world, yet she felt the layer of hardness in him, of self-control and of self-discipline, her own virtues.[61]

Rosemary's close study of Dick's physiognomy – of his 'reddish' complexion, fair hair and 'bright, hard blue' eyes – recalls the racial stereotyping employed by Tom Buchanan in *The Great Gatsby* in relation to Lothrop Stoddard's *The Rising Tide of Color Against White-World Supremacy*,[62] aligning Dick with an ideal of a (strawberry) blonde, 'Nordic' Irishman rather than with the 'black Irish' with whom Fitzgerald associates himself scornfully in his letter to O'Hara.[63] Fitzgerald's 'Irish' characters, like his fictionalised 'Chevalier O'Keefe', have 'reddish hair';[64] they are not dark, swarthy outcasts like Gatsby or like the 'irredeemably alienated', 'black Irish' Fitzgerald of his letters, as Paul Giles describes him.[65]

In the rest of *Tender is the Night*, 'Irish' comes to be associated with something romantic and alluring but also mysterious and possibly dangerous. Rosemary's growing insecurity in Dick's presence becomes wrapped up in what she perceives as the 'Irish' side of his character – the side that is not hard, self-controlled and self-disciplined like she is. This can be seen in an episode in which Rosemary presumptuously arranges a screen-test for Dick, to the embarrassment of Dick and his friends: 'Rosemary watched Dick comprehend what she meant, his face moving first in an Irish way; simultaneously she realized that she had made some mistake in the playing of her trump and she still she did not suspect that the card was at fault'. Dick's wife Nicole is also unsure of Dick's unpredictable 'Irish' side. During their uncertain courtship, Nicole scrutinises Dick in a manner that recalls Rosemary's observations in the early stage of their relationship: 'That part of him which seemed to fit his reddish Irish colouring she knew least; she was afraid of it, yet more anxious to explore – this was his more masculine side: the other part, the trained part, the consideration in the polite eyes, she expropriated without question, as most women did'.

Throughout the novel, then, 'Irish' becomes a by-word for that which is not quite understood in characters' readings of each other. Even Dick uses the adjective to describe that part of Rosemary that he simultaneously feels most attracted to and fails quite to grasp. In conversation with Rosemary's mother Mrs Speers, he claims: '"The wisdom she got from you is all moulded up into her persona, into the mask she faces the world with. She doesn't think; her real depths are Irish and romantic and illogical"'.[66] What is fascinating is the inconsistency with which the term 'Irish' is used in these three examples. In Rosemary's example, Dick's face is described as 'moving in an Irish way', perhaps to convey embarrassment or discomfort; in Nicole's view of Dick, it represents his unknowable, fearful, yet most masculine side – and is therefore tied to her fear of men in general; while in Dick's observation of Rosemary, it is linked to her 'real depths' of romance and illogic.

Fitzgerald's last, unfinished, novel, *The Last Tycoon* (1940), associates 'Irishness' increasingly with physical characteristics. The narrator of *The Last Tycoon*, Cecilia Brady, enters the office of her father – a 'chief executive' of a film studio – and describes him thus: 'Father can be very magnetic – he had a tough jaw and an Irish smile'. Although there is the implication that with the surname Brady, Cecilia's father might be Irish, this is the only explicit reference in the novel, apart from her earlier description of the 'tip-tilted Irish redness around my father's nostrils'.[67] Later on in the novel, the 'wild green eyes of a bus' mirror the eyes of Kathleen Moore – the one character whom Robert Rhodes identifies as 'genuinely Irish' thanks to her adolescence in Ireland.[68] Here Cecilia recounts a meeting between the producer Monroe Stahr and Kathleen, with whom he is about to fall in love:

'You're Irish,' he said ... .
She nodded.
'I've lived in London a long time – I didn't think you could tell.'
The wild green eyes of a bus sped up the road in the darkness. They were silent until it went by.[69]

In each example, physical characteristics – a smile, nasal redness, wild green eyes – become shorthand for 'Irish' qualities of magnetism, romance or (in the case of Brady's nose) excess. Although, then, this use of shorthand has the effect of turning the characters themselves into clichés, the fact that Fitzgerald continues to use Irish characters up until his very last novel – and, indeed, that the names of Brady and Kathleen, originally 'Bradogue' and 'Thalia', were made more 'Irish' in the last version of *The Last Tycoon* – tells us that Fitzgerald saw 'Irish' qualities as continuing to hold a certain promise.

Noting the problems raised by *The Last Tycoon* – with the unfinished manuscript worked up into a hypothetical finished story by Edmund Wilson – Robert Rhodes refrains from commenting conclusively on Fitzgerald's use of Irish characters in the novel. Nevertheless he suggests, tentatively, that 'all we know is that at the end Fitzgerald was extending the range of his Irish characters, that he was no longer motivated primarily by considerations of class, and that, if they are not at center stage, neither are they bit-players hovering in the wings'.[70] It is clear that 'genuine' Irish characters have become more of the fabric of this novel than of Fitzgerald's previous works, so that they mingle with the Jewish figures such as Stahr. Rhodes sees in Fitzgerald's use of a range of Irish characters a sign that the author was becoming more comfortable with the two sides of his heritage – his 'aristocratic' American inheritance from his father, and his more 'common' Irish side. And it might in turn signal Fitzgerald's ultimate acquiescence to a more prosaic interpretation of 'Irishness', which sees it as a constituent of hybridised American culture.

Ron Ebest discusses at length what he terms Fitzgerald's 'Irish problem', paying particular attention to the ambiguous use of 'Irish' in *Tender is the Night*:

> If Diver is literally Irish, the fact is obscure: Fitzgerald imagined him the heir to an ante-bellum North Carolina aristocracy. Even more peculiar is the fact that Diver calls the object of his desire, Rosemary Hoyt, 'Irish and romantic and illogical'. In fact, the text of the novel makes it clear that Rosemary Hoyt is not Irish at all. The peculiar habit of using the adjective 'Irish' to describe non-Irish people may derive in part from the autobiographical nature of Fitzgerald's work.[71]

This autobiographical argument is initially persuasive: nearly all of Fitzgerald's male protagonists share his weakness for women, his problems with alcohol and his red hair. We might also recall the amount of autobiographical material that found its way into the published version of *This Side of Paradise*. But as we have already seen, despite his red hair Fitzgerald remained preoccupied with what he saw as his 'half black Irish' identity, as he described it in the letter to O'Hara just one year before the publication of *Tender is the Night*.[72] It is as if Fitzgerald was determined to remain at the fringes of things, like Gatsby, his most elusive and alienated character. At the same time Fitzgerald's use of the term 'Irish' in his novels – though with some signs of a change of direction in *The Last Tycoon* – sees the adjective become increasingly untethered.

Fanning, as previously noted, argues that Fitzgerald ignored 'the possibilities for fiction of the ethnic dimension';[73] this is borne out through Fitzgerald's lack of direct reference to questions of Irish-American ethnicity, through his own discomfort with his 'black Irish' origins, and through the slight distaste displayed in *The Beautiful and Damned* for narratives of exiles, for Irish maids, and for the 'Irish question'. But what *Tender is the Night* offers in particular is a notion of Irishness unburdened by questions of ethnicity or hybridity. Instead Fitzgerald creates in 'Irish' an adjectival ideal, untarnished by the perceived grubbiness of his own immigrant identity – and by the spoils of the modern world as a whole. While his pejorative dismissal of his own ethnic heritage (expressed in 1933, at the same time he was writing *Tender is the Night*) is in itself troubling, and links back to those very debates from which it tries to move away, the move towards an abstracted view of 'Irishness' does strike one as essentially modernist, signalling what Giles describes as a 'desire to pass beyond what is merely local and contingent' in order to instigate a rediscovery of 'ritual and myth'.[74] By taking solace in the 'Irish and romantic and illogical', Fitzgerald comes closer to countering the rational fear, expressed through the mouthpiece of Amory at the end of *This Side of Paradise*, that modernity sees 'all Gods dead, all wars fought, all faiths in man shaken'.[75] This version of 'Irishness', completely fictional and entirely illusory, is derived from a mythology of Fitzgerald's own making. But does this matter, if entertaining such illusions aids Fitzgerald, in his quest for enchantment, to escape the creeping ennui … and write?

John Steinbeck (1902–68)

What Ebest describes as 'the autobiographical nature of Fitzgerald's work' is paralleled by the strong autobiographical strain of those of John Steinbeck's writings that engage with his Irish heritage or his interest in Irish culture.[76] In discussing Steinbeck's early drafts for his 1952 novel *East of Eden*, Jackson J. Benson relates the writer's interest in his Irish background to the development of his craft in the 1950s: 'At one point in his preliminary work … he had determined to write a nonfiction history, but then debated with himself about fictionalizing the family history. His work on *Burning Bright*, however, led him into thinking more and more about an extensive personal allegory'. This 'extensive personal allegory', *East of Eden*, was, according to Benson, not 'a departure in a new direction', but in fact 'both an outgrowth of and a culmination to' everything that Steinbeck had written before.[77]

But while the 'culmination' of Steinbeck's personal interest in the Irish side of his heritage is evident in *East of Eden* and in the travel essay 'I go back to Ireland' written during the same period, the specific 'personal allegory' that relates to Steinbeck's fascination with Ireland extends back much further, to the beginning of his career: it is even clear in his first published novel, *Cup of Gold* (1929). The 'personal allegory' that emerges from the writer's relationship with Ireland mediates between his rational and romantic – and factual and fictional – selves, so that the idea of autobiography functions literally and metaphorically within these texts. Although Steinbeck acknowledges that his reliance on Irish models, stories and forms can hinder his critical expression, or hamper his literary goals, there is a sense that he just cannot leave Ireland alone. What emerges is a tentative, and sometimes perilous, balancing act between Steinbeck, Ireland and autobiography that threatens to subsume the other presences – be they plot, language, structure or narrative voice – in these texts, while simultaneously helping us to unravel Steinbeck's complex, often contradictory relationship with the country of his maternal grandparents.[78]

Although it would be incorrect to label Steinbeck as an Irish American – he stressed his paternal German heritage in addition to his maternal Irish side – Ebest's idea of 'personal and social imagination' as related to Irish ethnicity is very useful, as Steinbeck's complex view of Ireland in terms of his idea of autobiography arguably involves a highly imaginative strain.[79] Steinbeck's assertions of his Irish ethnicity are complicated, however, by his pejorative attitude towards southern Irish people. In a letter to his literary representative Elizabeth Otis, sent in November 1935 – in which he refers to the Censorship of Publications Act first passed in Ireland in 1929 – Steinbeck appears concerned to stress his 'pure Ulster' heritage and his distaste for the 'dirty rednecks' of the Irish Free State:

> It is funny that the Irish Free State has me on the censored list. If they knew that my parentage was pure Ulster, they would all the more. The dirty rednecks. Let them be reading their beads and their stomachs full of whiskey, and let them parade under the sun with the cheeks of them stuck out and their knives between the shoulders of good men and the dark come. What did they but run off the stern tip of Ireland like the rats they are and the Orange after them. Free State indeed, and ask any one of the itchy devils are they free of the gray crawlers under their shirts?[80]

Although clearly propelled by the Irish Free State's censorship of his works, Steinbeck shows a distaste for Irish nationalist politics that recalls Gloria's 'loathing' of her maid's glorification of Sinn Fein in Fitzgerald's *The Beautiful and Damned*. Yet while Steinbeck is dismissive and cruel about the southern Irish and their traditions – in a later letter sent to Otis in 1967 he even criticises the 'earnest sleaze of the New York Irish' who celebrate St Patrick's Day[81] – he writes often about his love for the Irish countryside, visits the American filmmaker John Huston in Galway in 1964, and even writes his travelogue essay, 'I go back to Ireland' (1952), which fuses nostalgia with dashed romantic hopes.

This complicated attitude is evident in a letter to his friend Joseph Bryan III, following his 1964 trip to Ireland:

> I would like to go back to Ireland next winter. I liked the west country just fine. Galway and Connemara really exist out of time. On the coast it's rocky poor country. A man has to make a reservation to plant a cabbage on the lee of a stone, but there's more peat – they call it sod or turf – than it needs to keep them warm. And the people are lovely warm people. I feel good there and I should because I guess I'm related to most of them. The west of Ireland is pure Celt, not black like the south. Past and Future have no meaning at all because they're all one, and an old lady is as much your daughter as she is your grandmother. And you know – I talk too much.[82]

Steinbeck seems to stress – or even invent – certain aspects of his heritage, and play down others, if and when it is convenient for him to do so; here he wishes to assert the 'Celtic' side of his inheritance while dismissing the 'south' of Ireland as 'black', referring to Irish of Mediterranean appearance. There are, of course, similarities between this description and Fitzgerald's description of himself as 'black Irish' in the letter to John O'Hara sent in the same year (1935).[83] Yet an Irish Protestant inheritance such as Steinbeck's is arguably much less 'Celtic' in an ethnic sense than a southern Irish, probably Catholic, one: as we have seen, Fitzgerald closely associated his 'Celtic' inheritance with his 'black Irish' side. Moreover, how can Steinbeck be 'related to most of' the Irish in the west of Ireland, when his grandfather hailed from Ulster and his grandmother was 'from Cork and a convert, which made her a fire-eating Protestant', as he claimed in another letter of 1965?[84]

The portrayal of Steinbeck's grandmother Liza in *East of Eden* tells us that she was a force to be reckoned with; in this context, some of his inherited anti-Catholic sentiments seem less surprising. Consider, for example, the extended description in Chapter 5:

> It is amazing how Liza stamped her children. ... She had no experience with men save only her husband, and that she looked upon as a tiresome and sometimes painful duty. A good part of her life was taken up with bearing and raising. Her total intellectual association was the Bible, except the talk of Samuel and her children, and to them she did not listen. In that one book she had her history and her poetry, her knowledge of people and things, her ethics, her morals, and her salvation.[85]

The Hibernian turn of phrase in 'save only her husband', and in the use of gerunds ('bearing and raising'), tells us that this is something of an imitation of Liza's actual words, as we imagine her scolding her extended brood. A significant part of this fierce personality derives from her attachment to the Bible, informing the 'iron zeal' with which she hates 'alcoholic liquors' (p. 45), and marking her out as a Protestant convert, unromantic and almost Calvinist in her 'ethics' and 'morals'. Throughout the novel, she is contrasted with her husband Samuel, who unlike his wife is remarkable for his 'education and his reading, the books he bought and borrowed, his knowledge of things', and 'his interest in poetry and his respect for good writing' (p. 40). We can almost see the two sides of Steinbeck's maternal inheritance – one romantic and poetic, the other dour and Presbyterian – battling for attention in the two (semi-fictionalised) accounts of his Irish grandparents. Nevertheless, Steinbeck's assertion of a 'Celtic' background does extend this dichotomy to near-implausible extremes.

If, though, we regard Steinbeck's 'Celtic' assertions as largely cultural and his 'Ulster' claims as largely ethnic, we can begin to unravel some of the complexities surrounding his affiliations and disaffiliations with Ireland. In the letters cited above, Steinbeck associates the idyllic and pastoral west, a place of magic and temporal and ancestral fusion, with the Celts; whereas he links the 'black Irish' to the southern, Catholic, nationalist population. Steinbeck provides evidence of his interest in ethnic categorisation through describing his own physical features in the essay 'E pluribus unum' from his *America and the Americans* collection. Here he notes that, 'My cheeks are florid, with the tiny vesicles showing through, so characteristic of the Scottish and the North Irish.

But in spite of all this, I have never been taken for a European. And a sensitive European knows instantly that I am an American'.[86] We might recall how Frye Jacobson notes that the aims of the immigration committee established in 1924 desired that immigrants '"looked exactly like Americans"',[87] and note the ways in which the Irish had been physically stereotyped in American periodicals. Consider, for example, the cover illustration of *Judge* magazine, November 1888, entitled 'Uncle Sam is a man of strong features', in which the face of Uncle Sam is constructed from various immigrant groups – and in which the Irishman is short and squat, with a wide face, sunken mischievous eyes and a broad nose.[88]

Whether consciously or unconsciously, Steinbeck's own comments extend the kinds of eugenicist arguments that associated physiognomy with hierarchies of ethnicity. By associating himself with a 'pure Ulster' heritage and dismissing what he perceives as the 'black Irish' of the south, Steinbeck can claim an affiliation with the apparently superior, lionised 'Scotch-Irish' group that is most successfully assimilated into American culture: the group that, according to Edward A. Ross, 'molded our national character'.[89] Although Steinbeck is probably not engaging directly with these arguments, their influence in the period must have led writers to think carefully about questions of ethnicity and assimilation. By allying himself closely with his Ulster side – while somewhat disingenuously incorporating a 'Celtic' inheritance that can provide cultural inspiration – Steinbeck can associate himself with that group that looks most like Americans. Thus he has ensured, to reference his own claims in 'E pluribus unum', that through ethnic and physiognomic coding one might know instantly that he is an American.

The complexities of Steinbeck's identification with Ireland can be traced back to his first efforts as a novelist. Benson notes how even during his college years at Stanford (1919-22), Steinbeck had a 'fondness for leprechauns', while his 'writing and conversation ... were burdened by his Irish whimsy'.[90] He also had a rather unfortunate affection for the parochial Irish-American writer Donn Byrne, author of such epic quest novels as *Messer Marco Polo* (1921).[91] Jay Parini describes the 'overwriting that marred [Steinbeck's] first novel', noting of *Cup of Gold* (1929) that one 'hears in the prose the odd, inflated style used by Donn Byrne'.[92] As a result, the quest narrative of the novel combines a Welsh hero, pirate Henry Morgan, with a grandmother who speaks with an Irish lilt and has the 'second sight'.[93] It follows then, as Benson reports, that Steinbeck's first wife Carol, whom he married in 1930, 'felt that she should discourage the Irish in her husband's writing – which she associated with sentimentality and rhetorical embellishment – and encourage the Prussian, the realistic and disciplined' side, which he derived from his paternal inheritance.[94]

Steinbeck's next significant foray into Irish culture came with his 'play-novelette' *Burning Bright,* performed (to poor critical acclaim) in 1950 and published in 1951, soon after his divorce from his second wife, Gwyn, following her infidelity. Benson stresses the autobiographical elements of *Burning Bright*, which recounts the story of an infertile older man, his young wife and her lover, noting that: 'It was a very dramatic story for him because it was based on his story. He had taken Gwyn's unpleasant revelation, the divorce, and his own breakdown and spent the summer neatly transposing the elements in order to universalize his experience and create a modern allegory'.[95] Steinbeck's personalising of the story is clear even in his reactions to the critics. In a letter to Eugene Solow, Steinbeck complains: 'The critics murdered us. I don't know how long we can stay open but I would not think it would be long. But there you are. I've had it before and I will survive'.[96] Again we have the autobiographical resonances that Benson identifies in Steinbeck's Irish writing, linked to the idea of a personal allegory. But in *Burning Bright* itself, the Irish allusions are literary rather than literal, more subtle than Steinbeck's earlier anecdotes about leprechauns or family quirks. As Benson points out, Steinbeck 'sought to develop a special language for his play, lyrical, and essentially literary, rather than colloquial'.[97]

Robert DeMott has identified Steinbeck's interest in the work of J. M. Synge,[98] which is less surprising when we consider that Donn Byrne also modelled Synge in his early work.[99] Benson, meanwhile, remarks in *The Short Novels of John Steinbeck* that: 'the prose of *Burning Bright* sounds very much like overdone Synge, and the experimental setting changes in the play – putting the same set of characters in three different settings of circus, farm, and sea – may remind us of the combination of farm and sea used by Synge as the setting in his *Riders to the Sea*' (1903).[100] In his essay 'The Play-novelette', which reads essentially as a defence of *Burning Bright* and is often published as a preface to it, Steinbeck describes this new literary form as a means of enabling a writer to set the 'tone' of his work in a more powerful way than he would with just the play form to work with. He notes that whereas George Bernard Shaw tends to 'use the introduction for this purpose', the combined function of the 'play-novelette' would 'integrate tone and play in one entity', giving a greater sense of wholeness to the work itself.[101] Irish drama was clearly in his mind while writing the play.

A close reading of *Burning Bright*, with its fitting subtitle '*A Play in Story Form*', reveals parallels with Synge's dramatic style, and particularly with the language and patterning of *Riders to the Sea*. T. R. Henn notes that, 'The language of *Riders to the Sea* is the simplest of that of any of the six plays [of Synge]... Adjectives are few, and they do their work ... The strength of writing is in the strong pattern of the prose, whose rhythm moulds itself organically to the dramatic pressures'. Henn also sees 'parallelism and balance' in Synge's language, identifying its 'elaborate triple structure, traditional in rhetoric', which is 'reinforced by the strong alliterations'.[102] A short section of dialogue from *Riders to the Sea* – in which Bartley, the one remaining son, discusses the possibility of his brother's body being washed up on the shore – helps to illustrate Henn's argument: 'How would it be washed up, and we after looking each day for nine days, and a strong wind blowing a while back from the west and south?'.[103] Here, the three-part question, a common trope in the play, emphasises the inevitability and circularity of experience – as Bartley will soon also be 'washed up' like his brother. This inevitability is emphasised by the alliterative 'w' sounds, which echo through 'would', 'washed up', 'wind', 'while back' and 'west' to suggest that the brother's fate (and his own) is as predictable as the west of Ireland's weather is cruel. Meanwhile, the paucity of descriptive adjectives – we are given 'strong' to describe the wind, and 'nine' to recall the number of days (again divisible by three) – adds to this haunting sense of inevitability, as if all the characters can do is await their own, unspectacular fate.

Looking closely at the text of *Burning Bright*, we can identify several of the features that Henn notes in *Riders to the Sea*. Firstly, Steinbeck, like Synge, uses few adjectives, and each 'does their work'. This parallel can be noted particularly in Steinbeck's use of colour, where the adjectival/noun pairings are always used in the same way ('black earth', 'white arms') and the same palette is adhered to throughout. *Riders to the Sea*, likewise, uses its own pairings consistently, such as 'white rocks', 'green head', 'grey pony', 'black hags', and 'red mare'.[104] In *Burning Bright* the colours used are green, grey, black, yellow, white, blue, red and brown, the exact palette which is used in *Riders*: surely not a coincidence? Moreover, the prose in *Burning Bright* is heavily patterned, employing an elaborate but not always successful 'triple structure' that also makes considerable use of 'strong alliterations' and parallelism. This can be seen clearly in one of the opening sentences of *Burning Bright*: 'The canvas walls of the dressing-tent were discoloured with brown water spots, with green grass stains and grey streaks of mildew, and the prickles of sun glittering came through'.[105] Judging by the tripartite structure of the sentence, the preponderance of d, g, and s sounds, and the saturation of adjectival/noun colour pairings – 'brown water spots', 'green grass stains', 'grey streaks of mildew' – we note Steinbeck's careful replication of Synge's patternings, which enable the allusions to Synge's play about love, loss and grief in a remote village off the west coast of Ireland to unite with Steinbeck's own feelings of loss and uncertainty following the breakdown of his marriage. However, and somewhat ironically, this same imitation of Synge, through which Steinbeck tries to reinforce the relationship between his personal autobiography, his maternal family history and his fascination with Irish culture, arguably comes at the expense of his own personal expression. Thus it comes perhaps as no surprise that Benson describes the prose of this highly autobiographical play-novelette as sounding like 'overdone Synge' rather than 'overdone Steinbeck'.[106]

Steinbeck once described *East of Eden* as 'two books – the story of my country and the story of me',[107] thus marking the culmination of the 'extended personal allegory' that he applies to his semi-autobiographical fiction – much of which is related to Ireland. In *Journal of a Novel*, the collection of letters that Steinbeck wrote to his friend and editor Pascal Covici while drafting *East of Eden*, Steinbeck includes a revealing passage about the autobiographical strand of his novel, which deals with his own family:

I can see no reason why I should not tell family stories. They are just as good as they ever were and maybe as I go I will remember more and more of them. But I know that I must put in all of the lore and anecdote I can. And many of the family stories amount to folklore and will be used for and by the boys. Then they will know their family. I think I will put [in] a good deal of my mother and my father also. It is time I wrote these things, else they will be gone because no one else will ever do them except me.[108]

This sentiment is translated to the opening passages of the novel itself which, although Steinbeck claims in *Journal of a Novel* that 'all of the Hamilton stories are true',[109] actually point to a combination of folklore and family history in the narration of the story of Steinbeck's grandfather, Samuel Hamilton: 'I must depend on hearsay, on old photographs, on stories told, and on memories which are hazy and mixed with fable in trying to tell you about the Hamiltons'.

Yet this sentence is closely followed by an assertive passage that rings with almost biblical authority while adopting a folkloric tone:

> Young Samuel Hamilton came from the north of Ireland and so did his wife. He was the son of small farmers, neither rich nor poor, who had lived on one landhold and in one stone house for many hundreds of years. The Hamiltons managed to be remarkably well educated and well read; and, as is so often true in that green country, they were connected and related to very great people and very small people, so that one cousin might be a baronet and another cousin a beggar. And of course they were descended from the ancient kings of Ireland, as every Irishman is.[110]

What is particularly ironic about this passage is that despite a slightly self-mocking conclusion, its combination of nostalgia and idealism for Ireland and the Irish betrays the same wistfulness that Steinbeck criticises elsewhere. For example, just four years after writing *East of Eden*, Steinbeck noted in a letter to Pascal Covici that, 'I think I told you that I want to leave the past and the nostalgic. It is the disease of modern writing';[111] while in the same letter, sent in 1967 to Elizabeth Otis, where he criticised the 'earnest sleaze' of the New York Irish, Steinbeck also mocked their homesickness 'for a place that never existed'.[112] Such a place certainly seems to exist in the folklore of *East of Eden*, while Steinbeck's eulogising of his Irish family – and particularly his grandfather – even extends famously to Samuel Hamilton's Chinese housekeeper, Lee. As Benson puts it, 'the blarney-philosophy of the Chinese houseboy Lee ... has become the particular target of academic sarcasm'.[113]

Steinbeck's 1952 travel essay 'I go back to Ireland' was published shortly after *East of Eden*, and has similar preoccupations. Describing a sort of pilgrimage that Steinbeck made to the north of Ireland to dig up his Irish roots, the essay includes the story of a sexton who gave Steinbeck a single rose taken from a grave of one of his ancestors. Steinbeck notes of this rose, 'And that's the seat of my culture and the origin of my being and the soil of my background, the one full-blown evidence of a thousand years of family. I have it pressed in a book'.[114] But of course Steinbeck has already pressed his family into a book – in a highly personal attempt, in *East of Eden*, to remember the Hamiltons; as Steinbeck claims in *Journal of a Novel*, 'It is time I wrote these things, else they will be gone because no one else will ever do them except me'.[115] Yet perhaps this personal conviction comes, to some extent, at the cost of literary self-awareness. Is it mere accident, for example, that *Cup of Gold* was a critical failure; that *Burning Bright* had the merest of runs;[116] and that the film version of *East of Eden* ignored almost entirely the story of the Hamiltons?[117] In some ways, then, Steinbeck's preoccupation with Ireland, and his continued enchantment with his maternal background, risked inhibiting his literary development – and his critical success.

Marianne Moore (1887–1972)

The subjective elements of Steinbeck's experience of Ireland – almost entirely related to his maternal family connections and his interests in specific Irish writers – might be compared with Marianne Moore's personal relationship with Irish literature and culture, and her quixotic approach to the idea of Irish ancestry. Fiona Green sums up this approach by noting that, 'The roots to which Moore traces her ancestry ... seem especially flexible'.[118] A recent biographical entry on Moore points out that although Moore is 'typically regarded as an American writer, she expresses a persistent affinity with the Ireland of her distant inheritance'.[119] Moore had first referred to this inheritance in a letter to Ezra Pound, written near the beginning of her poetic career on 9 January 1919. Pound had written to Moore, asking the younger poet to describe not only her background, but also her physical and racial characteristics.[120] She replied, by way of introduction: 'I am glad to give you personal data and hope that the bare facts I have to offer, may not cause work that I may do from time to time, utterly to fail in interest'. These 'bare facts' included that she was born in 1887 and brought up in the home of her grandfather, and that she 'was graduated from Bryn Mawr' in 1909. Moore added, in response to Pound's query concerning whether she was African in origin, like the elephant she describes in 'Black Earth' (1918), that the poem 'was written about an elephant that I have, named Melanchthon'; and that 'contrary to your impression, I am altogether a blond and have red hair'.[121]

But the 'personal data' and 'bare facts' of Moore's letter also include an oft-quoted, though somewhat unclear, description of her heritage: 'I am Irish by descent, possibly Scotch also, but purely Celtic'. Here 'possibly' and 'purely' seem to contradict each other, so that the reader is left unsure of exactly what Moore means by the adjectives 'Scotch' and 'Celtic'. In contrast, the 'I am' of 'I am Irish' appears strident, though it is undermined by the relative uncertainty of the apparent qualifiers that follow. This enlightening but evasive letter exposes Moore's precision concerning the 'bare facts' of her adolescence and adulthood when contrasted with her imprecise description of her racial and cultural inheritances. Discussing the letter, Cristanne Miller commends Moore's 'deliberate avoidance' of 'racist or nativist labels' such as 'white' or 'American', and suggests that Moore offers 'instead "Irish by descent" and "blond" (with red hair)'.[122] It is likely that Moore was embarrassed by having to respond to the racist question Pound had asked her in his letter, considering whether she was 'a jet-black Ethiopian, Othello-hued'; in a later letter he would admit to being relieved by her answer.[123] At the same time, however, Moore appears keen to please the older poet, and to gain his good opinion – after all, she had only been an established poet since 1915, when her poems were first published in *The Egoist*. Perhaps, then, Moore includes in her answer the descriptors 'purely Celtic' and 'altogether a blond' as a means of confirming that she is Caucasian, and therefore giving Pound the answer he expects, without addressing the question directly.

Despite Moore's claim that this information represents 'bare facts', investigations into Moore's family background point instead to her relatively weak connection to Ireland.[124] Moore's biographer Charles Molesworth discusses the poet's 1964 trip to Ireland, claiming that during her trip Moore visited 'the house their grandfather had been born in' in Merrion Square, Dublin: but this is incorrect.[125] In her memoir of Moore, Elizabeth Bishop recounts Moore's connection to Dublin: 'she liked being of Irish descent; her great-great-grandfather had run away from a house in Merrion Square, Dublin'.[126] Moore's diary records that she visited Merrion Square, taking photographs of 10 Merrion Square during a trip to Dublin on 7 October 1964.[127] Yet Moore's family connection with the address is historical rather than enduring. A typed 'Autobiography' written by Moore's great uncle Henry Warner, found among Moore's papers, gives further clues about the identity of Moore's distant Dublin relatives. Henry Warner describes his 'paternal grand-father', another Henry Warner, as 'an Irish gentleman of wealth and leisure who resided in the City of Dublin, Ireland'. In the 'Autobiography', Warner describes how his own father, the son of this Dublin gentleman, 'ran away and enlisted, as a common sailor before the mast' at the age of twelve, eventually travelling to America, and settling in Pittsburgh, Pennsylvania.[128] The evidence points to the fact that, as Bishop suggests, Moore's tearaway great-great-grandfather is her closest Dublin ancestor. Moore continued to celebrate her link to Merrion Square despite the weakness of the connection. In a letter sent to Moore by the Irish-American academic John L. Sweeney in 1959, regarding a lecture on American poetry that he was planning to give, he proposed 'to mention to the Dublin audience that Merrion Square is an ancestral association of yours'.[129] Why did Moore, then, according to Bishop, like 'being of Irish descent', and why did she celebrate her historical connections with Dublin?[130]

To understand the reasons behind Moore's self-description as detailed to Pound, we need to assess its value as a racial and cultural claim. According to the 'Autobiography' of Henry Warner, Moore's nearest Irish-born relative on her mother's side was her great grandfather, also named Henry Warner, who was born in Kells, County Meath, in 1795, while her maternal great-grandmother, Mary Riddle, was born in County Monaghan in 1803.[131] Moore's great-grandparents on the side of her maternal grandmother were William Craig (1794–1855) and Mary Vance Watson (1798–1878), both born in Pennsylvania. A book Moore kept in her library, *Five Typical Scotch-Irish Families of the Cumberland Valley* written by her cousin Mary Craig Shoemaker, describes how the Craig family emigrated from Ulster and settled in Pennsylvania, forming a settlement 'known as "Craigs" or "The Irish Settlement"'.[132] In *The Scotch-Irish in Pennsylvania and Kentucky*, Billy Kennedy traces the Craig family to eighteenth-century Philadelphia, and emphasises their Presbyterian background. It is likely that Moore's maternal grandmother, Jane Craig, was descended from this Presbyterian family. Kennedy also gives examples of the intermarriage of the Boyd and Craig families: this tradition continued to subsequent generations as Moore's maternal great-great-grandfather John Craig (d.1801) married Jean Boyd.[133]

Bearing this information in mind, it becomes difficult to see how Moore's racial inheritance might be described accurately as 'Irish by descent, possibly Scotch also, but purely Celtic'. Henry Warner traces the Warner family to Dublin, Kells and County Monaghan, while Mary Shoemaker and Billy Kennedy trace the Craig family back to Ulster, and possibly to Donegal. Geographically speaking, then, Moore's ancestry on her mother's side was Irish. Yet one might be tempted to describe this background, as it is largely Protestant on both sides, as a mixture of Anglo-Irish and Scotch-Irish.[134] A further complication arises upon investigating Moore's paternal background. A printed piece, a 'History of the Moore family', found among Moore's papers at the Rosenbach, describes the English ancestry of the Moore family. It explains how a distant ancestor 'Thomas More [sic] came over in a boat named the "Mary and John" from London, England, in 1630'.[135]

By deducing from the evidence that Moore's racial background is a mixture of Anglo-Irish, Ulster/Scots-Irish and English, and considering this alongside her own self-description as 'Irish by descent, possibly Scotch also, but purely Celtic', we can see how the latter represents a simplification of the racial and linguistic complexities that shape her inheritance. Indeed in Moore's claims there are echoes of Steinbeck's own confused racial and cultural claims of an Ulster descent and a 'Celtic' inheritance. But despite Moore's apparently oversimplified affiliations, Ireland played an important role in her familial and cultural lives. Tellingly, the part of Moore's ancestry that was southern Irish was that of her grandfather, Reverend John Riddle Warner, with whom Moore and her brother lived when they were growing up. A letter to the Reverend Warner from his sister Anne in 1854 describes an impending visit from family friends in Ireland, suggesting that the Warner family had immediate links with Ireland in the decades preceding Moore's birth.[136] These links, however tentative by the time Moore reached adulthood, would prove significant. Brian O'Doherty, summarising an interview with Moore for Dublin's *University Review* in 1956, explains how Moore stressed the importance of her Irish 'roots': 'She spoke … of poetry, of her Irish origins, which she felt important; "one must not forget one's roots" she said again and again'.[137] It is significant that Moore's 'Irish origins' were as important to her in 1956 as they had been back in 1919.

Moore's archive at the Rosenbach Museum and Library, Philadelphia, contains a wealth of books, letters and clippings from newspapers on Irish subjects. Her clippings files, for example, contain articles on Edmund Burke, James Joyce, George Moore, Shaw, James Stephens, Oscar Wilde and Yeats. Moreover her private library includes works by Joseph Campbell, Pádraic Colum, Maria Edgeworth, Oliver Goldsmith, Joyce, George Moore, Shaw, Stephens, L. A. G. Strong, Synge, Wilde and Yeats, many of which are first or collectors' editions.[138] Taking into account this enduring interest in Irish and Celtic culture, and her apparent self-identification with the Irish part of her background in particular, we might view Moore's claim of Irish, 'possibly' Scotch and 'purely' Celtic descent, made in 1919, as part of a process of cultural selection from within her racial inheritance that reflected her personal interests and poetic ideas. Moore would have been aware of the significance of such a process. On the one hand, affiliating herself with a particular culture would have meant acknowledging literary influence as a poet, while on the other an assertion of a particular racial inheritance would have meant accepting a qualifying antecedent to her American identity (such as 'Irish-' or 'Scottish-'). Moore maintained her interest in Ireland throughout her life thanks on the one hand to a loyalty to her maternal grandfather's southern Irish background, and on the other to a belief in the value of external cultural experiences to American writing. Cynthia Stamy contends that Moore 'corroborates the essential Americanness of what is garnered abroad', in order to apply this to her poetry.[139] Moore might be viewed, then, as a poet who actively creates an Irish inheritance for herself from which to 'garner' inspiration – in order to shape, and inflect, her distinctive American voice.

Eugene O'Neill (1888–1953)

Unlike Moore, whose claim of a 'purely Celtic' inheritance appears somewhat disingenuous in light of the facts of her family background, the Irish background of Eugene O'Neill is relatively uncontroversial: for, as he points out in a letter to W. B. Yeats in 1926, 'I am Irish on both sides of my family'.[140] In his letters, however, one can still find the same kind of racial language that permeates the correspondence of all the writers discussed in this chapter. For example, in a letter to the Northern Irish playwright St John Ervine sent in 1920, O'Neill describes himself as being 'of undiluted Irish blood on both sides of my family'; while in a 1938 letter to Harry Weinberger he notes that in contrast to his own 'pure Irish' background, his children are 'a weird mixture, racially speaking'.[141] Such language influenced the racial stereotyping of his plays, too. In an early draft of *A Touch of the Poet* we can find evidence of O'Neill toning down his depiction of the Irish Maloy in relation to his physical characteristics:

> [Mickey] Maloy is twenty-six, a typical Irish peasant, with a sturdy physique and an ~~flat, common,~~ amiable cunning, ^and the^ ~~and his~~ mouth ~~is~~ usually set in a half-leering grin ~~of would-be cynicism.~~[142]

Maloy is met by Jamie Cregan, 'As obviously Irish as Maloy'; O'Neill's description is indicative of his belief in the connections between physical and emotional qualities within the Irish character.

Moreover, for O'Neill the Irish and Catholic sides of his inheritance were permanently, and necessarily, entwined. Edward L. Shaughnessy relates this issue to O'Neill's constant awareness of his Irish family inheritance:

> Early and often Eugene O'Neill had been reminded of his Irish heritage. That, it is probably fair to say, was not much different from being

reminded of his Catholic heritage. If one's ethnic and religious origins often shape one's identity, this principle surely held true in the case of O'Neill. The Celtic background appealed to him. Indeed, he took considerable pride in the history of the O'Neills, especially that of the second Earl of Tyrone, Hugh O'Neill. But the Catholic influence of his formative years produced lifelong anguish. He could neither forget his part nor live comfortably in the knowledge of it.[143]

In their biography of O'Neill, Arthur and Barbara Gelb give details of O'Neill's Irish heritage: his father, the actor James O'Neill, was born in Kilkenny in 1846 and emigrated to upstate New York in 1855, while his mother, Ella Quinlan, was born in 1857, the daughter of Irish Catholics who had both immigrated from Ireland. As the Gelbs point out, O'Neill's father 'began to instil in his younger son a profound consciousness of and pride in his pure Irish ancestry from the moment of his birth by bestowing on him a traditional Gaelic name. Eugene is the Anglicization of Eoghan and Eoghan Rudha, or Owen Rae, was the greatest of the O'Neill soldiers to fight the Parliamentarians'.[144] In this context it comes perhaps as little surprise that O'Neill's older brother had been named Edmund Burke after the eighteenth-century Anglo-Irish statesman.

O'Neill's letters, meanwhile, contain many references to his Irish background: references that are often linked, somewhat lightheartedly, to anti-British, nationalistic ideals. Following a poor review of his career by St John Ervine, O'Neill comments in a letter to his dentist and friend J. O. Lief that: 'I am Irish enough at heart to love to see the English make damn fools of themselves, I guess. Ervine is an Orangeman. That makes it even more toothsome.'[145] O'Neill would wade into Irish politics more substantially in a letter to his son, Eugene O'Neill Junior, in 1940: 'Of course, if Ireland is invaded, I shall probably volunteer at once – or might if I was sure the great majority there wouldn't welcome the Nazis with howls of joy! Remembering the Black and Tan atrocities committed by the British not so many years ago, it would hardly be surprising. One might even call it justice'.[146] Such commentaries make it clear which side he is on.

However towards the end of his life, while suffering from Parkinson's disease, O'Neill takes a more reflective approach, his commentaries becoming more cultural and less political. Writing to Elizabeth Shepley Sergeant in 1944, O'Neill likens his illness to Celtic characteristics: 'The worst part of Parkinson's disease to me is the fits of extreme melancholia that go with it. God knows I have had enough of Celtic Twilight in my make-up without needing any more of the same. And this isn't the same.'[147] A late letter to his son is particularly poignant, as he comments on the 'melancholia' of his family situation:

> My family's quarrels and tragedy were within. To the outer world we maintained an indomitably united front and lied and lied for each other. A typical pure Irish family. The same loyalty occurs, of course, in all kinds of families, but there is, I think, among Irish still close to, or born in Ireland, a strange mixture of fight and hate and forgive, a clannish pride before the world, that is peculiarly its own.[148]

What each example cited here reveals is that throughout his life, O'Neill always related larger Irish concerns – politics, the Celtic Twilight, clannishness – to the peculiarities of his personal Irish Catholic background. Indeed in each case O'Neill makes an effort to enable historical, political and cultural aspects of the Irish experience to mirror his life and art.

It is fitting that Shaughnessy uses a dramatic metaphor to enact the relationship between O'Neill and his Irish background – describing how he could not 'forget his part' in the family history – because for O'Neill, as for Steinbeck, his art becomes at times an autobiographical extension of his concerns. This occurs despite O'Neill's constant protestations to the contrary; for example, a 1935 Press Release by the Theatre Guild, which discusses O'Neill's plans for his new (and ultimately ill-fated) play cycle, notes: 'O'Neill is particularly eager to deny one report that the new play is autobiographical. It is not, in any sense, autobiographical'.[149] Indeed Arthur and Barbara Gelb identify autobiographical elements in O'Neill's two most 'Irish' plays, *Long Day's Journey into Night* (written 1940–41, published posthumously in 1956) and *A Touch of the Poet* (completed 1942, first performed 1958). Of *Long Day's Journey*, they note:

> O'Neill had chosen [the name of] Tyrone to designate his surname because, steeped as he was in Gaelic history and intensely proud of his

undiluted Irish blood, he knew the name was derived from Tir-eoghain, meaning the land of Owen. Owen, who died in A.D. 465, was the ancestor of the O'Neills who for centuries ruled over a section of Ulster, including the part that later became County Tyrone.[150]

Similarities between the Tyrones of *Long Day's Journey* and the professional and personal set-up of the O'Neills are well known. The setting, a summer home in Connecticut, corresponds to the O'Neill family home in New London, Connecticut; despite a few name changes, the ages of the characters in the year of the play (1912) correspond to the ages of the O'Neill family in August 1912;[151] and James O'Neill, like the James Tyrone of the play, had been a promising young actor. Even the opening stage directions, which describe the shelves in the living room of 'James Tyrone's summer house' as containing 'several histories of Ireland' which all 'have the look of having been read and re-read', might have been recounting the reading practices of O'Neill and his father.[152] For instance, the Gelbs note how 'from early adolescence Eugene had been devouring the books in his father's library' including 'the Irish romantic, Charles Lever, and the volumes of Irish history with which James's library was studded'.[153] Paul Giles also identifies autobiographical strains in *Long Day's Journey*, identifying in the play a 'nostalgia for the European homeland', an 'attachment to the shaping spirit of ancestry' and 'a tendency toward alcoholism'.[154]

Less noted, however, are the similarities between *A Touch of the Poet* and O'Neill's own family background; but they are arguably just as difficult to ignore. In a review of a performance of the play in Stockholm in 1957, Alan Cole noted in the *New York Herald Tribune*, that, '[the main character] Cornelius Melody might be the grandfather of James O'Neill himself. In all of O'Neill's heroes … one senses a touch of the poet'. But Cole's review also opens a vein of argument that might mitigate some of the claims of autobiographical resonance, as he concludes that 'In Cornelius Melody one senses also a touch of the Irish and of the American, when that word was new'. He had opened the review with the comment that 'All [O'Neill's plays] together explain much about America to Americans, much that O'Neill wanted to sat about America's past and that of his own family's'.[155] For O'Neill, then, the story of his Irish-American family might have appeared to be the story of American families. Fascinatingly, this same argument was echoed by the Hollywood actress Katharine Hepburn, who starred as Mary Tyrone in the 1962 film version of *Long Day's Journey*: 'It's the best darned role I ever played', she claimed, 'But of course, it's the greatest American play ever written'.[156]

What the example of O'Neill tells us is that for some American writers of Irish descent, their family story was intrinsically connected, for them at least, to the story of America – as if his 'Irish family' could become a metonym for the American family. And in this light, it is possible even to see how O'Neill could deny the autobiographical bent of his stories: if we were to take Hepburn's argument as befitting O'Neill's desire, as a playwright, to write the great American play, we might see how in doing (or trying to do) this, in plays such as *Long Day's Journey* he might be telling the story of his archetypal American family – of which his family is merely a representation.

★

In Fitzgerald, Steinbeck, Moore and O'Neill we are presented with very different examples of how twentieth-century American writers engage with their familial Irish inheritance, and represent this 'family feeling' in their work.[157] In each case, however, as befits a period in which the idea of 'America' is being contested, and when there is growing suspicion about immigration and multiculturalism, each writer seems to sense a necessity to forge a cultural relationship with the Ireland of their forebears while disassociating themselves with those aspects of their heritage that they are less comfortable with. Even Fitzgerald and O'Neill, who are descended from Irish immigrant stock – Fitzgerald on his mother's side, O'Neill on both – adopt Irish stereotypes in their work, and attempt to separate themselves from the cliché of the drunken, boorish immigrant that was so ubiquitous during this period. Steinbeck, meanwhile, asserted a 'Celtic' inheritance that denied some of the facts of his Irish Protestant background in order to tap into a rich cultural vein of inspiration, while disassociating himself from the 'black' Irish and their associated politics. Moore, too, was attracted more to the cultural potential of a 'Celtic' inheritance than to the realities of a complex immigrant background, made up of Scotch-Irish, Anglo-Irish, Ulster and English inheritances.

For these writers, Irish cultural identity related on the whole to an idealised country over the Atlantic: and marked a somewhat naïve desire for separation from the racial and social questions that were being asked about Irish immigrants within their own country. However, this 'desire to pass beyond what is merely local and contingent' in order to instigate a rediscovery of 'ritual and myth', as Paul Giles puts it,[158] is strengthened by each writer's modernist aspirations: as in each case, their enchantment with Ireland – and the illusions of romance and possibility that this enchantment can provide – offers them an irresistible, and sometimes incurable, escape from the disillusionment of everyday life.

Notes

1 Louis MacNeice, *Autumn Journal*, XVI, ll. 65–6, in *Collected Poems*, ed. E. R. Dodds. London: Faber, 1966, pp. 101–53 (131–4).
2 Paul Giles, *American Catholic Arts and Fictions: Culture, Ideology, Aesthetics*. Cambridge: Cambridge University Press, 1992, p. 119. Giles quotes from p. 196 of *This Side of Paradise*. London: Penguin, 2000.
3 Marianne Moore to Ezra Pound, 9 January 1919, *The Selected Letters of Marianne Moore*, ed. Bonnie Costello, Celeste Goodridge and Cristanne Miller. London: Faber, 1998, pp. 122–5 (122).
4 Eugene O'Neill to Harry Weinberger, 8 March 1938, *Selected Letters of Eugene O'Neill*, ed. Travis Bogard and Jackson R. Bryer. New Haven and London: Yale University Press, 1988, pp. 475–6 (476).
5 Ron Ebest, *Private Histories: The Writing of Irish Americans, 1900–1935*. Notre Dame, Indiana: University of Notre Dame Press, 2005, p. 6.
6 F. Scott Fitzgerald to John O'Hara, 18 July 1935, *Letters of F. Scott Fitzgerald*, ed. Andrew Turnbull. Harmondsworth: Penguin, 1968, p. 522.
7 John Steinbeck to Elizabeth Otis, 3 November 1935, *Steinbeck: a Life in Letters*, ed. Elaine Steinbeck and Robert Wallsten. Harmondsworth: Penguin, 2001, pp. 116–17.
8 See Fitzgerald, *The Great Gatsby*, with an introduction by Tony Tanner. London: Penguin, 2000, p. 18.
9 Matthew Frye Jacobson, *Whiteness of a Different Colour: European Immigrants and the Alchemy of Race*. Cambridge, Massachusetts and London: Harvard University Press, 1998, p. 78.
10 Fitzgerald, *The Great Gatsby*, p. 18.

11 See Fitzgerald, *The Great Gatsby*, pp. 18, 12, 49, 51, 116.
12 Madison Grant, *The Passing of the Great Race*, introduction to fourth revised edition. London: G. Bell and Sons, Ltd., 1921, pp. xxxi, xxxii.
13 Edward A. Ross, *The Old World in the New: The Significance of Past and Present Immigration to the American People*. New York: The Century Co., 1914, pp. 13, 26–7.
14 W. Lloyd Warner and Leo Srole, *The Social Systems of American Ethnic Groups* (Yankee City Series, Vol. III). New Haven: Yale University Press, 1945, p. 290.
15 Grant, *The Passing of the Great Race*, table insert between pp. 122 and 123.
16 See *Oxford English Dictionary* online (www.oed.com): 'Irish: B1a.', elliptical uses of 'Irish'.
17 Fitzgerald to Edmund Wilson, 26 September 1917 and Fall 1917, *Letters*, pp. 337–9 (337), and pp. 339–41 (341).
18 Marianne Moore, 'Spenser's Ireland' (1941), *Complete Poems*, ed. Clive Driver. London: Faber, 1987, pp. 112–14, ll. 18–21.
19 Letter cited in Laura O'Connor, 'Flamboyant reticence: an Irish incognita', in *Critics and Poets on Marianne Moore: 'A Right Good Salvo of Barks'*, ed. Linda Leavell, Cristanne Miller, and Robin G. Schulze. Lewisburg: Bucknell University Press, 2005, pp. 165–83 (note 9, pp. 179–80).
20 Moore, 'Pym', first published in *Tipyn O'Bob*, 5 (January 1908), 13–17; reprinted in *The Complete Prose of Marianne Moore*, ed. Patricia Willis. London: Faber, 1987, pp. 12–16 (15).
21 Ruth Benedict, *Patterns of Culture*. First published 1934; London: Routledge and Kegan Paul, 1961, p. 11.
22 Frye Jacobson, *Whiteness of a Different Colour*, p. 96.
23 John F. Callahan, *The Illusions of a Nation: Myth and History in the Novels of F. Scott Fitzgerald*. London and Chicago: University of Illinois Press, 1972, p. 3.
24 Grant, *The Passing of the Great Race*, p. 58.
25 Callahan, *Illusions of a Nation*, p. 13.
26 Ben Howard, *The Pressed Melodeon: Essays on Modern Irish Writing*. Brownsville, Oregon: Story Line Press, 1996, p. xi.
27 Turnbull, *The Letters of Scott Fitzgerald*, p. 12.
28 See Fitzgerald, *The Beautiful and Damned*, ed. Alan Margolies. Oxford: Oxford University Press, 2009, note p. 350, and title page.
29 See Princeton University Library's list of books owned by F. Scott Fitzgerald. The list can be accessed at: http://infoshare1.princeton.edu/rbsc2/misc/Fitzgerald.pdf.

30 Fitzgerald to Leslie, February 1918, and Fitzgerald to Wilson, Fall 1917, *Letters*, pp. 393, 340.
31 See Fitzgerald, *This Side of Paradise*, with an introduction by Patrick O'Donnell. London: Penguin, 2000, pp. 147–8.
32 James L. West III, *The Making of This Side of Paradise*. Philadelphia: University of Pennsylvania Press, 1983, p. 56.
33 Father Sigourney Fay to Fitzgerald, 10 December 1917, in *Correspondence of F. Scott Fitzgerald*, ed. Matthew J. Bruccoli and Margaret M. Duggan. New York: Random House, 1980, pp. 23–4 (23).
34 Fitzgerald, *This Side of Paradise*, p. 145.
35 Leslie to Fitzgerald, 3 September 1920, *Correspondence*, pp. 66–7 (66).
36 Fitzgerald to Leslie, 17 September 1920, *Letters*, pp. 397–8.
37 Fitzgerald, *This Side of Paradise*, p. 192.
38 Jack Hendriksen, *This Side of Paradise as a Bildungsroman*. New York: Peter Lang, 1993, p. 130.
39 O'Donnell, introduction to *This Side of Paradise*, p. xii.
40 See Callahan, *Illusions of a Nation*, p. 4; Callahan refers to Fitzgerald's personal copy of *Dubliners*, archived in the Fitzgerald papers at Princeton.
41 O'Donnell, *This Side of Paradise*, p. xxii.
42 Fitzgerald, *This Side of Paradise*, pp. 259–60.
43 James Joyce, *A Portrait of the Artist as a Young Man*, with an introduction and notes by Seamus Deane. Harmondsworth: Penguin, 1992, pp. 275–6.
44 O'Donnell, *This Side of Paradise*, p. xxi.
45 Fitzgerald, *This Side of Paradise*, p. 260.
46 Giles, *American Catholic Arts and Fictions*, p. 119.
47 See Callahan, *Illusions of a Nation*, p. 4; Callahan refers to Fitzgerald's personal copy of *Dubliners*, archived in the Fitzgerald papers at Princeton University Library.
48 O'Donnell, *This Side of Paradise*, p. xxi.
49 Charles Fanning, *The Irish Voice in America: Irish-American Fiction from the 1760s to the 1980s*. Lexington, Kentucky: University of Kentucky Press, 1990, p. 248.
50 Giles, *American Catholic Arts and Fictions*, p. 179.
51 Callahan, *The Illusions of a Nation*, p. 60.
52 Fitzgerald to Edmund Wilson, January 1922, *Letters*, pp. 350–2 (351–2).
53 Edmund Wilson, 'F. Scott Fitzgerald', *Bookman*, 55 (March 1922), 20–5; collected in *The Shores of Light: A Literary Chronicle of the Twenties and Thirties* (London: W. H. Allen, 1952), pp. 27–35 (30–1). Wilson is actually quoting an Irish character, Doyle, who makes a speech on the

difference between the English and the Irish in Shaw's play *John Bull's Other Island* (1904).
54 Fitzgerald to John O'Hara, 18 July 1933, *Letters*, p. 522.
55 Arthur Mizener, citing Kenneth Eble (later author of *Scott Fitzgerald*, 1977), in *Scott Fitzgerald and His World*. London: Thames and Hudson, 1972, p. 5.
56 Fitzgerald, *The Beautiful and Damned*, p. 75.
57 See 'A lament for a foster son, and he going to the War against the King of foreign', in *This Side of Paradise*, pp. 147–8 (and discussions above).
58 Fanning, *The Irish Voice in America*, p. 252.
59 Fitzgerald, *The Beautiful and Damned*, p. 226.
60 Fitzgerald, *This Side of Paradise*, p. 192.
61 Fitzgerald, *Tender is the Night*, ed. Arnold Goldman. London: Penguin, 2000, p. 28. I use the original, non-chronological version of the story, rather than the revised, chronological version (1951), throughout this chapter.
62 Fitzgerald, *The Great Gatsby*, p. 18 (and see discussions above).
63 See Fitzgerald to John O'Hara, 18 July 1933, *Letters*, p. 522 (and discussions above).
64 See Fitzgerald, *The Beautiful and Damned*, p. 75 (and discussions above).
65 Giles, *American Catholic Arts and Fictions*, p. 179. Giles comments on the same letter from Fitzgerald to O'Hara (1933) that is discussed here.
66 Fitzgerald, *Tender is the Night*, pp. 81, 158, 181.
67 Fitzgerald, *The Last Tycoon*, ed. Edmund Wilson. London: Penguin, 2001, pp. 29, 9.
68 Robert E. Rhodes, 'F. Scott Fitzgerald: All my fathers', *Irish-American Fiction: Essays in Criticism*, ed. Daniel J. Casey and Robert E. Rhodes. New York: AMS Press, 1979, pp. 29–51 (47).
69 Fitzgerald, *The Last Tycoon*, p. 80.
70 Rhodes, 'All my fathers', p. 49.
71 Ebest, *Private Histories*, pp. 100–1.
72 Fitzgerald to John O'Hara, 18 July 1933, *Letters*, p. 522 (and see discussions above).
73 Fanning, *The Irish Voice in America*, p. 248.
74 Giles, *American Catholic Arts and Fictions*, pp. 119, 121.
75 See Fitzgerald, *Tender is the Night*, p. 181, *This Side of Paradise*, p. 260 (and discussions above).
76 Ebest, *Private Histories*, p. 101.
77 Jackson J. Benson, *The True Adventures of John Steinbeck, Writer* (London: Heinemann, 1984), pp. 666, 668.
78 Jackson J. Benson claims that although Steinbeck's grandfather Samuel Hamilton was born in Northern Ireland, his wife (Elizabeth Fayes) was

born in the USA, though her family was from the north; this appears to contradict Steinbeck's claim (cited below) that his grandmother hailed from Cork: see Benson, *True Adventures*, p. 15.
79 Ebest, *Private Histories*, p. 6 (and see fuller citation above).
80 Steinbeck to Elizabeth Otis, 3 November 1935, *A Life in Letters*, pp. 116–17.
81 Steinbeck to Elizabeth Otis, 18 March 1967, *A Life in Letters*, p. 846.
82 Steinbeck to Joseph Bryan III, 14 March 1965, *A Life in Letters*, pp. 815–16 (815).
83 Fitzgerald to O'Hara, 18 July 1935, *Letters of F. Scott Fitzgerald*, p. 522. See also discussions of 'black Irish' above.
84 Steinbeck to John Huston and Gladys Hill, 17 February 1965, *A Life in Letters*, pp. 807–8.
85 Steinbeck, *East of Eden*. First published 1952; London: Pan, 1963, p. 44.
86 Steinbeck, 'E Pluribus Unum', in *America and the Americans*, reprinted in *Of Men and their Making: The Selected Non-fiction of John Steinbeck*, ed. Susan Shillingshaw and Jackson J. Benson. London: Allen Lane/Penguin, 2002, pp. 319–29 (324).
87 Frye Jacobson, *Whiteness of a Different Colour*, p. 78 (and see fuller note above).
88 'Uncle Sam is a man of strong features', illustration in *Judge*, 35, no. 893 (26 November 1888).
89 Ross, *The Old World in the New*, p. 13.
90 Benson, *True Adventures*, p. 42.
91 See Donn Byrne, *Messer Marco Polo*. Charleston, South Carolina: Forgotten Books, 2008.
92 Jay Parini, *John Steinbeck: A Biography*. London: Heinemann, 1994, pp. 52, 106.
93 See, for example, the description of Henry's grandmother, 'holding her necromantic court': 'For many years, now, she had been practicing the second sight and taking pride in it': Steinbeck, *Cup of Gold – A Life of Henry Morgan, Buccaneer, With Occasional Reference to History*. New York: Robert M. McBride and Company, 1929, p. 3.
94 Benson, *True Adventures*, p. 20.
95 Ibid., p. 643.
96 Steinbeck to Eugene Sollow (adapter of *Of Mice and Men* for the screen), 21 October 1950, *A Life in Letters*, pp. 412–13 (412).
97 Benson, *True Adventures*, p. 647.
98 See Robert DeMott, *Steinbeck's Reading: A Catalogue of Books Owned and Borrowed*. New York and London: Garland Publishing, 1984. De Mott records that Steinbeck owned Synge's complete works (p. 108), and notes

that Steinbeck was making comparisons between Byrne and Synge in correspondence as early as 1928 (p. 175).
99 Charles Fanning, for example, discusses the realism of Byrne's early works, comparing his short story 'The Wake' with Synge's *In The Shadow of the Glen* (1903); see Fanning, *The Irish Voice in America*, p. 246.
100 Benson (ed.), *The Short Novels of John Steinbeck*. Durham and London: Duke University Press, 1990, p. 5.
101 See Steinbeck, 'The Play-novelette', in *Of Men and Their Making*, pp. 155–7 (155–6).
102 T. R. Henn, introduction to *Riders to the Sea* (in a joint volume with *In the Shadow of the Glen*) by J. M. Synge. London: Methuen, 1961, pp. 18–19, 19.
103 See Synge, *Riders to the Sea*, in *Collected Works, Volume III: Plays, Book I*, ed. Ann Saddlemyer. Gerrards Cross, Colin Smythe, 1982, p. 9.
104 See Synge, *Riders to the Sea*, whole play, pp. 1–27.
105 Steinbeck, *Burning Bright: A Play in Story Form* (first published 1951), in *Travels with Charley and Later Novels, 1947–1962*. New York: Library of America, 2007, pp. 229–96 (235).
106 See Benson, *Short Novels*, p. 5.
107 Steinbeck, *Journal of a Novel: The East of Eden Letters*. Harmondsworth: Penguin, 2001, p. 3.
108 Steinbeck, *Journal of a Novel*, pp. 8–9. 'The boys' refers to Steinbeck's two sons, Thom and John, with Gwyndolyn Conger.
109 Steinbeck, *Journal of a Novel*, p. 63.
110 Steinbeck, *East of Eden*, p. 2.
111 Steinbeck to Pascal Covici, February 1956, *Life in Letters*, p. 520.
112 Steinbeck, *Life in Letters*, p. 846.
113 Benson, *True Adventures*, p. 732.
114 John Steinbeck, 'I go back to Ireland', first published in *Collier's*, 31 January 1953, reprinted in *Of Men and their Making: The Selected Non-fiction of John Steinbeck*, ed. Susan Shillingshaw and Jackson J. Benson. London: Allen Lane/Penguin, 2002, pp. 262–9 (269).
115 Steinbeck, *Journal of a Novel*, pp. 8–9.
116 See also Steinbeck's responses to his critics in 'Critics, critics, burning bright', *Saturday Review of Literature* (11 November 1950), 20–1; and E. W. Tedlock and C. V. Wicker (eds), *Steinbeck and his Critics: A Record of Twenty-Five Years*. Albuquerque: University of New Mexico Press, 1957.
117 The film version of *East of Eden* was produced in 1955 and directed by Elia Kazan, starring James Dean, with a screenplay by Paul Osborn. It focuses on the story of brothers Cal and Aron and their wayward,

psychopathic mother Cathy. Samuel Hamilton has a small role, and there are some references to the Hamiltons as a 'family of inventors', but the family's 'Irish' heritage is downplayed and the other family members feature only briefly in the story.

118 Fiona Green, '"Your trouble is their trouble": Marianne Moore, Maria Edgeworth and Ireland', *Symbiosis: A Journal of Anglo-American Literary Relations*, 1.2 (October 1997), 173–85 (174).
119 Jo Gill, 'Moore, Marianne (1887–1972)', *Ireland and the Americas: Culture, Politics, and History*, ed. James P. Byrne, Philip Coleman, and Jason King. Santa Barbara: ABC-Clio, 2008, pp. 611–12.
120 Marianne Moore Archive, Rosenbach Museum and Library ['RML'], Philadelphia, USA, V:50:06, letter from Ezra Pound to Moore, 16 December 1918.
121 Moore to Pound, 9 January 1919, *Selected Letters*, pp. 122–5 (122).
122 Cristanne Miller, *Marianne Moore: Questions of Authority*. Cambridge, Massachusetts: Harvard University Press, 1995, p. 134.
123 Pound to Moore, 16 December 1918, RML V:50:06.
124 I elaborate on this topic further elsewhere; see Tara Stubbs, 'Irish by descent? Marianne Moore's American-Irish inheritance', *IJAS online*, June 2009: www.ijasonline.com/TARASTUBBS.html.
125 Charles Molesworth, *Marianne Moore: A Literary Life*. New York: Atheneum, 1990, p. 425.
126 Elizabeth Bishop, 'Efforts of affection: a memoir of Marianne Moore' (c. 1969), *Bishop: Poems, Prose, and Letters*. New York: Library of America, 2008, pp. 471–99 (481).
127 RML VIII:04:03, Daily Diary 1964, Wednesday 7 October. The diary records that Moore visited 12 Merrion Square but the photographs themselves are apparently of 10 Merrion Square: see RML XII:07:24a–25h.
128 RML, not catalogued, 'The Autobiography of Henry Warner – commenced November 30th 1870. Re-written 1875–76'.
129 RML V:64:37, Moore to John L. ('Jack') Sweeney, 22 January 1959.
130 Bishop, 'Efforts of affection', p. 481.
131 'Autobiography' of Henry Warner, p. 1.
132 Mary Craig Shoemaker, *Five Typical Scotch-Irish Families of the Cumberland Valley*. Pennsylvania: self-published, 1922, p. 45. Kept at Moore's private library at RML.
133 See Billy Kennedy, *The Scotch-Irish in Pennsylvania and Kentucky*. Belfast: Causeway Press, 1998, p. 37; and Shoemaker, p. 57.
134 I use the term 'Scotch-Irish' according to Mary Shoemaker's use of the label to describe families, including the Craigs, who came to America from Scotland by way of Ulster in the eighteenth century.

135 RML, not catalogued, 'History of the Moore Family' by Mittie Moore Sharpe (a distant cousin of Moore), p. 1.
136 RML VI:01:30, Family Correspondence February – June 1854, Annie Warner to John Riddle Warner, 26 May.
137 Brian O'Doherty, 'Poetry and paintings in New York', *University Review*, Dublin 1956: see RML V:46:18, Brian O'Doherty to Moore, 3 May 1958, and enclosed cutting.
138 See Moore's private library at the Rosenbach Museum and Archive ['RML']; and Moore's 'Clippings' files (RML XIV: Britain and Ireland, and Authors A–Z).
139 Cynthia Stamy, *Marianne Moore and China: Orientalism and a Writing of America*. Oxford: Oxford University Press, 1999, p. 33.
140 Eugene O'Neill to W. B. Yeats, 6 January 1926, *Selected Letters*, pp. 230–1 (231).
141 O'Neill to St. John Ervine, *Selected Letters*, p. 116; and to Harry Weinberger, 8 March 1938, *Selected Letters*, p. 436.
142 O'Neill, *A Touch of the Poet*: early draft, Beinecke Rare Book and Manuscript Library, Yale University, YCAL MSS 123, Box 46, folder 969, p. 1.
143 Edward L. Shaughnessy, *Down the Nights and Down the Days: Eugene O'Neill's Catholic Sensibility*. Notre Dame, Indiana: University of Notre Dame Press, 2000, p. 11.
144 Arthur and Barbara Gelb, *O'Neill*. London: Jonathan Cape, 1962, pp. 9, 57–8.
145 O'Neill to J. O. Lief, 7 August 1927, *Selected Letters*, pp. 250–1 (251). Ervine was known for his scathing reviews of O'Neill's work, which would culminate in a notorious commentary in *The Observer* in 1937: 'Mr. O'Neill is, in drama, very much what D. H. Lawrence is in the novel: force without direction. He lets off an immense amount of steam, but the train does not move: it still stands in the station from which it is supposed to be removing at the rate of seventy or eighty miles an hour' (St John Ervine, 'At the play', *The Observer*, 13 June 1937, p. 8).
146 O'Neill to Eugene O'Neill Jnr., 14 July 1940, *Selected Letters*, p. 509.
147 O'Neill to Elizabeth Shepley Sergeant, 4 December 1944, *Selected Letters*, pp. 565–6 (566).
148 O'Neill to Eugene O'Neill Jnr., 7 May 1945, *Selected Letters*, pp. 569–70 (569).
149 Press Release by the Theatre Guild, 1935 [?], Beinecke Rare Book and Music Library, Eugene O'Neill Papers, YCAL MSS 123, Box 44, Folder 946, p. 1.
150 Arthur and Barbara Geld, *O'Neill*, p. 8.

151 The surname, Tyrone, is obviously changed from O'Neill, but further subtle changes are also made: the names of the second and third sons (Edmund and Eugene) are reversed, and the name of O'Neill's mother, Mary Ellen ('Ella') Quinlan, is changed to 'Mary Cavan'.
152 O'Neill, *Long Day's Journey into Night*, in *O'Neill: Complete Plays 1932–1943*. New York: Library of America, 1988, p. 717.
153 Arthur and Barbara Geld, *O'Neill*, p. 88.
154 Giles, *American Catholic Arts and Fictions*, p. 130.
155 Alan Cole, '*A Touch of the Poet* Done in Stockholm', *New York Herald Tribune*, 7 April 1957, Beinecke YCAL MSS 123, Box 46, 982, clippings of reviews and advertisements of *A Touch of the Poet*, 1956–57.
156 Katharine Hepburn cited on a Press Release from Bill Doll & Company to Joseph E. Levine's Embassy Pictures, Beinecke YCAL MSS 124, Box 12, Folder 22.
157 This chapter has not covered in detail Moore's responses to Ireland within her work, as they will be discussed in subsequent chapters.
158 Giles, *American Catholic Arts and Fictions*, pp. 119, 121.

Chapter 2
American modernists and the Celtic Revival

> ... a world that never was,
> Baptised with fairy water[1]

MacNeice's sardonic claim that the 'real' Ireland contrasts with the idealised one – 'a world that never was' – provides a criticism of the mythmaking that surrounds the Celtic Revival, which portrays Ireland as a place 'Baptised with fairy water'. Such suspicion of Celticism had its followers. In *Intellectual America*, Oscar Cargill argues that the surge of Celtic-American idealism that followed Matthew Arnold's Oxford lectures on Celtic literature in the 1860s was later substituted by cynicism following Oscar Wilde's fall from grace.[2] The term 'Celtic Twilight' – as coined by Yeats in his story collection of the same name in 1893 – also came under scrutiny; in the *Oxford English Dictionary*, we find a somewhat mocking comment by Aldous Huxley in his 1923 work *On Margin*: 'If Mr. Yeats understood the Einstein theory ... he too could give us, out of the Celtic twilight, his lyrics of relativity'.[3] Clearly the Celtic Revivalists' lofty aims were drawing their doubters and critics. It is easy, particularly within contemporary critical circles, to dismiss Celticism as a fanciful, archaic construction: as Daniel G. Williams argues, nowadays '"Celticism" is either associated with an outmoded racial conception of identity, or is seen as an internalised form of colonial discourse established in the writings of Ernest Renan and Matthew Arnold'.[4]

But for some American modernist writers, the enchantment of Celticism – as conveyed and celebrated by the Revivalists – offered a certain promise despite, or even because of, its unreality. The efforts of W. B. Yeats, Lady Gregory, Douglas Hyde and J. M. Synge from the late 1880s onwards had done much to revive American writers' interest in

Celtic culture – and to establish a Celtic ideal that influenced different social groups. For example, Tracy Mishkin discusses the tangible effect of the Celtic Revival – as represented by the Abbey Theatre's efforts in America – on the efforts of the proponents of the Harlem Renaissance:

> [T]he Abbey's representations of Irish life caught the imagination of those Americans interested in exploring the various facets of their own identity, including several people, black and white, who went on to participate in the Harlem Renaissance of the 1920s. They noted the many similarities between Irish culture and history and those of the African Americans, and they advocated following the Irish model for literary renaissance and social change.

Mishkin goes on to argue that W. E. B. DuBois was inspired to found the Krigwa Players (later named the Negro Experimental Theatre) as part of the 'Little Theatre' movement that was itself inspired by the Abbey's American tours.[5] Similarly, James Weldon Johnson celebrated the Celtic Revivalists in his Preface to *The Book of American Negro Poetry* (1922): 'What the colored poet in the United States needs to do is something like what Synge did for the Irish; he needs to find a form that will express the racial spirit by symbols from within rather than symbols from without'.[6] An alternative, though racially essentialist, view is offered by James P. Cantrell's overview of southern literature, where he argues that 'Celtic folkways and heritage formed a significant basis in the development of white Southern culture', and notes the influence of Celtic culture on writing by Faulkner, Margaret Mitchell, Flannery O'Connor and others.[7] Yet we might offer a different reading by investigating the cultural interpretation of Celticisim that was pervasive in modernist circles, as writers like Moore, Steinbeck and Stevens became inspired by the folklore and history surrounding the Revival. This chapter, then, investigates some of the ways in which Celtic Revivalism shaped, and was in turn reshaped, by, the works of American modernist writers.

The Celtic Revival in the USA

Tracy Mishkin notes that 'Three of the elements important to those who wished to construct an Irish identity were the past, the peasants, and religion'. By emphasising these three elements, Irish nationalists and writers were able 'to distance themselves from what they perceived as the ugly, urban, material life of England'.⁸ The Celtic Revivalists' focus on storytelling played particularly on a love of the past (whether real or mythical), as it centred on stories that returned Ireland to an almost pre-lapsarian state. Lady Gregory, Yeats and Douglas Hyde all produced volumes of Irish stories and folklore from the 1880s onwards: Yeats's *Fairy and Folk Tales of the Irish Peasantry* (1888) and *The Celtic Twilight* (1893) were followed by Hyde's *Love Songs of Connacht* (1893) and Gregory's *Cuchulain of Muirthemne* (1902) and *Gods and Fighting Men* (1904).

In America, the 'pirate' publisher Thomas Bird Mosher (1856–1923) and the New York-based art collector, lawyer and patron John Quinn (1870–1924) promoted heavily the writings and ideals of the Celtic Revivalists. In the last decades of the nineteenth century, and the first of the twentieth, Maine publisher Mosher brought out pirated copies of, among many others, George Meredith's *Modern Love* (1891), Æ's *Homeward: Songs by the Way* (1895), Yeats's *The Land of Heart's Desire* (1903), Wilde's *The Ballad of Reading Gaol* (1904), Katharine Tynan Hinkson's *A Little Book of XXIV Carols* (1907), and two anthologies of poetry, *A Little Garland of Christmas Verse* (1905) and *A Little Garland of Celtic Verse* (1904). Meanwhile John Quinn made strenuous efforts on Yeats's behalf, organising the publication of his work and arranging lecture tours for him in 1903–4. He also promoted Dun Emer (later Cuala) crafts as part of an Irish Industrial Exhibition in New York in 1905; organised Douglas Hyde's tour of the United States in 1905–6; and arranged for the American publication of Lady Gregory's *Gods and Fighting Men*, together with small private editions of Synge's *The Well of the Saints*, *In the Shadow of the Glen*, and *The Playboy of the Western World*. Quinn was also personally responsible for publishing a limited edition of Synge's *Poems and Translations* from the Cuala Press edition following his death in 1909, and producing a limited American edition of Synge's *Deirdre of the Sorrows*. In addition, he was a patron of Dun Emer/Cuala, subscribing to many of their hand-printed volumes.⁹

The works of Yeats, Hyde and Gregory (among many others) were published by Elizabeth Yeats's Cuala Press, established as the Dun Emer Press in 1902 and renamed in 1908. The initial aim of the press was to produce the works of writers associated with the Revival, but in later years it became a kind of exporter of Irish art and culture – for example, a letter from W. B. Yeats's wife George to Irish poet and critic Thomas McGreevy in November 1925 discussed an exhibition of Cuala embroideries that were being shown at the Drapers Hall in London.[10] Margaret Mills Harper describes at length the appeal of private presses like the Cuala, noting how their limited print run was integral to their popularity:

> [I]n that the appeal of such books partakes of the romanticisation of the antique that swept Europe in the wake of industrialisation, exploration, and empire building, their rarity is a sign of the power of the consumer at least as significantly as it is the sign of the power of the artefact. Like ownership of ancient keeps or archaeological treasures, the possession of old knowledge, in old books, bestows value on the owner. So does the possession of newly written knowledge in limited editions, like the ... volumes printed by the Cuala Press. ... We should also note that such value is essentially religious or, more particularly, magical.[11]

Playing on the illustrious image of Celtic culture, and this contemporary desire for a limited edition bound up somehow with a notional 'magical' value, the Cuala Press – which published beautifully illustrated, expensively bound editions of Irish writings, and a subscription-only monthly 'Broadside' – managed to establish a small but loyal following in the United States. Elizabeth Yeats sent Wallace Stevens a Cuala Press edition and translation of the Italian philosopher Mario Rossi's travelogue about Ireland, *Pilgrimage in the West*, in 1934: Stevens mentions this book in several letters,[12] and his daughter Holly Stevens notes that 'private' printers – including the Cuala Press – 'rank high in the list of major correspondents' for Stevens in the mid-1930s.[13]

Stevens had already been in correspondence with the Cuala Press for two decades. Writing to Thomas McGreevy while researching an edition of her father's correspondence, Holly Stevens asked if he might point her in the direction of letters from Stevens to Elizabeth Yeats: 'Apparently my father first wrote to her in 1914, inquiring about the Cuala Press, for I have her note in response, together with some circulars, and a few other notes dating up to 1934'.[14] Meanwhile Marianne Moore wrote to Elizabeth in 1933, describing the lavish production values of the Cuala editions of her brother W. B. Yeats's work: 'NEW

STORIES OF MICHAEL ROBARTES came a week later; and I received from William Jackson poems for music. ... Sometime I hope I shall be asking for other things; the production alone is tempting enough – independent of content'.[15]

During this period Moore and others were displaying interest in the works of Irish short story writers like Joseph Campbell and Pádraic Colum, two Irish exports who, like the Cuala Press, were benefiting directly from the surge of interest in Celtic culture. Both writers gave lectures in New York on folklore and legend, and Colum in particular capitalised on American interests in Irish storytelling and Celtic legend by publishing countless volumes with Macmillan New York. These included *The Island of the Mighty: Being the Hero Stories of Celtic Britain, Retold from the Mabinogion by Pádraic Colum* (1924),[16] *King of Ireland's son* (1925), *The Legend of St. Columba* (1935), and several illustrated texts, which were collaborations with Boris Artzybasheff, such as *The Forge in the Forest* (1925), *The Fountain of Youth* (1927), and *The Frenzied Prince* (1943).

Taking as a source a lecture on Irish storytelling given by Colum entitled 'Story-telling to the Young and Ever Young', which she attended on 20 December 1937, Moore makes considerable use of Colum's stories in her 1941 poem 'Spenser's Ireland'. In a note to the poem, Moore refers to the lecture: 'Line 58: *Earl Gerald*. From a lecture by Padraic [sic] Colum'.[17] 'Earl Gerald' is the subject of the first section of the final stanza of 'Spenser's Ireland', which discusses how in Irish folklore 'Earl Gerald ... changed himself into a stag, into / a great green-eyed cat of the mountain' (ll. 58–61). In the poem, Moore uses Colum's tale of 'Earl Gerald' as the basis for her assertion that Ireland should embrace once again the power of its storytelling with the aim of 'reinstating/ the enchantment' (ll. 19–20). But Moore's notes to Colum's lecture also record how he describes a 'great big stag ... a cat of the mountain w[ith] great green eyes',[18] indicating how she has made further use of Colum's stories throughout the poem. In the second stanza, for example, where she hypothesises that 'in Ireland/ they play the harp backward at need' (ll. 13–14), this is borrowed from Colum's story of a 'Swineheard's son' who 'played the harp backward'. Similarly, Moore's description of the Irish, gathering 'at midday the seed/ of the fern' (ll. 15–16), is taken from Colum's comment that Earl Gerald 'had no sword for when you can't gather fern seed'.

Moore extended her admiration for Irish storytelling to Colum and Campbell during her period of editorship of *The Dial* between 1925 and 1929.[19] During this time, there was an overall increase in the number of Irish publications in the magazine.[20] Moore's interest in Irish writing distinguished her from her predecessor at *The Dial*, Scofield Thayer. George Bornstein notes the changes Moore made: '[she] took particular care to strengthen the Irish component of the magazine. Besides Yeats and Colum, she also printed work by Daniel Corkery, John Eglinton (William Magee), Thomas McGreevy, Frank O'Connor, Seán O'Faoláin, and Liam O'Flaherty'.[21] Moore also published lesser-known writers including Shaemas O'Sheel, Margaret O'Leary and L. A. G. Strong. Her criticism and 'Comments' also often focused on Irish subjects. This marked a significant departure in attitude and tone from the magazine of her predecessors.

In August 1925, Campbell, recently arrived in New York, sent a letter to the editors of *The Dial* on headed notepaper from the New York School of Irish Studies, which he had founded that year. The letter, dated 30 August, asked whether the editors had had a chance to look at the poem he had submitted; but the headed notepaper was more telling, quoting from Joseph Dunn's 1922 work *The Need and Use of Celtic Philology*:

> Although the Celts no longer constitute a nation, and not one of the Celtic peoples enjoys complete political autonomy, the spiritual empire of the Celts is greater to-day than it ever was before their political unity was broken by Rome.
>
> Joseph Dunn, in 'Celtic Philology'.[22]

This was the clear cultural and political context against which Campbell submitted his work to *The Dial*. However, the editors were not dissuaded, choosing instead to be enchanted by Campbell's work. For example, writing to accept Campbell's poem 'The Cock' for publication in *The Dial* in May 1925, Moore noted that 'We shall always be delighted to see anything which you are willing to entrust to us', while in a letter sent to Campbell in July she described his lyric 'The star' as 'most beautifully refulgent'.[23] Moore also recounted a visit Colum and Campbell had made to *The Dial* offices in May 1925, during which they discussed Dutton's collection of *Ancient Irish Poetry*, a book that

Moore had since tried, unsuccessfully, to locate.[24] Meanwhile a review of Colum's work published in *The Dial*, by Llewellyn Powys, associated his writings directly with a Celtic ideal. Colum's stories, Powys argued, were 'poetical in the true Celtic sense of the word'.[25] Similarly, in a review of *Stories From The Dial* published in the magazine in January 1925, Paul Morand noted that Colum's story 'The Sad Sequel to Puss in Boots' was 'sprung from Irish fantasy', and described 'realism and fantasy' as 'the two wings of the Irish genius'.[26] Not to be outdone in praise of Colum's work, Moore wrote to him directly to ask him for a copy of his religious poem collection *The Way of the Cross*, as: 'The transporting perfection of some of the lines is such that one really hesitates to speak – even to seem grateful'.[27] Evidently still interested in Irish storytelling in 1928, Moore wrote to Colum in April to ask him to write an essay for *The Dial* on 'the book of James Stephens's stories' *Etched in Moonlight* – based on Irish fairy stories – 'of three pages – or four': a rather long piece for *The Dial*, which was known for the brevity of pieces such as its 'Briefer Mention' book reviews.[28] The promise of 'fairy water', sprinkled by the writings of Irish writers, clearly held a certain appeal for Moore during her time at the helm of *The Dial* – one she felt would be extended to her readership.

Though eugenicist critics such as Grant and Ross were keen to dispel the myth that there was such a thing as a Celtic race, even they acquiesced to the existence of a 'magical' Celtic culture within Irish immigrant communities. Ross, for example, having dismissed the Celtic drinker as 'quarrelsome and foolish', and the 'Celtic offender' as having 'weak control of impulses', goes on to describe at length the Celt's powers of imagination:

TRAITS OF THE CELT
With his Celtic imagination as a magic glass, the Irishman sees into the human heart and learns how to touch its strings. No one can wheedle like an Irish beggar or 'blarney' like an Irish ward boss. ... the Irish furnish stirring orators, persuasive stump-speakers, moving pleaders, and delightful after-dinner speech-makers[.]

Writing in 1914, Ross would also add that 'the peaks of Celtic superiority are poetry and eloquence', and that 'The word "brilliant" is oftener used for the Irish than for any other Aliens among us save the Hebrews'.²⁹ Even Madison Grant, writing in 1916, acknowledged grudgingly the existence of a '"Celtic" language and culture'³⁰ – underlining the pervasive, and persuasive, presence of Celticism in the first decades of the twentieth century.

Versions of Celticism: Bogan, Moore and Steinbeck

Discussions of Celtic culture and inheritance necessarily attract extreme opinions. For example, when writing about Faulkner, James P. Cantrell notes that 'Whatever the actual bloodlines, Faulkner's self-identity was Celtic, specifically Scottish'.³¹ This all-inclusive reading of a 'Celtic' inheritance, which extends even to Faulkner with his deep and historical southern roots, seems inherently opposed to the revivalist view of critic R. F. Garratt, who claims that in Ireland the 'rich Celtic inheritance' is 'inaccessible to the Irish Protestant community'.³² Both statements reflect ongoing debates about ethnic and cultural lines of affiliation concerning Irish-Catholic and Scotch-Irish/Protestant groups in Ireland and the Irish diaspora in America and beyond. And both are potentially problematic. Cantrell's thesis risks returning to the kinds of racial stereotyping that Kerby A. Miller identifies in early nineteenth-century America, where 'southern whites' would 'downplay internal differences for the sake of racial solidarity against the region's large and potentially rebellious slave population'; it is interesting, then, that Cantrell places Margaret Mitchell's 1936 civil war novel *Gone With The Wind* at the centre of his debates. On the other hand, Garratt's assertion of the 'inaccessibility' of Celtic culture reveals an exclusivity that risks ignoring the vast numbers of Americans of Irish descent who (as Miller puts it) 'share responsibility for Ireland's tragic past and troubled present', despite not having an Irish-Catholic background.³³

What is needed, then, is a balanced approach – one that acknowledges the potential pitfalls of extending 'Celtic' readings to a wide range of subjects, but is also aware of the potentially reductive reading of a Celtic inheritance as one to which only writers of an Irish-Catholic background can legitimately gain access. This approach also aligns itself more closely to the general tendency that Miller identifies among Americans with complex Irish histories – be they northern or southern, Protestant or Catholic or a mixture of all four – 'to regard themselves as inclusively, if vaguely, "Irish"'.[34] In the case of certain American modernists, what is clear is that their understanding of the reach of Celticism went beyond 'bloodlines', and extended past a reading of 'Celtic' as 'Irish' and 'Catholic'. For example, the poet and critic Louise Bogan displayed a keen awareness of her inheritance, a mixture of Ulster Catholic on her father's side and Dublin Catholic on her mother's. In letters to Allen Tate, though, she revealed a complex attitude towards her family background. In an early letter she claimed she had 'never been certain' that 'Bogan' was 'a definitely Irish stem', while in a later letter she asserted that 'all my talent comes from my mother's side'.[35] Thus what Bogan described in a 1939 questionnaire for the *Partisan Review* as a 'Celtic gift for language, and talent in the form of a remarkable sense of energy, on the maternal side of my family' was something that she clearly associated with her southern Irish, Dublin family rather than with her Northern Irish side: this despite the fact that her parents were both Catholic, and that she was brought up in the Roman Catholic Church – leading her to be treated as a '"Mick"' 'all during' her adolescence.[36]

This somewhat unresolved attitude towards Ireland extends to Bogan's interest in the Protestant inheritance, which she contrasts with the 'Celtic', Catholic background that endowed upon her a 'gift for language'. Thus Bogan describes herself, in her questionnaire for the *Partisan Review*, as one who 'was exposed to real liturgy' in the Catholic Church, 'instead of the dreary "services" and the dreadful hymnody of the Protestant churches'.[37] But in a review of Marianne Moore published in the *Quarterly Review of Literature* in 1948, Bogan identifies what she sees as Moore's Irish Protestantism – where 'Miss Moore is a descendant not of Swiss or Scotch, but of Irish presbyters' – as a key component in her 'value' as a poet. Moore's Protestantism, in Bogan's view, allows her to be 'a moralist (though a gentle one) and a stern – though flexible – technician': thus 'The tone of her poems often derives from her "other", Protestant, inheritance'. This allows her to stand out among the other modernists, as: 'Alive to the meaning of variation, Miss Moore can examine what the modern world displays, with an unmodern eye. This is her value to us'.[38]

It is interesting, in this context, to note that Moore, who asserted a claim to a 'possibly Scotch' inheritance,[39] extended her interest in

Celticism beyond Ireland to Scotland. Thus while Bogan ascribed her own Celtic powers to her maternal Dublin inheritance, and sought to critique her contemporary Moore as an Irish Presbyterian whose 'sensibilities are Counter-Reformation' and 'against whose vigor the vigor of the Baroque was actively opposed',[40] Moore melded her 'possibly' Scotch, Presbyterian background to an interest in Scots language and culture. Clippings that she took from newspapers included poetry by the Scots dialect poet Tom Scott with Moore's notes on the 'Scottish vernacular' scribbled on it, and an article entitled 'Some Notes on Old Scots and Melodic Line in Verse' taken from the *Shenandoah Review* in spring 1955.[41] Moore was also fascinated by the Scottish national poet Robert Burns, to which her extensive notes on *The Songs of Robert Burns* by James C. Dick, and her transcriptions of various poems by Burns, in a reading notebook from 1938–42 attest.[42] In an earlier notebook from around 1907, she had also copied out a less well-known verse from Burns's poem 'Auld Lang Syne', and had given the publication details of a book of *Scottish Songs and Ballads* by James Hogg, the 'Ettrick shepherd'.[43] Moore's investigations into the culture of another province of the Celtic fringe[44] – itself a site of cultural and religious division – tells us that she expressed an affiliation with Scotland even if the details of her own connections to the country had not quite been established.

Steinbeck's attraction to Celtic folklore extended even further – pursuing similar lines of investigation that had seen Matthew Arnold asserting in the 1860s the importance of English culture to Celtic identity.[45] Working on a translation of Malory later on in his life, in 1959, Steinbeck wrote to the Malory scholar Eugène Vinaver describing the area of Somerset in which he was working. Tellingly, he links what he perceives as the Anglo-Saxon/Celtic mix of the Mendip Hills with his own apparently Celtic/German background:

> The Somerset speech is Anglo-Saxon with a lacing of Celtic – it is even pronounced in that way. For right here the two met and fought and later mingled. The Norman never really took hold here. I feel at home and why-? My mother was of pure Celtic stock if there is any such [sic] and my name Steinbeck is not German in the modern sense. The two bloods meet in me just as they met here in the Mendip Hills and so there is every reason for me to feel that I have come home.[46]

Steinbeck's desire for discovering 'home' amongst a part-Celtic community recalls his attribution of restlessness and dissatisfaction to the American people in his essay 'Paradox and dream' while, tellingly, applying not Ireland but instead 'a lacing of Celtic' and his mother's apparently 'pure Celtic stock' (a near-echo of Moore's claim of a 'purely Celtic' inheritance) to his feelings of satisfaction at having 'come home'.[47]

Steinbeck's labelling is intriguing, because in using the terms 'Norman' and 'Anglo-Saxon' he is borrowing from the rhetoric of the American civil war, in which the 'Norman' south battled against the 'Saxon' north. This shows a further instance of muddling within Steinbeck's views of his Celtic inheritance. In civil war rhetoric, it is the southern 'Normans' who are associated with the Celts, and the northern 'Saxons' who are believed to be descended from the English: thus leading to a paradigm described by Richie Devon Watson Jr. as one in which the old rhetoric of 'Puritan and Cavalier' is replaced by 'Saxon and Norman' and then replaced by '*English* and *Celt*'.[48] Thus in describing the Mendip Hills as a place where the Anglo-Saxons and Celts 'fought' and 'later mingled', but also as a place where the 'Norman' never really took hold, Steinbeck is aiming to separate the 'Norman' from the 'Celt' and instead yoke the 'Celt' more closely to the 'Saxon'. We can see why this might appeal – as the Puritan inheritance he has gained from his maternal grandmother (an Irish convert to Protestantism), and possibly also from his German ancestors on his father's side, might therefore be yoked to the 'pure Celtic stock' of myth and folklore he feels he has gained through his mother. In turn this might find connections with the hybrid 'Anglo-Saxon' and 'Celtic' atmosphere of Somerset. Yet this desire for cultural and racial 'mingling', combined with Steinbeck's use of civil war rhetoric, signals an idealised meeting of bloodlines, translated uncertainly across the Atlantic – and back in time.

Steinbeck's somewhat muddled fascination with Celtic culture might be extended to his systems of belief, which also tended to gloss over the inconsistencies of his hybrid Celtic/German/Protestant inheritance. Ten years before writing this letter, Steinbeck had written to his future wife Elaine on the subject of a 'Celtic or Gaelic cross' that he was planning to send her – which he had 'spent the afternoon pleasantly making'. Later in the letter he adds, 'I don't know why I made a Celtic cross and inscribed it in Gaelic. Just felt like it I guess'.[49] In a letter to his sister, Jean Anderson Boone, Steinbeck had written:

> I believe that everyone needs something outside himself to cling to. Actually such a thing as I have in mind is not outside yourself but rather a physical symbol that you are all right inside yourself. So I have made you this little cross to wear, to hold in your hand, to rub between your fingers and to feel against your cheek. I hope it can be that symbol of your own inner safety.[50]

The spirituality and promise of safety embodied in Steinbeck's Celtic cross, inscribed in Gaelic, link the rituals of ancient Gaelic tradition to Steinbeck's personal belief systems. While it is debatable whether the Celtic cross is itself Catholic in origin, the Celtic Revival had reasserted the importance of the cross to Catholic events – and particularly to funerals – while the way that Steinbeck describes the cross in terms of something to 'rub between your fingers and feel against your cheek' recalls the ritualistic comfort of rosary beads. Interestingly, then, both the devout Presbyterian Moore and the Ulster-affiliated Protestant Steinbeck align themselves, at various points, with a Celtic tradition that owes a considerable amount of its modern identity to Catholicism. Yet of course, and once again, we find a precedent for such blurred religious and cultural affiliations in the figures of the Celtic Revivalists themselves, most of whom came from Protestant backgrounds.

The place of the peasant

Steinbeck's preoccupation with Celticism links the three facets that Mishkin locates at the heart of the appeal of the Revival: the past, the peasants, and religion. In Steinbeck's Celtic cross we can see a commingling of the past and religion, while in his portrayals of the lowly Welsh stowaway-cum- naval hero in the character of Sir Henry Morgan in *Cup of Gold* (1929), and in the eternally poor inventor Samuel Hamilton in *East of Eden* (1952),[51] the Celtic peasant is reimagined variously as a Welsh sea captain and an Irish immigrant to the American west. Of course the image of the peasant had become something of a calling card of the Irish Renaissance. Indeed, as discussed in the previous chapter, Steinbeck was inspired by J. M. Synge's depiction of Aran island peasants in *Riders to the Sea* (1903) when writing his own 'play-novelette' *Burning Bright* (1952), which transposed the Atlantic coast location of Synge's play to the three settings of circus, farm and ship.

The Revivalists' portrayals of peasants, which saw them alternately as spiritual visionaries or uncouth symbols of the 'real' Ireland, garnered popularity and controversy. Yeats comments in *Dramatis Personae* how his playwright patron and friend Lady Gregory 'was born to see the glory of the world in a peasant mirror';[52] meanwhile Jacqueline Genet has noted how, for Yeats, the peasant is associated with 'the old Celtic civilisation and with the universal collective memory where the legends which turn Ireland into a "holy land" of the imagination are stored'.[53] Yeats placed the peasant at the centre of his Celtic Revivalist discourse, as evidenced by his works *Fairy and Folk Tales of the Irish Peasantry* (1888) and *The Celtic Twilight* (1893); and he envied what he saw as the peasants' connection to the spirit world. This is emphasised by a well-known passage from his essay 'Away' (1902), in which Yeats tells stories of Irish country people, and their preoccupation with 'those men and women and children [who] are said to be "away"' – people who are constantly in the company of fairies and go about their daily lives as if in a dream.[54] Indeed Yeats comes to associate his spiritual endeavours as an artist with the otherworldly powers of the peasant: as Genet notes, in *A Vision* (1925, revised 1937) 'Yeats systematizes the perception of the relationship between the artist and the peasant', as '[t]he man of phase 17 (Yeats himself, Shelley, Dante and other artists) derives his mask from phase 3, the peasant'.[55] Thus the poet and peasant exist, according to Yeats's systems, in perpetual symbiosis.

Discussing Yeats's depiction of the Irish peasantry in his writings, however, Genet comments that '[t]he peasant is close to the child whose non-temporal, non-historical innocence he possesses, in opposition to the sophistication of the townsman';[56] in order for a romantic ideal of innocence to be preserved, then, the peasant has to be regarded both as sage and child. Yet when writers tried to move away from such idealised images of the peasant, they ran the risk of censure. For example, J. M. Synge's depiction of the Irish peasantry in *The Playboy of the Western World* (1907) famously caused uproar, thanks to its depiction of a group of incredulous peasants, living in a village on the west coast of County Mayo, who hero-worship an unknown visitor because of his claims of patricide. But the 'Playboy Riots' of 1907 had precedents in Ireland and America; indeed, as James Kilroy has pointed out, there had already been protests triggered by 'alleged attacks on Ireland or offensive representations of the Irish character' following performances of Irish plays in St Louis, Missouri, while in the same week as the Dublin riots a similar scene 'forced the Russell brothers off the stage of Hammerstein's Victoria Theatre in New York for their alleged ridicule of the Irish' in their famous 'Irish servant girl' routine, which had previously been a hit with Irish America.[57] Accordingly, in the days following the first performance of *Playboy* in Dublin (Saturday 26 June 1907), the inevitable backlash began – with the *Freeman's Journal* launching the first attack: 'A strong protest must ... be entered against this unmitigated, protracted libel upon Irish peasant men and, worse still, among Irish peasant girlhood'.[58]

In his Preface to *Playboy*, Synge anticipated such accusations of 'libel' in his depiction of Irish peasant life, defending its accuracy following his several trips to the west of Ireland, and the recordings he had made there: 'Anyone who has lived in real intimacy with the Irish peasantry will know that the wildest sayings and ideas in this play are tame indeed, compared with the fancies one may hear in any little hillside cabin in Geesala, or Carraroe, or Dingle Bay'.[59] This, after all, was a writer who claimed to 'have the wildest admiration for the Irish peasants'.[60] The question of how to portray the Irish peasantry in art, if at all, lay at the heart of the initial debates surrounding *Playboy*. On the one hand, the nationalist contingent in Ireland worried that the play perpetuated the same stereotypes that had seen the 'stage Irishman' marauded on the English stage for years; the initial review from the *Freeman's Journal* noted that 'The worse specimen of stage Irishman of the past is a refined, acceptable fellow compared with that imagined by Mr. Synge',[61] which sparked a sardonic response by a reviewer for the *Irish Times*: 'the *Sinn Fein* shouters ... have founded their objections on a theory of Celtic impeccability which is absurd in principle, and intolerable, when it is sought to be rigidly imposed as a canon of art'.[62] On the other hand, a more open-minded (though arguably patronising) reviewer saw the play as a useful critique of rural Ireland, asking whether the 'Western peasantry' could have a 'truer friend than the one who exhibits to criticism and to condemnation the forces affecting their lives'.[63] Stranger still was the notion expressed in a letter to the *Irish Times* that 'The question remains whether unrelieved peasant human nature is a legitimate subject for drama', revealing an opinion that was by turns belittling and protective in its attitude towards the peasant classes.⁶⁴

The Dublin riots extended for the whole of the play's first run in 1907; but after the storm had long died down in Ireland, riots greeted the Abbey Players in New York and America on their first American tour in late 1911 to early 1912. By then such responses seemed curiously outmoded: indeed even in America the riots were not widespread, while the city of Chicago was famously receptive to the Abbey, with the 1912 tour leading to the establishment of Maurice Browne's 'Little Theatre', which opened with works by Yeats and Synge.⁶⁵ Following the arrest of the Abbey Players, including Lady Gregory, in Philadelphia in January 1912, the *Irish Times* noted that, 'American citizens of Irish descent persist in regarding the Irish players as producing works which do not reflect glory upon the Irish race'. Citing a statement made on the arrests by Yeats, the *Irish Times* piece continued:

> They have looked for a source of offence in a quarter where the considered judgement of the United States has decided that there is none. They have carried prudery to the extreme where it defeats its own purpose. We prefer, with Mr. W. B. Yeats, to find the explanation in the fact that literary and dramatic opinion in Irish America, or, at least in that class of Irish America which the 'Playboy's' critics represent, is twenty years behind Ireland.⁶⁶

Despite the time-lag, nationalist 'Irish America' was determined to object to Synge's challenge to the romantic ideal in his representation of the Irish peasant, thus reflecting a desire shared with its brothers over the Atlantic to protect its vision of 'Celtic impeccability': one that saw peasants as innocent and blameless – and incapable of using the kind of colourful language that Synge had them speak in his play.⁶⁷

American Celticism: Donn Byrne (1889–1928)

The desire within Irish-American nationalist circles in the early part of the twentieth century to preserve 'Celtic impeccability', particularly in the image of Ireland that was transmitted to the outside world, helps in part to explain the curious popularity of the Irish-American novelist and writer Donn Byrne, who saw himself as the 'last traditional Irish novelist', following on from Goldsmith and Sterne.[68] Having been educated by Douglas Hyde at University College Dublin, Byrne had been strongly affected by Hyde's passion for Irish ballads and the Irish Gaelic language (Byrne grew up speaking Irish and English). Hyde was famous for his *Songs of Raftery*, a translation of the work of the Irish balladeer Anthony Raftery (1784–1835), and Byrne would follow this with his novel *Blind Raftery* (1924), in which Raftery is resurrected as an icon for modern Ireland.[69] However the works of Hyde, and Byrne after him, are markedly different from those of Synge, Yeats and (to a lesser extent) Gregory in that they remain preoccupied with the past, and with the Irish language, as facets of Irish culture that should not be tampered with. Rather than represent the Irish as they actually speak, with whatever 'wildness' this incorporates (as Synge attempted), Hyde and Byrne remained loyal to the view that a traditional representation of Irish life was the most powerful method of representing the Irish character and its accompanying Celtic culture.

Famous for his fantastical novels, and for his obsession with Irish idiom and the Irish peasantry, Byrne has now been dismissed as a largely comical, highly parochial author. Nevertheless, Ron Ebest argues that Byrne's influence on American culture during the early part of the twentieth century cannot be overstated: 'because he was the last great "American Celticist"', Ebest contends, Byrne 'represents the end of a literary tradition, a fact he recognized and lamented'. Yet: 'despite the fact that his work is now forgotten, Donn Byrne in his time was arguably the most financially, critically and popularly successful novelist in the Irish-American canon'. Ebest even explains how 'in 1923, Donn Byrne's writing was taught at Columbia University, on the grounds that his book *Changeling* was the best short story collection in four decades. And Sir Shane Leslie compared W. B. Yeats and James Joyce unfavourably to [him]'.[70] Shane Leslie's approval is hardly surprising, when we consider the extent of his efforts to persuade a young and impressionable Fitzgerald into Celticism in the early part of his career;[71] nevertheless the extent of Byrne's appeal tells us that at this time American writers were hungry for Byrne's romanticised views of Ireland and Irish folklore. As Ebest notes, Byrne's stories were 'sought by journals across the popular spectrum', including *Smart Set* and *Harper's Monthly*, and American writers as diverse as Stephen Vincent Benet, James Branch Cabell, Joseph Devlin, Frank Harris, Joyce Kilmer and Amy Lowell read his work.[72] Byrne sent Kilmer a presentation copy of his 1915 collection *Stories Without Women*, and inscribed a second printing of *Messer Marco Polo* (1921) to Amy Lowell;[73] while Cabell in *The Nation* reviewed *Messer Marco Polo* as a 'very magically beautiful book', despite the author's apparent lack of 'effort or shame'.[74] The most famous example is probably Steinbeck, however, who read Byrne's works avidly when he was starting out as a writer, and was quizzed on his use of Byrne in his work, emphasising its flavour rather than its content: 'the words didn't have to mean much', Steinbeck said; 'when I'd get what they had to give I knew what I wanted to do'.[75] Nevertheless Steinbeck's first wife Carol and his biographer Jackson J. Benson viewed his reliance on Byrne as sufficiently strong to stilt his literary development in the early years of his career, particularly in shaping the mock-heroic fable *Cup of Gold* (1929), which took Steinbeck years to complete.[76]

But even some of those who read Byrne during the height of his popularity were suspicious of his depictions of Irish life. For example, in her 1941 poem 'Spenser's Ireland' Marianne Moore made extensive, but somewhat comical, use of Byrne's travelogue *Ireland: The Rock Whence I Was Hewn*. Byrne's work, first published in *National Geographic* in March 1927 alongside photographs of Irish peasants, displayed such a romanticised – and condescending – view of Irish life that even the editor of the 1929 edition, the journalist and Irish nationalist MP T. P. O'Connor, felt the need to disassociate himself from it.[77] In his introduction, O'Connor declares:

> Personally, I am afraid I am a little too much of a realist and have seen too much in political controversy of the dark as well as the good side of Ireland, for Donn Byrne's pictures of that country to make the same appeal to me as those who know it less from the inside. The land bathed in poetry and universal good-will was not quite the Ireland that was brought home to me – especially by the bitter controversy in its politics, in which unwillingly I had to take part – and I could not accept as a complete picture of Ireland this land of wandering and popular bards and romantic love.[78]

Though Ebest mentions O'Connor as a reader of Byrne,[79] and though even here O'Connor is writing an introduction to one of Byrne's works, his suspicion of Byrne's motives rings through. Henry S. Bannister points out Byrne's lack of interest in the 'political troubles' in Ireland, as emphasised by his publication, in 1916, of the fanciful story of Irish life, 'A Woman of the Shee'; while Paul Mellon noted in 1926 that in each of Byrne's works 'There is a certain mythical, magic beauty to Ireland'.[80] This focus on an ideal of Celtic beauty at the expense of considering political realities is derived from Byrne's outsider's perspective: for although Donn Byrne was Irish, he had spent much of his life in America and Europe.

The title of Moore's poem – 'Spenser's Ireland' – refers to the poet Edmund Spenser (1552–99), who served under the Lord Deputy in Ireland from 1580; he was later awarded land in Cork for his services. Spenser's unpopular colonial treatise *A View of the Present State of Ireland* (1598) – with its aim of 'turning' the Irish soil 'to good uses, and reducing that savage nation to better government and civility'[81] – might seem crueller than Byrne's fanciful though patronising view of the Irish peasantry in *Ireland: The Rock Whence I Was Hewn*; yet in Moore's poem they are read together as texts that express narrow and outmoded views of Ireland. Byrne's text informs the opening and concluding stanzas of 'Spenser's Ireland'.[82] In a paragraph discussing the loquaciousness and mannerisms of the Irish, Byrne notes, 'The only discipline you can use is to forebear speaking to them for some days. This is torture'.[83] Moore relocates Byrne's statement in the middle section of the opening stanza:

> Spenser's Ireland
> has not altered; –
> a place as kind as it is green,
> the greenest place I've never seen.
> Every name is a tune.
> Denunciations do not affect
> the culprit; nor blows, but it
> is torture to him to not be spoken to. (ll. 1–8)

Like Byrne and Spenser before him, Moore is claiming that the country 'has not altered', but it is only Moore's speaker who knows better, as she is aware of the possible consequences of viewing Ireland in this way. Thus Moore's speaker is a reader of texts about Ireland who is constructing her impression of it from the words she reads, rather than from seeing it for herself, but who knows what she is doing: it's 'the greenest place I've never seen' (l. 4).

In these opening lines, Moore subtly mocks Byrne's simultaneous association and disassociation with native Irishmen. In Byrne's text he complains that 'no tongue-thrashing will affect' the 'carelessness' of a peasant, 'which drives a sane man mad';[84] superficially then, the 'culprit' of these lines is the Irishman whom 'Denunciations' and 'blows' do not affect (ll. 6, 7). Nevertheless, it is also possible to see the 'culprit' as Byrne himself: a writer who is guilty of perpetuating incorrect myths about Ireland. In lines 7 and 8, Byrne's 'This is torture' is physically disjointed over the line break – 'it/ is torture to him to not be spoken to' – and verbally displaced into a Hibernian turn of phrase that luxuriates in the loquacious expressiveness of the triple use of 'to'. Moore, then, reverses the superior, almost colonial tone of Byrne's statement, with its controlled, Germanic sentence structure, by reshaping it as a loose, Hibernian expression that is humorous rather than sterile. Through this act of reversal, Moore questions whether it is the peasants of Byrne's narrative or the self-important writer himself for whom it is torture 'to not be spoken to'. In assuming the speech patterns of native Irish speakers, Moore allies herself with the same 'Irish' whom Byrne teases.

Moore parodies Byrne's model further in the concluding lines to 'Spenser's Ireland'. In a section about Aran islanders in *Ireland: The Rock Whence I Was Hewn,* Byrne notes: 'I know of nothing more dignified than an Aran islander – than, indeed, any Irish peasant. When they are young they are supple as a larch. When they are old they have the kindness and sanity of a gnarled apple tree. Always, your trouble is their trouble and your joy theirs. We are a giving people'.[85] But in 'Spenser's Ireland' Moore mocks Byrne's naïve and self-praising celebration of community by isolating 'your trouble is their trouble' to give it a cynical twist:

> The Irish say your trouble is their
> trouble and your
> joy their joy? I wish

I could believe it;
I am troubled, I'm dissatisfied, I'm Irish. (ll. 63–7)

Whereas Byrne answers 'your trouble is their trouble and your joy theirs' with 'We are a giving people', Moore adds a question mark, so that her answer, centred on the pronoun 'I', creates a sense of deflation: 'I wish/ I could believe it'. The last line of the poem – 'I am troubled, I'm dissatisfied, I'm Irish' – argues that Irish life is far removed from Byrne's ideal. Meanwhile the fastidious rhythm of 'dissatisfied' emphasises the joylessness and discomfort that can underline the Irish experience. As George Bornstein puts it, 'the ending stakes a claim to being Irish not by adhering to the sentimental stereotypes promoted by Byrne but by a level-headed clarity that values accuracy of perception as both a poetic and political starting point'.[86] Thus for Moore, an upholding of the magical and literary potential of Celtic culture – as epitomised by Colum's 'great green-eyed cat of the mountain' (l. 61) – is counterbalanced by a warning that, as in the case of Byrne, and Spenser before him, 'Celticism' can become suffocated by parochialism and caricature. It is fitting, then, that 'Spenser's Ireland' takes its sources from Colum and Byrne (among others) to provide a nuanced picture of the possible readings of Celticism within modernist discourse.[87]

Transatlantic Celticism: Stevens and McGreevy

Another modernist writer whose interest in Celtic culture informed the direction of his work was Wallace Stevens. He developed a strong attraction towards Celticism at the end of his career, which was initiated, shaped and influenced by his eight-year correspondence with the Irish poet Thomas McGreevy, lasting from 1948 to 1955.[88] But this attraction had been simmering for a while; Daniel Tobin notes, for example, that Stevens's acquisition in 1934 of the Italian philosopher Mario Rossi's Irish travelogue *Pilgrimage in the West* from the Cuala Press 'provides evidence' of Stevens's 'perception of Ireland as a metaphor for the imagination'. Quoting Rossi's text, Tobin remarks on its 'racially infused conception of Ireland and the Irish', which describes '"Irish Celticism"' as '"the obstinate permanence of an original spirit athwart all the modern superstructures, athwart mingling of blood, and variations of language and religions'".[89] That Stevens was not unduly perturbed by Rossi's contentions, and that he was still fascinated by the imaginative potential of Ireland when he was introduced to McGreevy some fifteen years later, illustrates the enduring power of Celticism, for Stevens, as an escape from unimaginative modernity.

Although McGreevy is now relatively unknown – his legacy felt only in a single volume of *Poems* (1934)[90] – he was a close correspondent of many major figures of the modernist period, including Beckett and Joyce, and was Director of the National Gallery, Dublin, from 1950 to 1963. Désirée Hirst has described McGreevy as 'an impressive survivor of the early twentieth century movement' that pre-dated the political and literary turbulence of Ireland from the 1930s onwards.[91] Meanwhile, Mary Joan Egan notes how McGreevy 'was an Irish Irishman, familiar with Gaelic language and story, seeking both to inform Ireland with the finest that the rest of the world could offer to bring it out of its insularity and make Irish thought and sensibility internationally recognised'.[92] Thus McGreevy provides an interesting counterpoint to Donn Byrne in his aims to celebrate the traditions of 'Irishness' as essentially Celtic and Catholic and simultaneously to create in 'Irish thought and sensibility' something that might be seen outside Ireland as modern and cosmopolitan.

For Stevens, McGreevy was an influential figure at an important time in his life.[93] When he was introduced (by letter) to McGreevy in 1948, Stevens had just suffered the loss of his close correspondent, Henry Church. Lee Jenkins has noted that 'it is tempting to speculate that his Irish-Catholic friend [McGreevy] played some part in Stevens's alleged deathbed conversion to Catholicism', and Egan has argued that '[i]t is safe to speculate that McGreevy's ebullient devotion to a kind and generous God contributed to [Stevens's] confidence about taking that step'.[94] The most striking souvenir of Stevens's correspondence with McGreevy is Stevens's late poem, 'Our Stars Come From Ireland' (published in *The Auroras of Autumn* in 1950). In a letter to Barbara Church dated 19 August 1948, Stevens revealed the spiritual way in which he viewed his new Irish correspondent: 'I need not say that if you go to Dublin I should like to be remembered to Mr. McGreevy and all his saints. He sent me a cable and also a letter and he is a blessed creature. He is entitled, however, to more than thanks and that must somehow come about and I don't know how. I should of course write to him and shall'.[95] Stevens's relations with McGreevy helped shape his opinions of Ireland in intriguing, but sometimes unsettling, ways. In September 1948, for example, writing to Barbara Church, Stevens decided, on reading an Irish newspaper McGreevy had sent him, that he 'was interested to see that they have sausages in Eire [sic]', as 'it doesn't seem quite Celtic'.[96] Such an attitude recalls Byrne's comment in *Ireland: The Rock Whence I Was Hewn* that 'What a peasant in his cottage wants electricity for, I cannot say',[97] and points to Stevens's idealism, and parochialism, concerning Ireland.

In his correspondence with McGreevy, Stevens openly acknowledges the influence of the spiritual Irish poet. For example, in a letter to McGreevy of May 1948, Stevens cites McGreevy's poem 'Homage to Hieronymus Bosch': 'Last night I read your poems [–] "High above the bank of Ireland / Unearthly music sounded, / Passing westwards"'.[98] Compare this with lines from the first section of Stevens's 1950 poem 'Our Stars Come From Ireland', entitled '*Tom McGreevy, in America, Thinks of Himself as a Boy*':

> Over the top of the Bank of Ireland,
> The wind blows quaintly
> Its thin-stringed music,
> As he heard it in Tarbert.
>
> These things were made of him
> And out of myself.
> He stayed in Kerry, died there.
> I live in Pennsylvania.[99]

William Fogarty has noted how, in citing and subsequently reusing McGreevy's words for his poem, Stevens has focused neither on the political context of the original poem – the hanging of National University student Kevin Barry during the Irish War of Independence in November 1920[100] – nor on McGreevy's 'surrealism and his Boschian grotesquerie'. Instead, McGreevy's lines are reconfigured in relation to Stevens's 'poetics of reality and imagination':[101] it is their 'Irish' qualities, related to a kind of covert spiritualism, and entwined with an enticing 'westwardness', that appeal to Stevens.

Joan Richardson notes how McGreevy's 'religious, mystical kind of perceptiveness, which led him to conceptualise his relationship with Stevens in terms of a quasi-mystical twinning, is replicated in "Our Stars Come From Ireland"'.[102] In only the third letter he wrote to Stevens, sent on 10 May 1948 (the first was written on 12 April), McGreevy encourages this 'twinning' while simultaneously affecting modesty concerning his own presumption: 'Wallace Stevens was born in Reading, Pa., on October 2, 1879, fourteen years and 24 days before Tom McGreevy was born in Tarbert, Co. Kerry, and yet the said Tom McGreevy gives himself the airs of a wise man in writing to Wallace Stevens. He'd like Wallace Stevens to forgive him. God's blessing. Please write again'.[103] Stevens's response to this almost enforced 'quasi-mystical twinning' is evident both in the title of the section of 'Our Stars Come From Ireland' –'*Tom McGreevy, in America, Thinks of Himself as a Boy*' – and in the fusion of 'him' and 'myself' in the above lines (9–10). But what is particularly intriguing is the way in which Stevens interprets this 'twinning'. Stevens not only imagines McGreevy as simultaneously in America and Ireland, implying a kind of symbiotic fusion between the two countries, but also hints that this fusion extends to him – as the American poet – and to McGreevy, as his Irish correspondent. The mystical potency of the memory of the 'wind' that passes west from the Bank of Ireland (in Dublin), to Tarbert in County Kerry, seems to have blown further still: to America itself, and specifically to where Stevens's speaker is living, in 'Pennsylvania' (l. 12), near the east coast. The east-west metaphor, linking Pennsylvania and Kerry, is made much of in the writers' correspondence: indeed, in an early letter, McGreevy had referred to the literal transit of their exchanges, noting how, 'The east-west post seems to be faster than the west-east'.[104]

The metaphorical inspiration from east to west is extended further in the second half of Stevens's poem, entitled 'The Westwardness of Everything'. A later letter from Stevens to McGreevy, in October 1948, credits the Irish poet with this section of the poem too:

> What you say in your letters about your westwardness as a result of living near the Shannon Estuary interested me. The house in which I was born and lived as a boy faced the west and wherever I have lived if the house faced any other way I have always been pulling it round on an axis

to get it straight. The poem which I sent you ... is on this very subject: the westwardness of things[.]¹⁰⁵

And in the resulting poem by Stevens, describing the 'stars' that he says 'are washing up from Ireland' (l. 17), we find:

> These are the ashes of fiery weather,
> Of nights full of the green stars from Ireland,
> Wet out of the sea, and luminously wet,
> Like beautiful and abandoned refugees.
>
> The whole habit of the mind is changed by them,
> These Gaeled and fitful-fangled darknesses
> Made suddenly luminous, themselves a change,
> An east in their compelling westwardness,¹⁰⁶

Stevens's vision of Ireland is, tellingly, a fusion of opposites – of 'fiery weather' counterbalanced by luminous wetness, of greenness and redness (from the fiery weather), of light and dark, of east and west. Ireland's influence on America, washing up on the shore, is both a balm and a source of power: the poet seems unsure what to make of 'These Gaeled and fitful-fangled darknesses' brought by Ireland, which can change 'The whole habit of the mind'. Like Moore and Steinbeck, Ireland seems to provide Stevens with a cure for cultural restlessness while representing a new and exciting – but possibly frightening – axis of inspiration. We can almost hear in Stevens's words an echo of W. B. Yeats's commingled awe and excitement in 'The Second Coming', as his 'rough beast ... / Slouches towards Bethlehem to be born';¹⁰⁷ but here Stevens's stars, in their 'Gaeled and fitful-fangled darknesses', are washing up in the Schuylkill river. Fittingly, in a later letter to McGreevy, sent following the publication of *The Auroras of Autumn* in 1950, Stevens describes the two parts of 'Our Stars Come From Ireland' as McGreevy's work: 'A copy of *The Auroras of Autumn* is now on its way to Dublin. ... You will have no difficulty in finding your own poems'.¹⁰⁸

Several critics have commented at length on the unusual relationship between McGreevy and Stevens. Peter Brazeau, for example, notes that the two poets met up just once, in New York, during nearly eight years of correspondence – with their mutual correspondent Barbara Church as a 'mediating presence and buffer', as Lee Jenkins puts it.[109] Describing the moment that Stevens received a copy of McGreevy's poems in May 1948, Brazeau comments that, 'As Stevens read these Irish pieces that spring, he experienced a notable sense of kinship with the County Kerry poet'. Brazeau is clearly attracted to the folklore that surrounds this particular correspondence: 'McGreevy was his necessary angel in Dublin, through whose sight he glimpsed an Ireland which, as Stevens once told his friend, he knew he would never actually visit'. This did not matter, though, as 'McGreevy seemed a man made out of words'.[110] Jenkins notes, indeed, that 'In Stevens's poem ['Our Stars Come From Ireland'], McGreevy and Stevens are presented in a mystical oneness (but with the Atlantic safely in between them)'.[111]

Of course, in 'Our Stars Come From Ireland' 'Tom McGreevy' is described as having 'stayed in Kerry, died there' – despite the real McGreevy being perfectly alive, and living in Dublin, at the time of composition – so that 'Kerry' functions as an enduring symbol of the west of Ireland rather than as a real location.[112] Stevens's use of 'Pennsylvania' (l. 12) as his speaker's location is similarly symbolic, as Pennsylvania is associated with Stevens's place of birth, and with his ancestors – whom he seeks out in Tulpehocken, Pennsylvania in his 1951 essay and memoir collection *The Necessary Angel* – rather than with his actual home of Hartford, Connecticut.[113] This reinforces the characters' respective entwinement with their somewhat fictionalised, if not fully fictive, locations – and cements the poem's myth of transatlantic 'twinning', in which a poetic and spiritual fusion is predicated on a distance being forged between character and person, between place and idea, and between ideal and reality. In *The Necessary Angel*, first published in the same period as his 'Irish' poems, Stevens urges the poet to resist the 'pressure of reality' in order to access his powers of 'extraordinary imagination'. The poet, Stevens argues, 'must be able to abstract himself and also to abstract reality, which he does by placing it in his imagination'.[114] Thus if Stevens were to portray himself and McGreevy just as they were, and to acknowledge the 'reality' of events behind the construction of his poem, he would risk converting the poetry back into the prose of their correspondence – and leaving his imagination behind.

Unsurprisingly, Stevens avoided meeting McGreevy until it was absolutely necessary; a couple of excruciating letters, in which Stevens notes he cannot accommodate McGreevy because of all the chaos and dust in his house, and to which McGreevy replies by claiming that he would never have wanted to put Stevens out in the first place ('I am delighted that there is dust on the piano'), are testament to this.[115] Moreover Stevens's first poem about McGreevy was written very early in their relationship, before he could get a real sense of his new Irish correspondent. Although 'Our Stars Come From Ireland' would not be published until 1950, Stevens sent McGreevy a draft of the poem on 28 July 1948; the draft is identical to the published version.[116] Stevens explained the situation as follows:

> Do you mind if I use the enclosed poem? It might be published in England. I cannot use another name [other than 'Tom McGreevy'] because of the references to your poetry. The abbreviation of your name will either justify itself or nothing else will. I hope that I have spelled Tarbert correctly. When we look back, at least when I look back, I do not really remember myself but the places in which I lived and things there with which I was familiar.[117]

Significantly, this letter was only the fifth Stevens had sent to McGreevy – and followed only four he had received from the Irish poet.[118] During this time, Stevens had made overtures to McGreevy regarding Ireland and his idea of it. For example, in his first letter to the Irish poet, dated 20 April 1948 – written in response to McGreevy's first letter to him, which he had received the day before – it is Stevens who brings up the question of Ireland. He notes: 'Ireland is rather often in mind over here. Somehow the image of it is growing fresher and stronger'.[119] In his next letter to McGreevy, Stevens brings up Ireland again, discussing McGreevy's poetry and noting, in relation to their correspondence, that, 'The air mail brings you surprisingly close. Dublin seems much nearer'. Here, Stevens consciously romanticises his idea of Ireland, suggesting that 'While it seems to be merely a phrase to say that the lamp in Mr. Yeats's studio is like something not far away, yet it is more than a phrase' (Stevens refers to the 'standard lamp' that McGreevy had mentioned in Jack B. Yeats's studio, which had shed a flattering light on him as Yeats sketched his portrait for Stevens).[120]

In each of these exchanges, Stevens is trying out his images of
Ireland; indeed a pattern emerges in which Stevens hypothesises,
McGreevy indulges, and Stevens hypothesises again. It is as if Stevens
has discovered a sounding board upon which he can rehearse his ideas
of Ireland – ideas that, while clearly encouraged by McGreevy, Stevens
appears to have thought about before this correspondence began.
Again, it is the ideas themselves, rather than the reality, that seem to
appeal to Stevens in his vision of Ireland: and McGreevy in his replies
seems to understand his function – to indulge, and not to shatter, the
illusions of his American correspondent.

Though used to his role as cultural sounding board, McGreevy
appears stunned to receive Stevens's poem ('Our Stars Come From
Ireland') after such a brief correspondence – a poem, moreover, that
places him centre stage. Writing on 4 August 1948, McGreevy seems
touched, humbled, and even a little confused, by Stevens's actions:

> You ask me do I mind if you use the poem. It would be a poor answer
> if I said 'I don't mind', wouldn't it? And to say I should feel honoured
> would be inadequate because there is more than feeling honoured to it.
> The true answer would be a poem. Say a prayer that I may write it some
> day. ... Use it (in so far as I have any right to presume to tell you you
> may use it). And use my name by all means. It seems to me to be – to
> be a poem – there aren't any other words when a poem is a poem.[121]

Tellingly McGreevy notes, later in the letter, his incredulity at Stevens's
using Tarbert as a location for the poem: 'The only word in the poem
that surprised me was "Tarbert". Where in God's name did you get
it? Is it that in our short correspondence I have talked about myself as
much as that? But of course it belongs there all right. The whole poem
was like myself talking to myself – about Wallace Stevens maybe'. In
fact, it is Stevens who first idealises McGreevy's hometown. The Irish
poet is content to play along, though, noting in his next letter, sent
from Tarbert, that: 'It is fitting that I send you a word from here since
you have been here too – yesterday'.[122] This geographical 'twinning'
is something that Stevens has actively encouraged: but it is McGreevy,
again, who takes this up and runs with it, noting that, 'I had no America.
But now I have an America and if ever I go – which is not really very
likely – I have somewhere to go. I'll go to Swatara and Schuylkill.

And it will be to find the myself that was Wallace Stevens there'; and adding in a subsequent letter how, during his trip to Tarbert, 'I was quite by myself when, as was of course bound to happen, I thought of Swatara and Schuylkill, and the sense of inner content, of something indistinguishable from absolute peace, came naturally and sweetly'.[123]

It is interesting, then, that while Stevens takes the first step towards familiarity, it is the more sociable McGreevy who continues to take delight in this, whereas Stevens barely refers to the poem in future correspondence. Similarly following their eventual meeting in New York in 1954, it is McGreevy who continues to express excitement, and Stevens who barely mentions the occasion.[124] What is clear from studying these few letters is that it was the 'ideal' image of 'Tom McGreevy' – twinned to his hometown, sitting on the rocks in Tarbert – which appealed to Stevens, rather than the actual poet. In reality, McGreevy was a cosmopolitan poet and critic, spending extended periods of time in London and Paris in particular – and settling eventually not in Tarbert but in Dublin; indeed, unlike the 'Tom McGreevy' of Stevens's poem, who 'stayed' in Tarbert and 'died there',[125] McGreevy actually died in Dublin, a few years after retiring as Director of the National Gallery.[126]

Frank Kermode perhaps puts it best when he surmises of Stevens that he 'had no comparable English friend' to McGreevy: what Stevens took most joy from, in his Irish friend, was his Irish identity. But this is partly the point. As Kermode puts it, McGreevy was 'the sort of man Stevens might admire not only for his verses or the paintings in his charge but for his idiosyncratic style, [and] his individual relationship to Catholicism and to Irish nationalism'.[127] For Stevens, all of this was bound up in a Celtic parcel of irresistible allure, which was linked necessarily to the imagination rather than to reality.

★

There appears to be so much goodwill towards Celtic writers and the Celtic imagination amongst American intellectuals during this period that we might be surprised to see a distinctly anti-Celtic message in a piece by Ezra Pound, who himself would admit in 1954 to having being 'drunk with Celticism' in the early part of the twentieth century.[128] Yet back in 1914, in an essay published in *The Egoist* in which he celebrated Joyce's achievements in *Dubliners*, Pound had launched into a tirade against Ireland and its Celtic associations:

> It is surprising that Mr. Joyce is Irish. One is so tired of the Irish or 'Celtic' imagination (or 'phantasy' as I think they call it) flopping about. Mr. Joyce does not flop about. He defines. He is not an institution for the promotion of Irish peasant industries. He accepts an international standard of prose writing and lives up to it. He gives Dublin as it presumably is. ... Erase the local names and a few specifically local allusions, and a few historic events of the past, and substitute a few different local names, allusions and events, and these stories could be retold in any town. ... He does not bank on 'Irish character'.

Pound's analysis of Joyce's work relies on its everyday qualities – what later in the essay he describes as dealing with 'normal things and normal people'[129] – and its facility for being 'retold in any town'. Pound advocates abandoning the emphasis that the Irish Renaissance writers placed on location, preferring instead Joyce's work, which does not make its author 'an institution for the promotion of Irish peasant industries'. Louise Bogan reads Joyce's works similarly, commenting on *Finnegans Wake* for a 1944 review that: 'Into a limited locale (at its largest, Dublin, on the island of Ireland) are brought all ages of man and some of nature'.[130] Meanwhile, in his 1922 essay 'The three provincialities', Eliot had distinguished between Yeats and Synge as 'Irish' writers and, on the other hand, Joyce as a European – and as a writer 'of international value'.[131]

The possibility of substituting one 'locale' for another in Joyce's works, or their international value, is not what writers such as Moore, Steinbeck or Stevens look for in 'Celtic' stories – they are attracted instead to the extraordinary qualities of Celtic myth and folklore, which are linked intrinsically to an 'Irish' ideal, located in an 'Irish' location. Though Moore's 'Spenser's Ireland' warns against the extremes of parochialism in views of Ireland, the same poem takes solace in the 'enchantment' of Irish culture, through reading and hearing Colum's folk tales; meanwhile Stevens derives more inspiration from a 'Tom McGreevy' of his imagination, sitting on the rocks at Tarbert, than from the real McGreevy – a well-travelled, well-connected, modern figure. Steinbeck, lastly, derives inspiration from a range of Celtic writing, moving from Malory to Synge to Byrne in his search for expression. The idea of 'the international standard of prose writing', which Pound promotes here, is far removed from this particular locus of literary inspiration.

Notes

1 Louis MacNeice, *Autumn Journal*, XVI, ll.63–4, in *Collected Poems*, ed. E. R. Dodds. London: Faber, 1966, pp. 101–53 (131–4).
2 *See* Oscar Cargill, *Intellectual America: Ideas on the March*. First published 1941; New York: Macmillan, 1959, section on 'Celtic-American cynicism', in Chapter 6: 'The intelligentsia: the birth of pessimism'.
3 *Oxford English Dictionary* online (www.oed.com): 'Celtic', 2d.; 'Celtic Twilight'.
4 Daniel G. Williams, 'Introduction: Celticism and the Black Atlantic', *Comparative American Studies*, 8.2 (June 2010), 81–7 (81).
5 Tracy Mishkin, *The Harlem and Irish Renaissances: Language, Identity and Representation*. Gainesville, Florida: University Press of Florida, 1998, pp. 1, 14. Mishkin's study provides a useful introduction to the critical movement that examines the impact of Irish writing and culture on African-American writing in the twentieth century. The present study does not cover this area of investigation in any depth, because (space constraints aside) Mishkin and others have amply treated this elsewhere.
6 James Weldon Johnson, Preface, *The Book of American Negro Poetry*. New York: Hartcourt, Brace & Co., 1922, pp. xl-xli.
7 James P. Cantrell, *How Celtic Culture Invented Southern Literature*. Greta, Louisiana: Pelican Press, 2006, p. 9.
8 Mishkin, *The Harlem and Irish Renaissances*, pp. 69, 71.
9 Robert Keating O'Neill discusses the efforts of Mosher and Quinn at length in 'The Irish book in the United States', *The Oxford History of the Irish Book, Volume V: The Irish Book In English, 1891–2000*, ed. Clare Hutton and Patrick Walsh. Oxford: Oxford University Press, 2011, pp. 413–39 (see especially pp. 422–7).
10 George Yeats to Thomas M[a]cGreevy, envelope dated 3 November 1925, Trinity College Dublin ['TCD'] MS 8104/63; accessed through the MacGreevy archive at www.macgreevy.org.
11 Margaret Mills Harper, *Wisdom of Two: The Spiritual and Literary Collaboration of George and W. B. Yeats*. Oxford: Oxford University Press, 2006, p. 58.

12 Stevens mentions Rossi's book (published in Dublin by the Cuala Press in 1933) in letters to Hi Simons on 9 January 1940, to Barbara Church on 12 August 1947, and to Thomas McGreevy on 25 August 1948; see *Letters of Wallace Stevens*, ed. Holly Stevens. Berkeley: University of California Press, 1996, pp. 347, 564, 611.
13 Holly Stevens, in *Letters of Wallace Stevens*, p. 257.
14 Holly Stevens to Thomas McGreevy, 13 November 1964, TCD 8123/51.
15 Rosenbach Museum and Library ['RML'] V:79:20, Correspondence between Moore and Elizabeth C. Yeats, MM to ECY, 13 April 1933.
16 The 'Mabinogion' is the title given to a collection of 11 prose stories collected from the medieval Welsh. Yeats makes frequent mention of it in 'The Celtic Element in Literature' (1897), collected in *Ideas of Good and Evil* (Dublin: Maunsel & Co., 1905), pp. 270–95. In an additional note to the 1897 essay, written in 1902, Yeats adds that 'I could have written this essay with much more precision and have much better illustrated my meaning if I had waited until Lady Gregory had finished her books of legends, *Cuchulain of Muirthemne*, a book to set beside the *Morte D'Arthur* and the *Mabinogion*' (*Ideas of Good and Evil*, p. 295).
17 Moore, 'Notes' to 'Spenser's Ireland', *Complete Poems*, ed. Clive Driver. London: Faber, 1984, final note, p. 280. Moore began accompanying her poems with 'Notes' from her collection *Observations* (1924) onwards. See also Colum, *The Big Tree of Bunlahy – Stories of My Own Countryside* (New York, 1933), which contains several of the stories mentioned. I have excluded this source from the discussion, as there is no clear evidence that Moore read this work. Her private library at RML does contain two works by Colum, however: *Roofs of Gold: Poems to Read Aloud* (New York, 1964), #MML 02.08; and *Storytelling new and old* (New York, 1967), #MML 0284.
18 RML VII:06:03, Lecture notes 1937–1941, 'Story-telling to the Young and Ever Young', lecture given by Pádraic Colum, 20 December 1937, pp. 2r–6r.
19 Moore became Assistant Editor of *The Dial* in April 1925, then Acting Editor in July 1925, and finally Editor in July 1926, remaining in that position until the magazine closed in September 1929.
20 For example, in 1923 there were eleven pieces published in *The Dial* by Irish writers or on Irish subjects; while in the seven issues of the magazine published between January and July 1929 (before the magazine folded in August), there are thirty-two pieces by Irish, Anglo-Irish or Irish-American writers or artists. See also Barbara Zingman, *The Dial: An Author Index*. New York: Whitston, 1975.

21 George Bornstein, *Material Modernism: The Politics of the Page*. Cambridge: Cambridge University Press, 2001, p. 91.
22 Joseph Campbell to *The Dial*, 30 August 1926, Berg Collection, Beinecke Rare Book and Music Library, Dial Scofield Thayer Papers, YCAL MSS 34, Box 1, f. 33.
23 Letters from Marianne Moore to Joseph Campbell, 19 May and 23 July 1925, Beinecke YCAL MSS34, Box 1, folder 30: Joseph Campbell.
24 RML V:65:04, Correspondence between Moore and Scofield Thayer, MM to ST, 15 May 1925.
25 Llewellyn Powys, review of *The Island of the Mighty* by Pádraic Colum, *The Dial*, 78.4 (April 1925), 336–40 (336).
26 Paul Morand, review of *Stories from the Dial*, ed. Lincoln MacVeagh, *The Dial*, 78.1 (January 1925), 52.
27 Moore to Pádraic Colum, 18 December 1926, Beinecke YCAL MSS34, Box 1, folder 37: Padraic [sic] Colum 1926–October 1927.
28 Moore to Colum, 18 April 1928, Beinecke YCAL MSS34, Box 1, folder 38: Padraic [sic] Colum November 1927–July 1928.
29 Edward A. Ross, *The Old World in the New: The Significance of Past and Present Immigration to the American People*. New York: The Century Co., 1914, pp. 40, 39, 44.
30 Madison Grant, *The Passing of the Great Race*. First published 1916; London: G. Bell and Sons, Ltd., 1921, p. 63.
31 Cantrell, *How Celtic Culture Invented Southern Literature*, p. 132.
32 R. F. Garratt, *Modern Irish Poetry: Tradition and Continuity from Yeats to Heaney*. Berkeley: University of California Press, 1986, p. 10.
33 Kerby A. Miller, '"Scotch-Irish" myths and Irish identities in eighteenth- and nineteenth-century America', in *New Perspectives on the Irish Diaspora*, ed. Charles Fanning. Carbondale and Edwardsville: Southern Illinois University Press, 2000, pp. 75–92 (82, 88).
34 Miller, '"Scotch-Irish" myths and Irish identities', p. 87.
35 Taken from extracts of letters from Louise Bogan to Allen Tate, February 1927 and March 1941, collected in *A Poet's Prose: Selected Writings of Louise Bogan*, ed. Mary Kinzie. Athens, Ohio: Swallow Press / Ohio University Press, pp. 59–60.
36 From a selection of Bogan's responses to a questionnaire from the *Partisan Review*, 1939, collected in *A Poet's Prose*, pp. 60–2.
37 Ibid., p. 60.
38 Bogan, 'Marianne Moore, American to her backbone', first published in the *Quarterly Review of Literature*, 4.2 (1948), collected in *A Poet's Prose*, pp. 320–2.

39 As she claimed in a letter to Ezra Pound in 1919; see Moore to Pound, 9 January 1919, in *The Selected Letters of Marianne Moore*, ed. Bonnie Costello, Celeste Goodridge and Cristanne Miller. London: Faber, 1998, pp. 122–5 (122).
40 Bogan, 'Marianne Moore', pp. 320, 321.
41 RML XIV: Clippings files. See Authors A-Z, 'S', for all clippings mentioned.
42 RML VII:02:03, Reading notebook 1250/7: AMS 1938–1942, p. 28 onwards.
43 RML VII:01:01, Reading notebook 1250/1: AMS 1882–1915.
44 I use the term 'Celtic fringe' cautiously here, aware of its possible pejorative connotations, to mean '(the land of) the Scots, Welsh, Irish and Cornish, regarded as occupying the fringe or outlying edge of the British Isles'. See OED online: 'Celtic', definition 2c: 'Celtic fringe'.
45 For example, Arnold had urged: 'And, whether our Celtic partners will consider this or no, at any rate let us … remove the main ground of the Celt's alienation from the Englishman, by substituting, in place of that type of Englishman with whom alone the Celt has too long been familiar, a new type, more intelligent, more gracious, and more humane'. See Matthew Arnold, *On the Study of Celtic Literature*. London: Smith, Elder & Co., 1867, p. 7.
46 John Steinbeck to Eugène Vinaver, 23 March 1959, *Steinbeck: A Life in Letters*, ed. Elaine Steinbeck and Robert Wallsten. Harmondsworth: Penguin, 2001, pp. 619–20 (619).
47 Steinbeck notes, 'we are a restless, a dissatisfied, a searching people', in 'Paradox and dream', in *America and the Americans*, reprinted in *Of Men and Their Making: The Selected Non-fiction of John Steinbeck*, ed. Susan Shillingshaw and Jackson J. Benson. London: Allen Lane, 2002, pp. 330–8 (330). See also Moore to Pound, 9 January 1919, *Selected Letters*, p. 122 (and discussions in Chapter 1).
48 Ritchie Devon Watson, Jr., *Normans and Saxons: Southern Race Mythology and the Intellectual History of the American Civil War*. Baton Rouge: Louisiana State University Press, 2008, p. 250.
49 Steinbeck to Elaine Scott, 20–24 June 1949, *A Life in Letters*, pp. 361–5 (363).
50 Cited in Steinbeck, *A Life in Letters*, pp. 363–4.
51 See Steinbeck, *Cup of Gold: A Life of Henry Morgan, Buccaneer, with Occasional Reference to History*. New York: Robert M. McBride and Company, 1929; and *East of Eden*. First published 1952; London: Pan, 1963.
52 W. B. Yeats, *Dramatis Personae*, in *Autobiographies*. London: Macmillan, 1966, p. 457.

53 Jacqueline Genet, introduction, *Rural Ireland, Real Ireland?* Gerrards Cross: Colin Smythe, 1996, pp. 9–17 (13).
54 W. B. Yeats, 'Away', first published in the *Fortnightly Review* (April 1902), 267–82, reprinted in *Uncollected Prose by W. B. Yeats*, ed. J. P. Frayne and C. Johnson. London: Macmillan, 1975, p. 267. I discuss further this connection between Yeats's spiritualist practices and his interest in the powers of the Irish peasantry elsewhere; see Tara Stubbs, 'W. B. Yeats and the Ghost Club', *Irish Writing London, Volume 1: Revival to Emergency*, ed. Tom Herron. New York and London: Bloomsbury, 2013, pp. 21–33.
55 Genet, 'Yeats and the myth of rural Ireland', *Rural Ireland, Real Ireland?*, pp. 139–57 (152).
56 Ibid., p. 141.
57 James Kilroy, *The Playboy Riots*. Dublin: Dolmen Press, 1971, p. 6.
58 *Freeman's Journal*, 28 January 1907, p. 10; cited in Kilroy, *The Playboy Riots*, p. 7.
59 Synge, Preface, *The Playboy of the Western World*, in *Collected Works, Volume IV: Plays, II*, ed. Ann Saddlemyer. Gerrards Cross: Colin Smythe, 1982, p. 53.
60 J. M. Synge, letter to Stephen MacKenna, 9 April 1907, *Collected Works, Volume II: Prose*, ed. A. Price. London: Oxford University Press, 1966, p. 283.
61 *Freeman's Journal*, 28 January 1907, p. 10; cited in Kilroy, *The Playboy Riots*, p. 9.
62 *Irish Times*, 30 January 1907, p. 6; cited in Kilroy, *The Playboy Riots*, p. 36.
63 *Irish Times*, 30 January 1907, p. 9; cited in Kilroy, *The Playboy Riots*, p. 39.
64 *Irish Times*, 31 January 1907, p. 5; cited in Kilroy, *The Playboy Riots*, p. 56.
65 See Terence Diggory, *Yeats and American Poetry: The Tradition of the Self*. Princeton: Princeton University Press, 1983, pp. 64–5.
66 *Irish Times*, 20 January 1912, pp. 8, 6.
67 Debates ranged, for example, over whether peasant women would ever use the word 'shift' to refer to a piece of underwear, or whether country people would use words such as 'bloody'; even more open-minded reviewers questioned what they saw as Synge's over-use of bad language in the play: see Kilroy, *The Playboy Riots*, for further discussion.
68 Donn Byrne, Preface to *Hangman's House* (1926), cited in Ron Ebest, 'Donn Byrne: Bard of Armagh', in *New Perspectives on the Irish Diaspora*, ed. Charles Fanning. Carbondale and Edwardsville: Southern Illinois University Press, 2000, pp. 266–80 (271).
69 See Donn Byrne, *Blind Raftery and His Wife, Hilaria* (New York: Century, 1924).

70 Ron Ebest, 'Donn Byrne: Bard of Armagh', p. 266. Byrne inscribed a copy of his 1930 reprint of *Brother Saul* (1927) to Leslie, with an Irish Gaelic inscription; see Winthrop Wetherbee Jnr., *Donn Byrne: A Bibliography*. New York: New York Public Library, 1949, p. 25.
71 For more on Leslie and Fitzgerald, see discussions in Chapter 1.
72 Ebest, 'Donn Byrne: Bard of Armagh', p. 266. Bannister also discusses Byrne's friendship with Kilmer, Harris and Christopher Morley: see *Donn Byrne: A Descriptive Bibliography*, p. xx. For full publication details of Byrne's stories, see Wetherbee Jnr., *Donn Byrne: A Bibliography*.
73 See Wetherbee Jnr., *Donn Byrne: A Bibliography*, pp. 3, 10.
74 Cabell, review of *Messer Marco Polo*, *Nation* (2 November 1921), cited in *The Book Review Digest: Reviews of 1921 Books*, ed. Marion A. Knight and Mertice M. James (New York: H. W. Wilson Company, 1922), p. 67.
75 Steinbeck interviewed by Robert Van Gelder, 1974, *Conversations with John Steinbeck*, ed. Thomas Fensch. Jackson and London: University Press of Mississippi, 1988, p. 44.
76 See Jackson J. Benson's comments on this in *The True Adventures of John Steinbeck, Writer*. London: Heinemann, 1984, p. 20 (and discussions in Chapter 1).
77 For the full publication history of *Ireland: The Rock Whence I Was Hewn*, see Wetherbee Jnr., *Donn Byrne: A Bibliography*, p. 31.
78 T. P. O'Connor, introduction to Donn Byrne, *Ireland: The Rock Whence I was Hewn*. London: Sampson Low, Marston and Co., Ltd., 1929, pp. ix–x.
79 See Ebest, 'Donn Byrne: Bard of Armagh', p. 266.
80 Henry S. Bannister, *Donn Byrne: A Descriptive Bibliography 1912–1935*. Garland: New York and London, 1982, pp. xx; and foreword by Paul Mellon (1926), p. xi. Ebest describes how Byrne planned a film biography of Parnell 'at some point in 1918', thus providing evidence of Byrne's association with Irish politics; yet as Ebest points out, the portrayal of Parnell was to be of a 'Victorian gentleman', and Byrne later 'repudiated' Parnell as 'not the last figure of a great age but the first figure of a debauched one': see Ebest, 'Donn Byrne: Bard of Armagh', pp. 276–8.
81 Edmund Spenser, *A View of the Present State of Ireland*. First published c. 1598, ed. W. L. Renwick. Oxford: Clarendon Press, 1970, p. 1.
82 See Moore's first 'Note' to 'Spenser's Ireland', *Complete Poems*, p. 280: 'Lines 5, 7–8, 51, 63–4: "*Every name is a tune*," "*It is torture*," "*ancient jewelry*," "*Your trouble is their trouble*." See "Ireland: the rock whence I was hewn" by Don [sic] Byrne, *National Geographic Magazine*, March 1927.'
83 Byrne (1929), p. 8.

84   Ibid., p. 8.
85   Ibid., p. 7.
86   George Bornstein, *Material Modernism*, p. 109.
87   Moore also uses, as sources for the poem, Maria Edgeworth's novel *The Absentee* (1812), and the Cork-born poet Denis Sullivan's collection *Happy Memories of Glengarriff* (1930). See also Moore's 'Notes' to 'Spenser's Ireland', *Complete Poems*, p. 280.
88   Thomas McGreevy changed the official spelling of his surname to 'MacGreevy' in 1941; I have chosen to keep the original spelling for the purposes of my discussion, however, as this is the spelling that his American correspondents (including Stevens) used.
89   Daniel Tobin, 'The westwardness of everything: Irishness in the poetry of Wallace Stevens', in *Awake in America: On Irish American Poetry*. Notre Dame, Indiana: University of Notre Dame Press, 2011, pp. 87–112 (95, 94). Tobin cites a passage from Mario Rossi, *Pilgrimage in the West*, trans. J. M. Hone. Dublin: Cuala Press, 1933, p. 14.
90   See Thomas McGreevy, *Poems*. London: Heinemann, 1934; and Susan Schreibman, ed., *Collected Poems of Thomas MacGreevy: An Annotated Edition*. Dublin and Washington, D.C.: Anna Livia Press and Catholic University of America Press, 1991.
91   Désirée Hirst, 'The Sequel to "the Irish Renaissance"', *Canadian Journal of Irish Studies*, 13.1 (June 1987), 17–42 (19).
92   Mary Joan Egan, 'Thomas McGreevy and Wallace Stevens: A correspondence', *The Wallace Stevens Journal*, 18.2 (Fall 1994), 123–45 (124).
93   I discuss in greater detail elsewhere the important role McGreevy played in bringing Irish culture to his American modernist correspondents Moore, Stevens and Deutsch: see Tara Stubbs, '"So kind you are, to bring me this gift": Thomas MacGreevy, American modernists, and the "gift" of Irishness', *The Life and Work of Thomas MacGreevy: A Critical Reappraisal*, ed. Susan Schreibman. New York and London: Continuum, 2013, pp. 227–41.
94   Lee Jenkins, *Wallace Stevens: Rage for Order*. Brighton and Portland: Sussex Academic Press, 2000, p. 96; Egan, 'Thomas McGreevy and Wallace Stevens', p. 142.
95   Stevens to Church, 19 August 1948, *Letters*, pp. 609–10 (610).
96   Wallace Stevens to Barbara Church, 15 and 7 September 1948, *Letters*, p. 616.
97   Byrne, (1929), p. 87.
98   Stevens to McGreevy, 6 May 1948, *Letters* (1996), pp. 650–1 (650). McGreevy had sent Stevens a copy of his *Poems* (London: Heinemann,

1934), in April. See also McGreevy, 'Homage to Hieronymus Bosch', in *Poems*, pp. 13–15.
99   Stevens, 'Our Stars Come From Ireland', *Wallace Stevens: Collected Poems*. London: Faber and Faber, 2006, pp. 397–8 (397), I, ll. 5–12.
100 McGreevy explained the political and social context of the poem in a letter to M. E. Barber, reprinted in *Collected Poems*, ed. Schreibman, p. 104.
101 William Fogarty, 'Wallace Stevens, in America, thinks of himself as Tom MacGreevy', *Wallace Stevens Journal*, 35.1 (Spring 2011), 56–78 (62).
102 Joan Richardson, *Wallace Stevens: The Later Years, 1923–1955*. New York: Beech Tree Books, 1988, p. 312.
103 McGreevy to Stevens, 10 May 1948, Huntington Library, San Marino, California: WAS 143.
104 Ibid., WAS 143.
105 Stevens to McGreevy, 7 October 1948, *Letters*, pp. 617–19 (618).
106 Stevens, 'Our Stars Come From Ireland', II, ll. 1–8.
107 See W. B. Yeats, 'The Second Coming', *The Variorum Edition of the Poems of W.B. Yeats*, ed. Peter Allt and Russell K. Alspach. New York: Macmillan, 1966, pp. 401–2, ll. 21–2.
108 Stevens to McGreevy, 25 August 1950, *Letters*, p. 690.
109 Jenkins, *Wallace Stevens: Rage for Order*, p. 102.
110 Peter Brazeau, 'The Irish connection: Wallace Stevens and Thomas McGreevy', *The Southern Review*, 17.3 (Summer 1981), 533–41 (534, 538).
111 Jenkins, *Wallace Stevens: Rage for Order*, pp. 102–3.
112 See Stevens, 'Our Stars Come From Ireland', l. 11.
113 McGreevy mentions Stevens's birthplace as 'Reading, Pa.' in a letter dated 10 May 1948 (Huntington: WAS 143), while Stevens describes his visit to 'the old Zeller house in Tulpehocken, in Pennsylvania', in 'About one of Marianne Moore's poems', *The Necessary Angel: Essays on Reality and the Imagination*. First published 1951; London: Faber, 1984, pp. 93–103 (99).
114 Stevens, 'The noble rider and the sound of words', *The Necessary Angel*, pp. 3–36 (20, 23).
115 See letter from Stevens to McGreevy post-dated 2 November 1953, TCD MS 9123/32, and McGreevy's reply of 4 December 1953 (Huntington: WAS 174).
116 This enclosed draft is not cited in Holly Stevens's *Letters of Wallace Stevens*, but it can be found in the original manuscript: see Stevens to McGreevy, 28 July 1948, TCD 8123/5, f. 3.

117 Stevens to McGreevy, 28 July 1948, *Letters*, p. 608.
118 Stevens's first four letters were dated 20 April, 6 May, 12 May and 15 June 1948: see *Letters* pp. 586–7, 596–7, 597 and 600; while McGreevy's were dated 12 April, 27 April, 10 May and 26 May (Huntington: WAS 141, 142, 143, 144).
119 Stevens to McGreevy, 20 August 1948, *Letters*, pp. 586–7.
120 Stevens to McGreevy, 6 May 1948, *Letters*, pp. 596–7 (597); and McGreevy to Stevens, 27 April 1948 (Huntington: WAS 142).
121 McGreevy to Stevens, 4 August 1948 (Huntington: WAS 145).
122 McGreevy to Stevens, 21 August 1948 (Huntington: WAS 146).
123 McGreevy to Stevens, 4 and 21 August 1948 (WAS 145, 146).
124 Compare, for example, McGreevy's letter to Stevens, 7 March 1954 (WAS: 176) and Stevens to McGreevy, 19 April 1954, *Letters*, pp. 827–8. Stevens does not mention the meeting – though he does mention McGreevy's response to meeting him in a letter to Barbara Church dated 15 March (*Letters*, pp. 824–5).
125 See Stevens, 'Our Stars Come From Ireland', l. 11.
126 For further information on McGreevy's life, please refer to the 'Bibliographic Essay' found in the MacGreevy archive, ed. Susan Schreibman: see www.macgreevy.org/about.jsp#bioessay.
127 Frank Kermode, Preface, *Wallace Stevens Across the Atlantic*, ed. Bart Eeckhart and Edward Ragg. Basingstoke: Palgrave Macmillan, 2008, p. xvii.
128 Ezra Pound, *Literary Essays of Ezra Pound*, ed. with an introduction by T. S. Eliot. London: Faber and Faber, 1954, p. 287.
129 Ezra Pound, '*Dubliners* and Mr. James Joyce', *The Egoist*, l. 14 (15 July 1914), 267.
130 Louise Bogan, 'Approaching ur', review of *A Skeleton Key to Finnegans Wake* by Joseph Campbell and Henry Morton Robinson, first published in *The Nation* (19 August 1944), collected in *A Poet's Prose*, pp. 269–71 (269).
131 T. S. Eliot, 'The three provincialities' (first published 1922), *Essays in Criticism*, 1.1 (January 1951), 38–41 (38).

Chapter 3
Rural Ireland, mythmaking and transatlantic translation

> a place as kind as it is green
> the greenest place I've never seen.[1]

In her poem 'Spenser's Ireland', Marianne Moore asserts (with some self-mockery) a practice that was becoming ever more common within the work of her contemporaries – an idealisation of the Irish landscape from afar, despite an awareness of this act. Fintan O'Toole theorises that the 'invention of modern Ireland was driven by the Romantic search for a culture organically rooted in an authentic landscape. What was to be read in that cultural quest was the landscape itself'.[2] Yet certain American modernist writers, inspired by the focus placed on rural Ireland by the Celtic Revivalists, romanticised the Irish landscape that they read about in books or newspapers, or saw depicted in postcards or paintings – with the result that this landscape was not necessarily 'authentic', at least in terms of its relation to reality. In turn, the 'culture' that they found within this landscape was not necessarily authentic either. The 'landscape itself' was read into this 'cultural quest', then, but not quite in the way that O'Toole envisages it: as what was sought, and found, by these writers was a landscape that confirmed their own preconceptions of Irish culture. In the above lines from 'Spenser's Ireland', Moore is clearly aware of this somewhat flawed 'quest'; yet the end-rhyme between 'green' and 'seen' reveals her delight in the 'greenness' of Ireland despite her own suspicions that this might not be quite the whole truth. Like Moore, certain American modernist writers during this period – including Stevens and Steinbeck – became involved in an act of recreative translation, reimagining the Irish landscape through a search for 'authenticity' that was rooted in the writing and visual depiction of the landscape, and their readings of it, rather than in the reality of that landscape: a situation that was made even more complex when – in Moore's and Steinbeck's case, at least – they came to visit the country itself.

The efforts of the Celtic Revivalists had done much to persuade American writers that Ireland was a rural idyll – even if this was largely due to a fantastic reading of the Irish countryside and its inhabitants. Jacqueline Genet points out that in fact 'Ireland's rural population declined throughout the whole latter part of the nineteenth century' as a result of the potato famine and the consequent mass emigration, and that by 1961 'the rural population became the minority population in the country';[3] therefore, by the early twentieth century, country life might already have seemed in need of preservation. Genet argues that Irish writers first created and then perpetuated what she calls the 'rural myth' of Ireland – numbering among their ranks Yeats, Lady Gregory, J. M. Synge, Douglas Hyde, and Daniel Corkery, but also tracing the tradition back to 'Romantic' Irish novelists Maria Edgeworth and Lady Morgan (Sydney Owenson). Tied up with this rural idealisation, Genet notes, was a 'rejection of the town' and a refusal of 'the industrial world, the modern world'. But, as Genet also points out, this myth – based as it is on shaky foundations, with the peasant and his land in rural harmony – risks exploding, just as in the literature itself '[t]he peasant-poets often complain about their painful life'.[4] When American modernists turn to the Irish landscape in their writing, we find a contemplation of this rural myth of Ireland that is by turns naïve and knowing, enchanted by the promise of a bucolic haven and either indulging knowingly in the construction of the myth or deriving pleasure from its unreality.

In some ways, this turn to the Irish landscape within the work of certain American modernists can be paralleled with a similar impulse in other American writing during the period: for example, Sherwood Anderson's short story cycle *Winesburg Ohio: A Group of Tales of Ohio Small-Town Life* (1919) retreated into a pre-industrial past; while Steinbeck's cycle *The Pastures of Heaven* (1932) focused on the overlapping lives of agricultural workers in a remote Californian valley. These short story cycles rejected epic narratives, both in form and content, in favour of a regionalised and de-urbanised approach to storytelling, which could allow for a focus on the lives of individuals. In Ireland were emerging stories with a similar focus, composed by writers such as Liam O'Flaherty, Seán O'Faoláin and Frank O'Connor – some of which were published in American periodicals like *The Dial*, *The Bookman* and *Harper's*.[5] Most of these stories dealt with rural or small-town subjects; for example, the titles of the O'Flaherty stories published in *The Dial* in 1925 were 'The Conger Eel', 'The Foolish Butterfly', 'The Wild Goat's Kid', and 'Milking Time', while O'Flaherty published another story, 'The Little White Dog', in *The Bookman* in 1928.[6] Interestingly, too, the works by O'Flaherty and O'Faoláin that were banned in their native Ireland often found publication in the USA. For example, the March 1927 issue of *The Dial* included O'Faoláin's story 'The Bomb-Shop', which was about a group of Republicans making bombs for terrorist activities; yet the collection from which the story was taken, *Midsummer Night Madness*, was banned in Ireland following its publication in 1932.[7] In his critical work on the short story, *The Lonely Voice* (1963), Frank O'Connor links Irish and American stories in terms of their regionalism and their determination to shed light on minority voices or isolated communities;[8] but we can also see how these tendencies mark a wider modernist turn toward the agrarian and the rural. The efforts of the Celtic Revivalists to promote a rural idyll of Ireland, the publication of short stories by Irish writers in American periodicals, the turn towards the rural within 'local' American literature, and the syntheses between Irish and American stories as perceived by critics like Frank O'Connor all help to explain why American modernists turned to the Irish landscape at this time as a source of inspiration.

The preference for the rural over the urban, modelled by Synge, Yeats and others, and which influenced the attitudes of writers in America, has arguably continued into contemporary times. Eamonn Wall, an Irish poet living in America at the turn of the millennium, identified a similar trend within his American contemporaries migrating to Ireland:

> One important aspect of Ireland which these migrant poets have ignored, for the most part, is urban Ireland. Like Synge and Yeats, they have been almost exclusively concerned with exploring the natural beauties of Ireland. ... Ironically, these American poets are flocking to areas of Ireland which the Irish people have been deserting in droves for generations.[9]

While Wall's tone is strong, and his claims generalistic – for instance, Yeats's civic poems such as 'The Municipal Gallery Revisited' and 'Among School Children' might go some way to countering Wall's claim that Yeats's works focus just on the rural side of Irish life[10] – we can see how the efforts of the Revivalists put in motion a turn of events that saw the Irish countryside idealised and the urban largely dismissed within the work of American modernist writers. This chapter will underline the ways in which this preoccupation with the rural, and disinterest (or even disgust) in the urban, shaped the ways in which American modernists responded to, and translated, the Irish landscape within their works.

Questions of travel: Bishop and Moore

The easiest way to explode a myth is, of course, to expose the reality behind it. By visiting the place in question, we cannot help but have our fantasies challenged – or destroyed. Elizabeth Bishop, herself a constant traveller, would question the value of making trips at all. In her late poem 'Questions of Travel', the titular poem to her 1965 collection, Bishop describes the surfeit of experience that sometimes accompanies trips to faraway places:

> There are too many waterfalls here; the crowded streams
> hurry too rapidly down to the sea,
> and the pressure of so many clouds on the mountaintops
> makes them spill over the sides in soft slow-motion,
> turning to waterfalls under our very eyes.

As if in conclusion to such thoughts, the next stanza opines, 'Think of the long trip home. / Should we have stayed at home and thought of here?'.[11] Bishop visited Ireland just once, in 1937, and there is similarly just one reference to Ireland in her poems. In 'Over 2000 Illustrations and a Complete Concordance' she includes an anecdote from a visit to County Kerry amidst a list-like compilation of glimpses from places visited around the world: 'In Dingle harbor a golden length of evening / the rotting hulks held up their dripping plush'.[12] The lack of prepositions and verbs – is the verb that applies to the 'golden length of evening' missing, or does the poet mean that the 'hulks held up their dripping plush' *during* a 'golden length of evening'? – muddies the imagined beauty of the scene with more unpleasant, uncertain elements. This muddiness is extended by the unidentified attribution of the 'rotting hulks'; presumably, the poet is referring to boats, but what is their 'dripping plush'? Just as the waterfalls and clouds merge indistinctly – and somewhat uncomfortably – in 'Questions of Travel', here we have a merging of pictures that makes the scene alienating and oddly disturbing: a parody, perhaps, of a picture postcard scene.

It is perhaps not surprising, then, that in a memoir of Marianne Moore, entitled 'Efforts of affection', Elizabeth Bishop recalled Moore's delight in seeing a poem of hers bound in 'Irish green' while clearly distancing herself from this kind of sentiment.[13] A few years earlier Bishop had discussed the same topic in a review that she entitled 'A sentimental tribute'. Reviewing the 1962 Viking Reader of Moore's poems, Bishop concludes: 'Also, I don't like a bright orange jacket for someone whose great-great grandfather came from Merrian [sic] Square, Dublin'.[14] The sentimental association between colour and nationality is simultaneously upheld as significant and lightly mocked as (im)material. Indeed, in her much earlier poem 'The Map', Bishop had hinted at the disparity between 'the map-makers' colors' and the colours of places they depict, noting that where 'Land lies in water', 'it is shadowed green';[15] likewise 'Irish green' is more likely to be found on a paint palette label than to share any resemblance with the actual green of the Irish landscape.

Unlike Bishop, Moore was not disappointed when she finally visited Ireland in 1964 during her late seventies: even though it was a place, to coin Bishop's phrasing in 'Questions of Travel', of almost 'too much' green. During her visit to Ireland, Moore purchased several postcards as souvenirs, which depict poetic, romanticised or iconic subjects from Ireland's cultural history: these include the Lake Isle of Innisfree in County Sligo, turf cutting in County Mayo, O'Connell Street in Dublin, three different representations of the Book of Kells, and traditional cloaks worn by women of West Cork.[16] Moore's descriptions of her trip, meanwhile, are littered with heavily poeticised phrases. For example, in her 'Daily Diary' from 1964, Moore recounts arriving at Cork on the *Sylvania* following a long journey at sea: 'Wednesday 5 August … Ireland – verdant shore – Gulls – excited'; recalls a conversation on 27 September, 'Ireland is a *lovely* country – peaceful poetical'; and, on reaching Dublin on 5 October, notes: 'arrived 5:45 – Stephen's *green* green', referring to the famous Stephen's Green in the fashionable south side of the city. Moreover, in an entry dated 8 October, Moore draws a picture of three hills labelled as 'blue/ tan/ blue', adding above, 'another blue hill, paler silver'; while even her bedspread at the hotel in Cork, where she arrived on 9 October, becomes transformed into an artefact from Irish myth: 'emerald wool, dragons ... other side tomato red'.[17] It appears clear that Moore does not want to relinquish her tourist view of Ireland, or indeed her belief that it is as green (and colourful) as she has previously imagined, because this idea of Ireland continues to inspire.

That this picture-perfect world bears little relation to political or social realities does not necessarily hinder Moore's attraction to it in her role of visiting Ireland as a tourist for the first time. Pointedly, Moore's descriptions from her visit do not mention divisions between north and south, or make even a passing comparison between them, despite her visiting Belfast, County Down, Dublin and Cork. Although the early 1960s marked a period of relative stability in Northern Ireland, an abortive IRA campaign had been waged in the 1950s, and 1966 would bring the re-establishment of the Ulster Volunteer Force in response to a perceived revival of the IRA to commemorate the fiftieth anniversary of the Easter Rising. It is perhaps surprising that as someone who had written two poems, 'Sojourn in the Whale' (1917) and 'Spenser's Ireland' (1941), partly in reaction to events in Ireland, Moore chooses not to comment on the political situation during her visit.

Moore's idealised, apolitical stance is less surprising if we acknowledge that the septuagenarian American poet was satisfying a life-long wish to visit Ireland. Moreover, as Fiona Green points out, the period 1954 to 1964 had seen Moore 'turning to comedy and visiting Ireland as a tourist at a time when American and Irish histories [were] no longer so intimately entwined'.[18] 'Turning to comedy' refers to Moore's single 'Irish' output during the same period, her comedy *The Absentee* (written 1954, performed 1962). A dramatic adaptation of Maria Edgeworth's Anglo-Irish post-Union novel of 1812, Moore's play glosses over most of the political and social commentaries of Edgeworth's original and instead plays for laughs, engaging in particular with Irish, Anglo-Irish and English stereotypes that give the piece the air of a Restoration comedy rather than a mid-twentieth century satire.[19] A further reason for Moore's idealised, 'tourist' view of Ireland might be found in the sheer imaginative potential that Moore consciously derives from the Irish landscape and from the places she visits during her tour. As Nicola J. Watson points out, describing American tourists' tendencies when visiting cultural hotspots in particular, 'literary locations' can represent a 'fictive landscape awaiting imaginative (re)possession and (re)discovery'.[20] This rhetoric is not far removed from Moore's own plea in 'Spenser's Ireland' for 'reinstating / the enchantment' by reawakening Ireland to the richness of its cultural landscape. Though the poem describes a 'troubled' Ireland – concluding 'I am troubled, I'm dissatisfied, I'm Irish' – this dissatisfaction is challenged by the hope that Ireland might yet be reinvigorated by its own ability to delight: as 'a place as kind as it is green', where 'every name is a tune'.[21]

This hopeful view of Ireland as a place of enchantment and possibility, rooted in the greenness of its landscape, provides Moore with a locus of inspiration that is necessarily separate from America – and from New York in particular. In an undated draft of a letter to the Abbey Theatre playwright and director Lennox Robinson, Moore thanks Robinson for a picture she has received from him, presumably on a Christmas card, of an Irish scene. Writing on New Year's Day, and having begun with Christmas greetings – noting particularly the 'gift day of my Irish ancestors' (St. Stephen's Day) – Moore continues:

> I naturally thank you the more for y[ou]r holding me in remembrance, and for giving me a picture of so beautiful a spot in y[ou]r country. Such flowers & such outlook [with the?] sound of the sea – the very imagining of it enriches one. N. Y. has no such allurement [.][22]

The contrast between Ireland and New York, where Ireland is 'enriching' merely through the act of imagining it but New York 'has no such allurement', feeds into an ideal of Ireland as a natural paradise away from urban sprawl. Indeed, later in the same letter Moore notes that 'after the *Dial* was discontinued we [Moore and her mother] removed to an apartment in Brooklyn, where conditions are more healthful'. It is clearly a pastoral image of Ireland, rather than of a similarly less 'healthful' Dublin, that Moore has in mind here: and one that reflects the Celtic Revivalists' projection of the 'rural myth' in which, as Genet puts it, 'The town, which is essentially bad, is opposed to the country, which is essentially good'.²³

A similarly deliberate contrast can be found in a letter from Wallace Stevens to Thomas McGreevy in June 1953, in which Stevens comments on a picture of Maud Gonne that he has received from his Irish correspondent:

> The second paper which you sent me contained a most dramatic picture of Maud Gonne – the one with the dog. I am glad that you have sent these papers because they called attention to a character who will never be duplicated in American life. Her mere existence implies the vast difference between the two countries. For instance, I cannot even imagine the existence of that secluded garden in this country, if it was a garden: the brick wall. Many thanks again.²⁴

The strident language that informs Stevens's comparison – the affirmation that such a strong character as Gonne 'will never be duplicated in American life', and that her 'mere existence implies the vast difference' between Ireland and America – seeks to underline the necessity of the contrast itself. Indeed, the faintly ridiculous claim that such a 'secluded garden' could not exist in America confirms the extent to which Stevens is unwilling to relinquish his picture of Ireland as rural, protected – and necessarily different from home.

Ireland at a distance: Whitman and Stevens

'Stevens wrote of Ireland from a distance: it was a country explored through letters, books, and visual images which fed his imagination' – as Eamonn Wall notes.²⁵ For while Moore (and Bishop) did eventually visit Ireland, Stevens never did: his views of Ireland were informed by reading and thinking about it as an obstinate non-tourist. In a letter to the art patron Barbara Church in September 1948, Stevens describes an imagined visit to the Irish countryside, which contrasts with the relative grimness of Dublin: 'But the country could be more than that. I like natives: people in civilised countries whose only civilisation is that of their own land. Not that I have met any: it is merely an idea. Yet it would be nice to meet an idea like that driving a donkey cart, stopping to talk about the rain.'[26] Although Stevens's view of Ireland is arguably more romanticised, and condescending, than Moore's, his delight in the prospect of meeting 'an idea like that' fuels his poetic imagination in much the same way as the 'greenness' of Ireland delights Moore. As Fiona Green points out, commenting on another sound-bite from Stevens: '"Ireland, green as it is, seems to me much greener than it is", wrote Wallace Stevens in a letter to the Irish poet Thomas McGreevy; Stevens chose the "postcard imagination" as the most comfortable resort for an American poet who had never seen the country itself'.[27] Stevens's expression 'postcard imagination' and Green's phrase 'the most comfortable resort' are equally telling. The first points to Stevens's self-awareness that his interest in Ireland benefits from the distance between destination and source and the postcard's ability to present an idealised, visual representation of a place. Meanwhile Green reminds us that 'comfort' is at the centre of Stevens's idealisation of Ireland, and notes that a 'resort' is both an alternative and a created, even perfected, location for a holiday. Stevens's 'postcard imagination' with regard to Ireland represents a view of the country that is derived from staying at home and thinking of *there*, rather than actually making a visit to it.

The Irish-American Harvard librarian John L. ('Jack') Sweeney famously sent Stevens the postcard that informed his 1953 poem 'The Irish Cliffs of Moher'; he also sent Moore postcards of Irish scenes. In 1950 he sent Moore a postcard of 'Moore's Tree. Vale of Avoca. Co. Wicklow'; the reference to the Irish folk poet, and possible cultural forebear, Tom Moore, is surely intentional.[28] In another letter, from 1959, Sweeney asked Moore to explain her 'ancestral association' with Merrion Square for a lecture he was planning to give in Dublin on American poetry.[29] During her visit to Ireland in 1964 Moore took fifteen very detailed photographs of 10 Merrion Square, where her great-great grandfather had lived, accompanied by an inventory detailing the specific feature highlighted, such as the '18th c. stucco work detailed on first floor landing'.[30]

This anthropological, geographical, and even architectural idealisation of Ireland makes it unsurprising that American writers like Moore and Stevens indulged in a transatlantic translation of the Irish landscape, which risked glossing over the political realities of a country whose land had become synonymous with civil struggle. As Eamonn Wall notes, discussing Stevens's particular interest in Ireland:

> [S]uch concerns as contemporary Irish politics, family, religion, and the diaspora are generally outside his range of interest. It is the literary and physical esthetic which draws him to Ireland, and also the notion, which he felt strongly, that in Ireland the imagination is allowed freer play. It is ironic, of course, given the pervasive censoring of creative works in the 1940s and 1950s by the Irish Censorship Board, that Stevens would have chosen these decades to become interested in Ireland.[31]

As discussed in the previous chapter, Stevens's correspondence with Thomas McGreevy significantly shaped his attitudes to Ireland – with McGreevy encouraging Stevens's idealisation of Ireland from afar. Nevertheless even McGreevy was cautious in his praise of the present state of things in Ireland, even discussing in his first letter to Stevens the 'censors being difficult with books' there.[32] But Stevens chooses to interpret his view of Ireland from the more 'aesthetic' elements of their discussions. Inspired by letters from McGreevy, which expanded upon the synthesis of the natural and spiritual worlds within Irish culture, Stevens's poem 'Our Stars Come From Ireland' describes 'nights full of the green stars from Ireland'; thus Ireland becomes a poetic location rather than an actual place, a place of natural magic rather than of everyday life.[33] Stevens's use of the County Kerry-born McGreevy as a character in his poem reveals his desire to emulate McGreevy's deep spiritual connection to his hometown of Tarbert. As McGreevy explains in a letter to William Tindall of Columbia University, in 'Our Stars Come From Ireland' Stevens had done him 'the honour of thinking of himself as a Tom McGreevy of America'. But this substitution was predicated on the fact of Stevens's never having visited Ireland – as McGreevy noted in the same letter, 'Stevens was never, so far as I know, on this side of the Atlantic'.[34]

In a 1951 letter to McGreevy, Stevens explains this necessary distance between source and poem by noting, of the image of Tarbert he holds in his head, that 'I do not pretend even to myself that the image in any way looks like Tarbert because it consists largely of rocks with yourself seated on one of them, looking at a vast perspective of sea and cloud'.[35] Stevens merely picks out from the scene the elements that are most valuable to him. Stevens, then, pre-empts Bishop's question, 'Should we have stayed at home and thought of here?' by never travelling to the Ireland that he idealises: so that his image of Ireland can remain unsullied. For Stevens, the Irish landscape is not necessarily 'authentic' in the sense of being true to its topographical reality, but rather in the sense of being true to his poetic imagination.

As Stevens had no family connections to Ireland, and was actually of Dutch ancestry,[36] it would be inaccurate to read his poems about Ireland as essentially 'Irish American' in flavour: as Wall notes, 'it would be ridiculous to claim Wallace Stevens as an Irish American on the basis of his correspondence with Thomas McGreevy and because he wrote a few poems about Ireland'.[37] Daniel Tobin points out in his essay 'Irish-American poetry and the question of tradition' that the issue of Irish-American poets addressing Irish-American themes 'becomes even more murky when one considers those American poets for whom Ireland has no ancestral allure, and who yet have taken Ireland as inspiration for their own imaginative work'.[38] Thus the discussion of American poets using Ireland imaginatively requires a new approach, incorporating what Wall describes as the tendency in writers without a 'relational pull to Ireland' to 'bypass Irish America entirely'.[39]

This situation is made particularly complex in poems that use Ireland as a geographical locus of inspiration, but fuse this idea of Ireland with a consideration of American identity. Tobin notes, for example, how in Walt Whitman's poem 'Old Ireland' 'the iconography of the Irish emigrant experience becomes assimilated into the cosmos of Whitman's America';[40] this despite the fact that Whitman was of English and Dutch ancestry.[41] 'Old Ireland' establishes a kind of geographical shorthand for Ireland in contrast to the young, exciting America – thus almost predating the Irish-American immigrant experience in its iconographic reading of transatlantic emigration during the Famine years. The poem imagines 'Old Ireland' as an ageing, grey woman, 'Far hence amid an isle of wondrous beauty', mourning the loss of her son. But the poet consoles her:

> The Lord is not dead, he is risen again young and strong in another country,
> Even while you wept there by your fallen harp by the grave,
> What you wept for was translated, pass'd from the grave,

> The winds favor'd and the sea sail'd it,
> And now with rosy and new blood,
> Moves to-day in a new country.[42]

Here, then, Ireland is at once an 'isle of wondrous beauty', necessarily 'far' away; a place of mournful harps and more mournful graves; and a land of winds and water from which the son is blown westward to the 'new country' of America. 'What you wept for was translated', Whitman notes, as if he is conscious of the extent of his transatlantic translation of old for new – and young. But Whitman uses 'translated' in the biblical sense, meaning 'To carry or convey to heaven without death', as well as in the original sense of 'To bear, convey, or remove from one person, place or condition to another; to transfer, transport',[43] so that the loss to 'Old Ireland' of the young 'Lord' is reimagined not as a death, nor even as a resurrection, but instead as an ecstatic journey to an alternative 'heaven'. Yet the poet de-personalises the subject of the old woman's weeping so that while we might have been given 'Who you wept for was translated' – referring to the son – instead we are given 'What you wept for', to imply that it is perhaps the death itself, and the possibility of new life, that the woman weeps (and prays) for. Instead of ascending to heaven after 'death', however, the son is 'translated' across the Atlantic through his actual journey to America, which the 'winds favor'd and the seas sail'd'; while as a 'Lord', he reaches the new 'heaven' across the sea by virtue of a spiritual, symbolic 'translation'. In the *Bible*, such 'translations' are reserved for prophets like Elijah, who ascends to heaven in a whirlwind (in *2 Kings*: 1–11). Perhaps, then, we might see the 'son' of 'Old Ireland' as a kind of contemporary prophet, preaching a new life in an alternative world across the Atlantic.

Tobin links Whitman's poem to Stevens's late poems 'Our Stars Come From Ireland' and 'The Irish Cliffs of Moher', as in these works 'Ireland once again becomes a prism through which an American poet at once envisions and defines his work'.[44] In these poems Stevens is, like Whitman, keen to play on the geographical situations of Ireland and America: as if recalling Whitman's earlier poem, Stevens's 'Our Stars Come From Ireland' has a section entitled 'The Westwardness of Everything'.[45] Yet Stevens's 'Irish' poems look back towards Ireland from America: as if Whitman's metaphor of 'translation' has reversed its direction, and Ireland is instead the new and hopeful destination towards which the poet is transported. Stevens commented on this idea of Ireland in letters to McGreevy. On a postcard dated 2 November 1953, Stevens remarks how 'In recent years, thanks to a good many things, my conception of Ireland has changed a good deal. What used to seem a venerable land now looks young and fresh in the mind's eye. On the contrary, this country: the United States, while it never seemed venerable, has picked up a certain maturity and an appearance of being at least middle-aged'.[46] Stevens's first letter to McGreevy, in April 1948, had already established similar views: 'Ireland is rather often in mind over here. Somehow the image of it is growing fresher and stronger. In any case, the picture one had of it when I was a boy is no longer the present picture. It is something much more modern and vigorous'.[47] Such views of Ireland as a 'young and fresh', 'modern and vigorous' country are far removed from Whitman's presentation of 'Old Ireland' as an ageing mother mourning by a grave, her harp (an eternal, though arguably clichéd, symbol of Irish culture) left abandoned. Nevertheless, Stevens is careful to emphasise that his projections of Ireland are merely that: a 'conception' of 'the mind's eye', a 'picture' of the imagination.

It is unsurprising, then, that in 'The Irish Cliffs of Moher' Ireland is itself 'translated', poeticised according to the poet's own projections. The poem – whose subject is, fittingly, situated on a westerly point in Ireland, on the coast of County Clare – tells us much about the ways in which Stevens translates the Irish landscape in order to suit his own poetic imaginings, while re-affirming the interplay between landscape and tradition that is also at the root of Whitman's earlier poem. In a letter to Barbara Church dated 10 September 1952, Stevens explained how he came to write 'The Irish Cliffs of Moher': 'Jack Sweeney ... sent me a post-card from County Clare the other day – the worn cliffs towering up over the Atlantic. It was like a gust of freedom, a return to the spacious, solitary world in which we used to exist!'[48] Then, in a later letter to Church, he noted that Sweeney had sent him 'a photo of the Cliffs of Moher in Ireland last summer which eventually became a poem'.[49]

The eventual poem combines Stevens's nostalgia for a 'spacious, solitary world in which we used to exist' with a consideration of the physical enormity of the Cliffs, 'rising out of the mist' as if exceeding spatial and temporal constraints:

> Who is my father in this world, in this house,
> At the spirit's base?
>
> My father's father, his father's father, his —
> Shadows like winds
>
> Go back to a parent before thought, before speech,
> At the head of the past.
>
> They go to the cliffs of Moher rising out of the mist,
> Above the real,
>
> Rising out of present time and place, above
> The wet, green grass.
>
> This is not landscape, full of the somnambulations
> Of poetry
>
> And the sea. This is my father, or, maybe
> It is as he was,
>
> A likeness, one of the race of fathers: earth
> And sea and air.[50]

Here, Stevens goes beyond Whitman's geographical reading of Ireland, with its winds and waters and graves, to deny Ireland the existence of an actual, active landscape. 'This is not landscape, full of the somnambulations / Of poetry // And the sea', he argues, therefore stripping the landscape even of a relatively passive, dream-like poetic potential. Instead the signposts of landscape — the 'cliffs of Moher rising out of the mist', the 'wet green grass' — are taken 'out of present time and place', 'Above the real', in order to suit the poet's imaginative need for a nostalgic return. Rather than cliffs, grass and sea, we are presented with a metaphor for inherited poetic inspiration — where a 'race of fathers' inspires the inspired poet — that necessarily predates and excludes the present moment.

This 'race of fathers' might include Wordsworth, arguably the father figure of the natural sublime. Yet Stevens's denial of a literal existence to the 'landscape' of the cliffs risks challenging the concept of the natural sublime even as it evokes it. And though we can find evidence in Stevens's late poems of a nostalgia for Romantic verse through its spiritual expectations for poetry, he continues to view the spiritual element as curiously stinted when applied to modern writing. In 'Of Modern Poetry', from his 1942 collection *Parts of a World*, Stevens comes close to establishing what his own theory of poetry might be – if only through inference of what it is not. At the beginning of the poem, Stevens positions the modern poet as charged with the task of creating 'The poem in the mind in the act of finding / What will suffice'.[51] Thus while the poet is self-consciously creating the poem, he is also searching for satisfactory images. But rather than the sublime, we have the satisfactory.

Then Stevens moves on to a contemplation of how the situation was before 'modern poetry', noting, with some nostalgia:

> It has not always had
> To find: the scene was set; it repeated what
> Was in the script. (ll. 2–4)

The poet sees himself looking back to a time when one did not have to find the sufficient image: when the framework and the method for poetry were both clear. Breaking the line in two, evoking Shakespeare's own method of caesura, Stevens extends the dramatic metaphor to enact the break with tradition –

> Then the theatre was changed
> To something else. Its past was a souvenir. (ll. 4–5)

This sense of the past as a 'souvenir' denotes a nostalgia for a time that can only be remembered – as if the modernists' tenets to 'make new' do not allow the past to be useful in a constructive way. 'Souvenir' is appropriate here, as like Moore's mementoes of Ireland, or Stevens's postcard of the Cliffs of Moher, the past can only be configured in the present – just as the ideal can only be configured in the reality – as a (re)construction.

No wonder, then, that the conclusion to 'Of Modern Poetry' seems so filled with despair, the poet-as-actor blindly feeling his way with his instrument, without the possibility of the sublime to give him hope:

> The actor is
> A metaphysician in the dark, twanging
> An instrument, twanging a wiry string that gives
> Sounds passing through sudden rightnesses, wholly
> Containing the mind, below which it cannot descend,
> Beyond which it has no will to rise.
>   It must
> Be the finding of a satisfaction, and may
> Be of a man skating, a woman dancing, a woman
> Combing. The poem of the act of the mind. (ll. 18–26)

Rather than the sublime, to which the actor/metaphysician has 'no will to rise', the poem aims for 'the finding of a satisfaction'. This idea, of course, contains Yeatsian echoes, as we recall Yeats's acquiescent speaker in 'Nineteen Hundred and Nineteen':

> Some moralist or mythological poet
> Compares the solitary soul to a swan;
> I am satisfied with that,
> Satisfied if a troubled mirror show it,
> Before that brief gleam of its life be gone,[52]

Stevens's 'finding of a satisfaction' incorporates the fleeting search for metaphor – in, fittingly, Yeatsian images of skating, dancing or combing – just as in Yeats's poem the speaker lightly mocks the 'moralist or mythological poet' who searches for a comparison only to lose it straight away, the 'brief gleam of its life' gone. But both poets resign themselves to seeking out 'satisfaction', rather than the sublime – as if this is all that the 'troubled mirror' of modern poetry is able to reveal.

For Stevens, then, the 'poem of the act of the mind' befits modern poetry in that it is true to itself, and to its own moment of creation – but while the modern poets expect alchemy in the exact combination of structure, form and content within the poem, this alchemy does not lead to a generation of the sublime. Instead we must be content with satisfaction. In another poem, 'The American Sublime' (1936), Stevens asks, with some sarcasm:

> How does one stand
> To behold the sublime,
> To confront the mockers [?][53]

It is as if culture has moved so far beyond the possibility of the sublime that all that is left is the potential to 'mock'.

But for Stevens, what we are always left with is the poetry itself. As he comments in the third and fourth stanza of 'The American Sublime':

> But how does one feel?
> One grows used to the weather,
> The landscape and that;
> And the sublime comes down
> To the spirit itself.
>
> The spirit and space,
> The empty spirit
> In vacant space.
> What wine does one drink?
> What bread does one eat? (ll. 11–20)

Michael T. Beehler notes that 'in Stevens the sublime, the Kantian moment of the impulsion toward the transcendent, marks not the fallen limitation of representation and metaphor, but rather their boundless pervasiveness'.[54] Thus even though within modern American poetry there is a dismissal of the idea of the sublime – a reduction of its effect to a mere consideration of the self-conscious act of beholding the sublime through deciding what wine to drink or what bread to eat – for Stevens the sublime will continue to exist, will still 'come down / To the spirit itself'. It is not the tools of poetry that need to be changed, but our attitude towards them. For Stevens this means moving beyond the restrictions imposed by modern poetry, to find a new place for discovering the sublime. Yet what is bypassed in the process is the landscape itself, as 'One grows used to the weather, /

The landscape and that' at the same moment that the sublime comes to meet its own self.

Perhaps, then, it is 'old' Ireland – introduced to the poet by McGreevy in the last years of his life – that provides Stevens with a new place to locate the sublime, despite the pressures of modern poetry to deny its existence. The 'venerable land' that Stevens once saw Ireland as has now become 'young and fresh in the mind's eye':[55] this combination of historical longevity and imagined renewal allowing Ireland, and its landscape, to be simultaneously timeless and timely, as old as the hills and ripe for poetic plunder. Thus in 'The Irish Cliffs of Moher' it is 'my father', or 'A likeness, one of the race of fathers', that the landscape represents.[56] Like his description to Church of the world 'in which we used to exist', Stevens's 'race of fathers' is collective and pre-historical, asserting an identity that transcends genealogical inheritance. And so in turn the 'earth / And sea and air' (ll. 15–16), which conclude the poem, are spiritual, imaginary – and likewise 'Above the real'. As ephemeral as 'Shadows like winds', these elements are instead part of a place that predates 'thought' and 'speech' – a place that is located at 'At the head of the past' (ll. 4–6).

'The Irish Cliffs of Moher' represents, in essence, a twist on Fintan O'Toole's description of a 'Romantic search for a culture organically rooted in an authentic landscape': through his search for the sublime, Stevens projects his desires for Irish culture as a gateway to the sublime onto the landscape, but in doing so denies the landscape an authentic identity. Thus the actual Cliffs of Moher become subject to a transatlantic translation, whereby they are removed from their Irish location and turned into an abstraction so that they are emphatically 'not landscape', but something above and beyond it: 'earth / And sea and air'.[57] It is Ireland that inspires Stevens's search for the sublime, but it is Ireland that ultimately gets left behind. This is emphasised by the masculine characteristics Stevens places upon the cliffs, which evoke an inheritance that inevitably reaches back to the poetic 'fathers' Whitman and Wordsworth.

The patriarchal lineage of 'The Irish Cliffs of Moher' recalls the masculine imagery of Stevens's 1942 poem 'Notes Towards a Supreme Fiction'. Here Stevens's poet/speaker emphasises the 'virile' qualities of his 'major man', who undertakes a search for that place 'From which the poem springs'.[58] Similarly the lineage evoked in 'Our Stars Come From Ireland' is masculine, with Stevens depicting his Irish counterpart, the unmarried and childless Thomas McGreevy, as simultaneously a 'man' and a 'boy'.[59] This is far from the traditional feminised, maternal figure of Ireland (or 'Erin') that is integral to Irish culture: a figure that Whitman adopts in 'Old Ireland', and which has remained persistent, though controversial, in the history of Irish poetry. Seamus Heaney has, famously, been criticised for his continuance of the depiction of Ireland in this female, nurturing (and ultimately fecund) role – and particularly for his comment in his essay 'Belfast' that: 'I suppose the feminine element for me involves the matter of Ireland, and the masculine strain is drawn from the involvement with English literature'.[60] For Stevens, by reconfiguring the Irish landscape as an ideological abstraction, and as a poetic fatherland rather than a cultural motherland, Ireland is rendered both all-powerful and impotent, both pregnant with imaginative potential and denuded of the roots of that potential. That he has derived all of this from a postcard tells us all we need to know about the relationship between the 'real' and the imagined in Stevens's vision, and poetic translation, of the Irish landscape.

Art and landscape: Stevens and Jack B. Yeats

Stevens's imaginative, abstracted reading of the Irish landscape extends to his responses to the paintings of Jack B. Yeats, to whose work he was introduced by McGreevy. Yeats (1871–1951), arguably the most important artist in Ireland during the period, saw his work exhibited in Dublin, London and New York during the 1940s and 1950s. His paintings and drawings were also published widely in collections of Irish poetry and folklore; interestingly, the Macmillan Company had to send an apology to Yeats in 1934 for the unauthorised use of his illustrations in the New York edition of Pádraic Colum's *The Big Tree of Bunlahy*, which had recently gone on sale in the UK.[61] Though Yeats's paintings changed in style throughout his long career, becoming more experimental and expressionistic, they continued to focus on the scenes of country and small-town life that he knew well: markets, race-days, travelling circuses and the Irish landscape were all popular subjects. Additionally he painted scenes from Celtic mythology, and illustrated books for the Cuala Press.

Thomas McGreevy, as Director of the National Gallery in Dublin from 1950 to 1963, and Jack B. Yeats's close personal friend, introduced Yeats's work to his American correspondents. To Babette Deutsch, for example, McGreevy made bold claims for his friend's paintings, while lending them an air of folkloric enchantment:

> He is a great painter – more I think our own man – I mean Ireland's own – than his father. I made a little book about him which I shall send you. It will at least remind you that there is to be an exhibition of his work in New York in February or March. Incidentally the boys will be sure to like it (the exhibition). Children tell themselves grand stories about his pictures.[62]

In his very first letter to Stevens, meanwhile, McGreevy mentions that 'There's a little book I did on Jack Yeats's pictures (with some fairly good prose in it I think) which I will send if this reaches you all right'. In subsequent letters they discuss a portrait of McGreevy that Yeats draws to send to Stevens, and McGreevy sends Stevens an invitation to an exhibition of Yeats's paintings at the Victor Waddington Galleries in Dublin on 6 October 1949, enclosing an exhibition catalogue.[63] In 1952, no doubt due to the enthusiasm of his Irish correspondent, Stevens attended an exhibition of Yeats's paintings at the National Academy of Design in New York. Stevens tells Barbara Church in May 1952 that he will attend the exhibition on its second week of opening, and that McGreevy 'had Yeats send me a card, a pleasant gesture': an indication of McGreevy's determination to persuade the famously antisocial Stevens to be flattered into going.[64]

But this is, arguably, where McGreevy's influence ends. While Deutsch savours the book on Jack Yeats that McGreevy sends her, she confesses that this is mainly because she is very interested in the life of his father, John Butler Yeats, and his poet brother; she also notes in a later letter that she did not attend the exhibition in New York.[65] Stevens, meanwhile, did attend the exhibition – but his reaction is far from McGreevy's ideal of Yeats as 'Ireland's own' painter. In fact his response to the exhibition displays similarities, in his view of the relationship between the real and the imagined within Irish culture, with 'The Irish Cliffs of Moher', which he composed during the same period. Stevens begins:

> Having no real familiarity with Mr. Yeats's work, I had rather expected pictures of small size dealing with subjects, which, because of their familiarity to you, for example, would mean most to you because of the way they were done, but which to me would mean most because they were Irish. They were not like that at all. They were not paintings of reality seen in the space of the imagination. But they were largely the spaces of the imagination itself with all sorts of real references, of course, but still essentially unreal. At least this is as I thought of them. At that they came generally out of the air and weather of Ireland and were full of affinities with poetry.[66]

As with the postcard of the cliffs in 'The Irish Cliffs of Moher', we see Stevens taking Yeats's paintings out of 'reality' into 'the spaces of the imagination itself': so that the pictures, despite containing 'all sorts of real references', are 'still essentially unreal'. Moreover, just as the Cliffs of Moher are seen as something derived from 'Earth / and sea and air',[67] and become representative of a poetic inheritance that somehow predates time, here Jack Yeats's paintings come 'generally out of the air and weather of Ireland' and 'are full of affinities with poetry'. Stevens's comment 'At least this is as I thought of them' stands simultaneously as a defence against a correspondent who is a published art critic and as a celebration of his own subjective view of the Irish landscape, which he projects onto postcard and painting alike. This dual projection is unsurprising, in the context of Stevens's essay on 'The relations between poetry and painting' published in *The Necessary Angel* during this same period (1951), where he argues: 'No poet can have failed to recognize how often a detail, a propos or remark, in respect to painting, applies also to poetry'.[68]

Stevens's defensive comment implies, nevertheless, that he may have realised that his reading of Yeats's paintings is unlike that of other admirers: in comparison, say, with an editorial 'Comment' in *The Dial* by Marianne Moore, which expresses the detail and purpose behind Yeats's scenes – which assert that 'they have not been based on nothing'[69] – or with McGreevy's comments on the seriousness with which Yeats depicts the Irish people. In a 1942 essay on 'Three historical paintings by Jack B. Yeats', McGreevy summarises what he sees as Yeats's project, his reading of Yeats's art having more in common with Moore's observation of the painter's purpose than with Stevens's reading of Yeats:

> Very early in his career Jack B. Yeats turned to the life of the people in Ireland for the material, the subject-matter, of his art. In point of time, he was the first painter to do so. Here and there, an English or Anglo-Irish artist had, in the course of his ramblings, seized on the pictorial, the mere aesthetic, possibilities of the Irish scene. But Jack Yeats's work showed a whole-hearted sympathy, what it is no exaggeration to describe as a sense of identity, with the life of the common people in Ireland which had not been perceptible in the work of any painter before him. Looking back now, it is evident that the statement in terms of painting of that sympathy and that sense of identity with the people, amounted in his case to a vocation. He has stuck to it consistently for forty years and more, since before the beginning of this century. And as he was a born artist, a man who had the mysterious gift of being able at all times to make line and colour expressive, it was inevitable that as his experience and understanding deepened and matured, his interpretations of Irish life should become more and more comprehensive, should, nationally speaking, 'signify', to an ever greater degree.[70]

McGreevy's views of Jack B. Yeats – as a painter who is essentially, seriously and representatively 'Irish', and who continuously pursues a 'vocation' to depict Irish life – are far removed from Stevens's abstracted readings of the same painter as portraying what he sees as 'essentially unreal', essentially poetic scenes.

This disparity is most clearly shown through Stevens's reading of Yeats's use of colour in his paintings. Where McGreevy notes that Yeats has always 'had the mysterious gift of being able ... to make line and colour expressive', Stevens claims:

> The color was the most surprising of all. One does not think of color in relation to Ireland. Perhaps one is largely dependent on it when one loses so much in the mist and the rain. I should like to see the churches of Ireland and their interiors, the altars and the lights, to see how much

significance they have from the point of view of color. No doubt the color expresses that which made Mr. Yeats a painter, that is to say, made him want to be, and all that is beyond being an Irish-man or a man living in Ireland. It discloses the well at the bottom of the whole thing.[71]

For McGreevy, Yeats's use of 'line and color' is central to his self-expression as an Irish poet, and to his life-long project to convert his Irish experience into an art that might 'signify' something, 'nationally speaking'; however for Stevens, Yeats's use of colour is linked instead to 'the well at the bottom of the whole thing' – to an artistic, perhaps even aesthetic, desire to go beyond his Irish identity. As noted above, in a letter sent to McGreevy during the following year, Stevens would claim that 'Ireland, green as it is, seems to me much greener than it is';[72] but in the context of this letter this statement reads as part of a general dismissal of Ireland as a colourless country – as if all that greenness, like Yeats's obsession with colour, is a mere cover-up for all the 'mist and the rain'; and as if for Stevens the green 'Ireland' of his poetry is necessarily a purely imaginative realm, separated and removed as it is from the dull reality of the country itself.

This acknowledgement of a poetic inspiration derived not from Irish reality, or from a sympathy 'with the life of the common people in Ireland', but from an imagined ideal of Irish landscape, in turn hints at a lack of belief in the possibility of any sort of inspiration being derived from the 'real' Ireland, and a cultural snobbery on Stevens's part that sets his 'Irish' poems apart from the Ireland that Jack B. Yeats wishes to represent. At the same time, however, Stevens's imagined idea of Ireland is central to his theories of 'reality' and the 'imagination', in which imagination is seen as 'the next greatest power to faith: the reigning prince'; thus for Stevens both poet and painter are involved in a search not for a realist mode but for 'the miraculous kind of reason that the imagination sometimes promotes'.[73] The distance between American poet and Irish artist, then, is essentially aesthetic, but through constructing this framework, a cultural distance is also established – as while for Stevens 'Ireland' is an imaginative realm, for Yeats Ireland is a place that it is his life-long 'vocation' to know and understand.

Going back to Ireland: Steinbeck and Bogan

In his 1952 essay 'I go back to Ireland', John Steinbeck provides an intriguing counterpoint to Stevens's deliberate separation of the imagined Ireland from the real one. Like Moore, Steinbeck does visit Ireland; but unlike her, he is hesitant about his trip. Making the journey with his wife, Elaine, in 1952, he admits that it is something that he has been avoiding for some time – as if he fears that the reality will not match up to his expectations. Yet earlier in the year he had published his saga *East of Eden*, which told the story of his maternal grandfather, Samuel Hamilton, a Northern Irish immigrant to America, alongside the main narrative of the sociopathic Cathy and her two sons. It seems that writing the novel gave Steinbeck a final push to make the trip. As he puts it in 'I go back to Ireland', 'I should have gone to visit a long time ago, but I didn't. During the war, I landed at various airports and could have gone, but some curious, powerful reluctance always came over me when I got close to the home place. … Last summer, my wife and I finally went there'. Steinbeck introduces the trip by describing how his family in America had presented Ireland to him:

> I guess the people of my family thought of Ireland as a green paradise, mother of heroes, where golden people sprang full-flowered from the sod. I don't remember my mother actually telling me these things, but she must have given me such an impression of delight. Only kings and heroes came from this Holy Island, and at the very top of the glittering pyramid was our family, the Hamiltons.[74]

Buried in Steinbeck's witticisms and sarcasm, however, is a fear of finding out that at least some of these things are not true: as if he does not really want the 'impression of delight' that he was given to leave him entirely.

During the article, Steinbeck recounts how he made the trip in order to find his ancestors in County Derry – but he first visits the city of Derry itself, finding it to be an unwelcoming place with unfriendly hotel staff and a puritanical attitude towards drinking: 'Then we crossed and came to Derry, and it's a dour, cold city to an outsider – dark, angular buildings and uncrowded streets, waiting for something – a city of protest against the rolling green of County Derry and the lovely hills of Donegal across Lough Foyle'. Meanwhile, the 'rolling green' of the landscape itself leaves less of an impression on him than he had expected: 'It's green, all right – but so is Scotland. It seemed to me a different green, but I wouldn't submit the two greens to a colour test'. After leaving Derry, Steinbeck eventually finds the farmhouse where his ancestors grew up, only to discover that his relatives are long gone, together with all local memories of them. The dispiriting episode in fact causes him to conclude that during the trip, 'reality was violating every inherited memory and I was saying to myself that if the old folks went away from here, maybe they had good reason'.[75] We might recall Whitman's view of the 'new world' that awaits the son who leaves Ireland for America; through the ancestor of a son of 'old Ireland', the translation has come full circle.

Louise Bogan also visited the city of Derry during a trip she made to Ireland in 1937 with funds left over from a Guggenheim Fellowship that she had been awarded in 1933[76] – though, interestingly enough, in her letters she refers to the city as 'Londonderry' despite her Irish-Catholic background. In a letter to Edmund Wilson, Bogan describes Derry as 'pretty awful, except for about three streets, and a lovely park', but this bleak urban scene contrasts with the description of the Irish landscape that she gives later in the same paragraph: 'The light is so lovely. Yesterday I spent in Portrush, watching the Atlantic drive in from Iceland, between the dark cliffs. The clouded light makes the water look magical, and the whole country lives under that clouded light'.[77] She expresses a similar delight in a letter to Morton Zabel sent from Dublin, where she notes of her first arrival in Ireland: 'From Cobh to Cork by bus. – It is all true: this is the loveliest country in the world. Where, anywhere else, terrible ugliness would stand, at the curve of the road, there is a long, low house in a garden, or a round tower, or a hedge with yellow gorse all over it. Never a mistake.'[78]

But this delight with the 'magic' of Ireland is confined, within Bogan's descriptions, to the outside world – and particularly to rural communities. Though initially she celebrates in her correspondence with Zabel the 'affect' [sic] of the city of Cork with its 'lovely, clean spacious' layout, its 'bow windows', its 'broad streets and gray stone', her tone changes when she comes to discuss the 'insides' of Dublin houses:

What is behind the façades, I hesitate to think. Irish clutter, probably.
– I saw some, along with Irish poor taste, through some windows. O
Morton, they can't clean a plate or a floor decently, or print a newspaper
properly, and yet they have nobleness in their grain! I had a plate of ham
served to me for lunch, with thumb-marks on it, by a slavey who might
have been a duchess...[79]

Aside from Bogan's snobbery regarding her view of 'Irish poor taste'
and 'Irish clutter' – and her association of this inferiority with an inability to 'print a newspaper properly' – we can sense her disappointment
in the realities of Irish culture 'behind the façades'. It is as if Bogan
feels betrayed by Ireland – by her first impressions of the country as
beautiful and magical, and as 'the loveliest country in the world' – and
so blames the everyday Irishman for getting on with their (sometimes
grubby) lives. Beyond this is a shocked, though problematic, reaction
to the paradox that Bogan sees at the heart of Irish life – where the
clean broad streets contain houses full of 'Irish clutter', or where 'a
slavey might have been a duchess'.

Bogan expands upon these paradoxes in her letter to Wilson, where
she describes Dublin as 'perfectly beautiful' but also 'cruel and shut-up
and full of conspirators': it is a place promising much but giving away
little. She talks of managing to 'get away, to Belfast (it seemed, for a
while, that I would be in Dublin for the rest of my life. I became so
petrified, physically and spiritually)', as if she has become infected with
the same paralysis that overcomes the characters of Joyce's *Dubliners*.
On the other hand, though, she contends that 'maybe a town has to
be like that, in order that great literature be bred in it': perhaps it needs
to be 'Full of hidden dissension'. The whole leads up to a description that symbolises everything she loves and fears about Ireland: 'It's
incredibly beautiful, as a country, but terribly frightening. America
set up, in the blood, some clarity and definition that is antipathetic
to all this. – I never felt such a coward before'.[80] Through visiting the
country itself she has been forced to peel away the façade: to turn
from a contemplation of an innocent imaginative ideal and confront
instead an Ireland fraught with complications. This lack of 'clarity and
definition' within Ireland, which Bogan opposes to the straightforward
nature of American life, is found in the mystery and magic of the rural
landscape, and in the conspiratorial, confused and dangerous pull of

the city. The former is an ideal that unravels as her trip continues; the latter is more menacing, and more exciting. Perhaps this is why Bogan describes herself as 'petrified, physically and spiritually' by Dublin – as she fears that it might just pull her down into the muddying, frightening vortex of its terrible beauty.

★

Laura O'Connor points out, quite rightly, that when read with regard to Ireland 'the hyperbolic "greenest" risks becoming pejorative', as 'green' might be viewed 'in the compounded sense of credulous and uncultured and Irish'. But she goes on to claim that in Moore's lines from 'Spenser's Ireland' – 'a place as kind as it is green / the greenest place I've never seen'[81] – 'the utterance rebounds to brand the speaker as herself the "greenest", the most incredulous and the greatest dupe'. Warming into her theme, O'Connor remarks: 'since one cannot logically assert that an unseen place is the greenest, the admission paradoxically authenticates her as an Irish autobiographer by uttering an Irish bull. The ingénue-speaker is an outsider, but Irish culture is inside her, secreted within her idiosyncratic English'.[82] But what if the clue to Moore's description lies in her conscious self-identification as outsider, and as willing ingénue? And what if we were to suggest, instead, that it is exactly because we have not seen a place that we can assert that it is the 'greenest', as we come to terms with, and possibly even take delight in, the sway our imagination holds over us?

Stevens clearly seemed to think in this way. As noted above, he explained in a letter to McGreevy that 'Ireland, green as it is, seems to be much greener than it is', while in another letter he describes how at his home in Connecticut 'The grass is still green and a nice Irish rain is falling', in a neat moment of pathetic fallacy.[83] In such examples, Ireland's 'green' qualities are associated with abundance, newness and innocence, rather than with a lack of culture. Similarly, 'credulous' is not necessarily a pejorative term; in the case of both Moore and Stevens, their very incredulousness with regard to Ireland is what inspires them, while even the more wary travellers Steinbeck and Bogan seem uncertain about relinquishing their dream of Ireland as a 'green paradise'.[84] When Moore finally does visit Ireland, her excited descriptions of the places she travels to – as epitomised by her note 'Stephen's *green* green'[85] – signal the delight of the tourist rather than the knowingness of the insider. Perhaps, then, Stevens has the right idea – to take comfort in the 'postcard imagination' that he constructs around Ireland, rather than facing the reality, in order to continue to enable that ideal to inspire his poems. For Moore, Steinbeck, Stevens and Bogan, Ireland is the 'greenest place I've never seen', not just because it is a place yet to be visited, but also because such a place does not ultimately exist. It might, however, continue to exist in the imagination.

Notes

1 Marianne Moore, 'Spenser's Ireland', *Complete Poems*, ed. Clive Driver. London: Faber, 1987, pp. 112–14 (112), ll. 3–4 (counting title as first line, as was Moore's practice).
2 Fintan O'Toole, *Ex-isle of Erin: Images of a Global Ireland*. Dublin: New Ireland Books, 1997, p. 164.
3 Jacqueline Genet, introduction, *Rural Ireland, Real Ireland?* Gerrards Cross: Colin Smythe, 1996, pp. 9–17 (9).
4 Ibid., pp. 13, 9.
5 For example, Liam O'Flaherty's stories 'The Tyrant', 'Prey' and 'The Little White Dog' were published in *The Bookman* 65.6 (August 1927), 691–4, 66.2 (October 1927), 193–5, and 67.2 (April 1928), 145–7; see also Frank O'Connor, 'The Martyr' and 'The Ladies of the House', *Harper's* February 1953, 41–5, and October 1954, 58–64.
6 'The Conger Eel' was published in *The Dial*, 78.1 (January 1925), 5–8; 'The Foolish Butterfly' in 78.5 (May 1925), 402–4; 'The Wild Goat's Kid' in 79.2 (August 1925), 137–43, and 'Milking Time' in 79.6 (December 1925), 491–4. See also O'Flaherty, 'The Little White Dog', *The Bookman* 67.2 (April 1928), 145–7.
7 'The Bomb-Shop' was published in *The Dial*, 82.3 (May 1927), 197–209; O'Faoláin's *Midsummer Night Madness and Other Stories* was first published by Jonathan Cape (London) in 1932.
8 See Frank O'Connor, *The Lonely Voice: A Study of the Short Story*. London: Macmillan, 1963.
9 Eamonn Wall, *From the Sin-é Café to the Black Hills: Notes on the New Irish*. Madison, Wisconsin and London: University of Wisconsin Press, 1999, pp. 56–7.

10   See W. B. Yeats, 'The Municipal Gallery Revisited' and 'Among School Children', *The Variorum Edition of the Poems of W. B. Yeats*, ed. Peter Allt and Russell K. Alspach. New York: Macmillan, 1966, pp. 601–4 and pp. 443–6.
11   Elizabeth Bishop, 'Questions of Travel', *Elizabeth Bishop: Complete Poems*. London: Chatto and Windus, 2004, pp. 93–4, ll. 1–5, 13–14.
12   Bishop, 'Over 2,000 Illustrations and a Complete Concordance', *Complete Poems*, pp. 57–9, ll. 45–6.
13   Bishop, 'Efforts of affection: a memoir of Marianne Moore' (c. 1969), *Bishop: Poems, Prose, and Letters*. New York: Library of America, 2008, pp. 471–99 (481).
14   Bishop, 'A sentimental tribute', *Bishop: Poems, Prose, and Letters*, pp. 707–11 (711).
15   Bishop, 'The Map', *Complete Poems*, p. 3, ll. 27, 1.
16   Rosenbach Museum and Library ['RML'] XIV, Clippings Files, Britain and Ireland, collection from Moore's trip to Britain and Ireland in 1964.
17   RML VIII:04:03, Daily Diary 1964, entries from August to October.
18   Fiona Green, '"Your trouble is their trouble": Marianne Moore, Maria Edgeworth and Ireland', *Symbiosis*, 1.2 (October 1997), 173–85 (181). Green refers to the political contexts of Moore's earlier 'Irish' poems 'Sojourn in the Whale' (1917) and 'Spenser's Ireland' (1941); for further discussion, see Chapter 4.
19   For further discussion of the ways in which Moore adapted *The Absentee*, and altered it from the original novel, see Tara Stubbs, 'One title, three works? Marianne Moore, Maria Edgeworth and *The Absentee*', *Romantic Ireland from Tone to Gonne: Fresh Perspectives on Nineteenth-Century Ireland*, ed. Paddy Lyons, Willy Maley and John Miller, *Volume 1: Literature*. Oxford: Peter Lang, 2013, pp. 12–19.
20   Nicola J. Watson, *The Literary Tourist: Readers and Places in Romantic and Victorian Britain*. Basingstoke: Palgrave Macmillan, 2006, p. 4.
21   Moore, 'Spenser's Ireland', ll. 19–20, 67, 3, 5.
22   Moore to Lennox Robinson, no date (but probably written in the early 1930s, as *The Dial* was discontinued and the Moores moved to Brooklyn at the end of 1929), pencil draft with crossings out, RML V:52:32.
23   Genet, 'Yeats and the myth of rural Ireland', *Rural Ireland, Real Ireland?*, pp. 139–57 (147).
24   Wallace Stevens to Thomas McGreevy, 19 June 1953, Trinity College Dublin ['TCD'] MS 8123/31.
25   Wall, *From the Sin-é Café to the Black Hills*, p. 47.

26 Wallace Stevens to Barbara Church, 7 September 1948, *Letters of Wallace Stevens*, ed. Holly Stevens. Berkeley and Los Angeles: University of California Press, 1996, p. 613.
27 Green, '"Your trouble is their trouble"', p. 173; Green refers to a letter sent from Stevens to McGreevy on 17 April 1953: see TCD 8123/29.
28 John L. ('Jack') Sweeney to Marianne Moore, August 1950, RML V:64:37.
29 Sweeney to Moore, 22 January 1959, RML V:64:37.
30 See RML XII:07:24a–25h.
31 Wall, *From the Sin-é Café to the Black Hills*, p. 47.
32 McGreevy to Stevens, 12 April 1948, Huntington Library, San Marino, California: WAS 141.
33 Wallace Stevens, 'Our Stars Come From Ireland', *Collected Poems*. London: Faber, 2006, pp. 397–8.
34 McGreevy to William Tindall, 13 January 1960, TCD 8123/46. Tindall was compiling a pamphlet on Stevens, and had asked McGreevy several questions about his correspondence with the American poet (see Tindall to McGreevy, 9 January 1960: TCD 8123/45). For a more detailed discussion of 'Our Stars Come From Ireland', see Chapter 2.
35 Stevens to McGreevy, 10 September 1951, TCD 8123/26.
36 Stevens expands upon this in *The Necessary Angel*, where a trip to Tuplehocken, Pennsylvania, leads to a consideration of his heritage. See Stevens, *The Necessary Angel: Essays on Reality and Imagination*. First published 1951; London: Faber, 1984, pp. 99–100. See also Stevens's poem 'Dutch Graves in Bucks County' where he describes the inhabitants of the graves as 'my semblables, in sooty residence', *Collected Poems*, pp. 253–6, l. 6.
37 Wall, *From the Sin-é Café to the Black Hills*, p. 57.
38 Daniel Tobin, 'Irish-American poetry and the question of tradition', *New Hibernia Review*, 3.4 (Winter, 1999), 143–54 (145).
39 Wall, *From the Sin-é Café to the Black Hills*, p. 50.
40 Tobin, 'Irish-American poetry and the question of tradition', p. 145.
41 Whitman discusses his English and Dutch ancestry in *Specimen Days*: see especially 'Answer to an Insisting Friend', and 'Genealogy – Van Velsor and Whitman', *Complete Prose Works*. Philadelphia: David McKay, 1892, pp. 8–10.
42 Walt Whitman, 'Old Ireland' (first published 1861), *Leaves of Grass*. Philadelphia: David McKay, 1891–92, p. 284, ll. 1, 13–18.
43 'translate' (verb), *Oxford English Dictionary* online (www.oed.com), definitions 1b and 1a.

44 Tobin, 'Irish-American poetry', p. 145.
45 'The Westwardness of Everything' is the title of the second section of 'Our Stars Come From Ireland': *Collected Poems*, pp. 397–8. This section is discussed in Chapter 2.
46 Stevens to McGreevy, 2 November 1953, TCD 8123/32; punctuation as original.
47 Stevens to McGreevy, 20 April 1948, *Letters*, pp. 586–7 (586).
48 Stevens to Church, 10 September 1952, *Letters*, pp. 760–1.
49 Stevens to Church, 28 January 1953, *Letters*, pp. 769–70.
50 Stevens, 'The Irish Cliffs of Moher', *Collected Poems*, p. 439, poem in full.
51 Stevens, 'Of Modern Poetry', *Collected Poems*, pp. 209–10, ll. 1–2.
52 Yeats, 'Nineteen Hundred and Nineteen', *Variorum Edition*, pp. 428–33, III, ll. 59–63.
53 Stevens, 'The American Sublime', *Collected Poems*, p. 112, ll. 1–3.
54 Michael T. Beehler, 'Kant and Stevens: The dynamics of the sublime and the dynamics of Poetry', *The American Sublime*, ed. Mary Arensberg. Philadelphia: Penn State University Press, 1986, pp. 131–52 (141).
55 Stevens to McGreevy, 2 November 1953, TCD 8123/32.
56 Stevens, 'The Irish Cliffs of Moher', ll. 13, 15.
57 Ibid., ll. 11, 15–16.
58 See Stevens, 'Notes Towards a Supreme Fiction', *Collected Poems*, pp. 331–56, and especially sections I, II, IV and VIII.
59 See, for example, the first section of 'Our Stars Come From Ireland', entitled '*Tom McGreevy, in America, Thinks of Himself as a Boy*', *Collected Poems*, p. 397.
60 See Seamus Heaney, *Preoccupations: Selected Prose 1968–1978*. London: Faber, 1980, p. 34. Fran Brearton critiques this posture in her essay 'Heaney and the feminine', *The Cambridge Companion to Seamus Heaney*, ed. Bernard O'Donoghue. Cambridge: Cambridge University Press, 2008, pp. 72–91.
61 British Library Macmillan papers, Add.5575, Letter Book 4 July to 3 August 1934, Macmillan to Jack B. Yeats, 16 July 1934.
62 McGreevy to Babette Deutsch, 18 January 1947 [signed as 1946], Washington University Libraries, Department of Special Collections, Missouri, MSS 034, Box 1: Folder 3. McGreevy refers to Jack Yeats's father, the painter John Butler Yeats (1839–1922), and to Deutsch's two sons. The 'little book' he has written is *Jack B. Yeats: An Appreciation and An Interpretation*. Dublin: Victor Waddington, 1945.
63 See McGreevy to Stevens, 12 April 1948, 27 April 1948, and 3 October 1949, Huntington: WAS 141, 142 and 157.
64 Stevens to Church, 21 May 1952, *Letters*, p. 751.

65   See Deutsch to McGreevy, 9 February 1947, and 12 March 1953: TCD MS 8120 (microform). For more on Deutsch, McGreevy and the Yeats family, see Chapter 5.
66   Stevens to McGreevy, 26 June 1952, TCD 8123/27.
67   Stevens, 'The Irish Cliffs of Moher', ll. 15–16.
68   Stevens, 'The relations between poetry and painting', *The Necessary Angel: Essays on Reality and the Imagination*. First published 1951; London: Faber, 1984, pp. 159–76 (160).
69   Moore, 'Comment', *The Dial*, May 1929, pp. 449–50 (449).
70   Thomas McGreevy, 'Three historical paintings by Jack B. Yeats', *The Capuchin Annual 1942* (Dublin, 1942), pp. 238–51 (239); accessed through the Thomas M[a]cGreevy Archive: www.macgreevy.org.
71   Stevens to McGreevy, 26 June 1952, TCD 8123/27.
72   Stevens to McGreevy, 17 April 1953, TCD 8123/ 29.
73   Stevens, 'The relations between poetry and painting', pp. 171, 165.
74   John Steinbeck, 'I go back to Ireland', first published in *Collier's*, 31 January 1953, reprinted in *Of Men and their Making: The Selected Non-fiction of John Steinbeck*, ed. Susan Shillingshaw and Jackson J. Benson. London: Allen Lane/Penguin, 2002, pp. 262–9 (263, 261).
75   Steinbeck, 'I go back to Ireland', pp. 263–4, 263, 265.
76   See Mary Kinzie's note in Kinzie (ed.), *A Poet's Prose: Selected Writings of Louise Bogan*. Athens, Ohio: Swallow Press / Ohio University Press, 2005, p. 148.
77   Bogan to Wilson, 21 April 1937, collected in *A Poet's Prose*, pp. 150–1 (151).
78   Bogan to Morton D. Zabel, 14 April 1937, collected in *A Poet's Prose*, pp. 147–8 (147).
79   Bogan to Zabel, 14 April 1937, *A Poet's Prose*, pp. 147–8.
80   Bogan to Wilson, 21 April 1937, *A Poet's Prose*, pp. 150–1.
81   Marianne Moore, 'Spenser's Ireland', ll. 3–4 (counting title as first line, as was Moore's practice).
82   Laura O'Connor, 'Flamboyant reticence: an Irish incognita', in *Critics and Poets on Marianne Moore: A Right Good Salvo of Barks*, ed. Linda Leavell, Cristanne Miller, and Robin G. Schulze. Lewisburg: Bucknell University Press, 2005, pp. 165–83 (170). O'Connor does some quite intensive work on what she sees as Moore's use of Irish bulls in her 'Irish' poems, linking this to Moore's sustained use of double negatives. However, I have found no concrete evidence that Moore knew of Irish bulls, or that she deliberately used them in her work; I think it more likely that through reading Irish literature Moore became familiar with Hibernian phrasing in a more general sense. Moreover, Elizabeth Bishop

attributes Moore's use of 'double or triple negatives' to her 'conversational style'. I find this argument more convincing: see Bishop, 'Efforts of affection', p. 477.
83 Stevens to McGreevy, 17 April 1953, TCD 8123/29; and 15 December 1954, TCD 8123/36.
84 Steinbeck, 'I go back to Ireland', p. 261.
85 Taken from RML VIII:04:03, Daily Diary 1964, entries from August to October.

Chapter 4
Enchantment and disenchantment in political poetry

> I write in out in a verse –
> MacDonagh and MacBride
> And Connolly and Pearse
> Now and in time to be,
> Wherever green is worn,
> Are changed, changed utterly:
> A terrible beauty is born.[1]

The refrain to W. B. Yeats's poem 'Easter 1916', with its paradox of poetic inspiration and political fear, reveals Yeats's attempt to gain a sense of understanding from events that he has not been directly involved in. Nevertheless, Yeats takes it upon himself to put the rebels' actions into words. But to bear the 'terrible beauty' that their actions have engendered means to change the way one writes about Ireland: the manner of utterance is changed, as the language itself becomes charged with political significance. Yet 'Easter 1916' also becomes an act of literary revenge over political action; as the leaders of the Rising have been executed, it is Yeats, the poet, who remains to 'write it out in a verse'. The awkward end-rhyme between 'verse' and 'Pearse', separating the executed rebel-poet Pádraic Pearse from the verse-making with which he was associated, serves as a small act of remonstration against the rebels' decision to proceed in a way that diverged from Yeats's dream of a cultural (and peaceful) Irish revival.

But what Yeats's poem also marks is a movement within his own work from a declared position of non-involvement with politics to one through which he writes himself into the rhetoric of events. Only the year before the Easter Rising, Yeats had famously abstained from commenting on the events of World War One with his poem 'On Being Asked for a War Poem' (initially entitled 'A Reason for Keeping Silent'):

> I think it better that in times like these
> A poet's mouth be silent, for in truth
> We have no gift to set a statesman right;
> He has had enough of meddling who can please
> A young girl in the indolence of her youth,
> Or an old man upon a winter's night.²

Though Yeats's reasons for declining to comment on the war are not as humble as they first appear – his last couplet disclaiming his suitability for writing a war poem on the grounds of wide appeal, through his ability to please both 'young girl' and 'old man' with his verse – the emphatic iambic pentameter of the third line ('We have no gift to set a statesman right') reveals his determination not to comment, and his sense of rightness concerning this decision. Yet by 'Easter 1916' (composed on 25 September 1916), we find instead a poet writing himself into events – 'I write it out in a verse' conveying an equally stubborn determination to record the events of the Easter Rising as if it is his duty, and as if only he can do it.³

Yeats's example raises questions of poetic responsibility that have extended throughout the twentieth century, troubling poets such as W. H. Auden and Seamus Heaney. Though in his elegy for Yeats, 'In Memory of W. B. Yeats' (1939), Auden criticises the Irish poet for becoming wrapped up in the political and cultural frenzy of his country ('mad Ireland hurt you into poetry'), he contradicts this by emphasising the importance of poetry as a tool for discussion and a statement of survival: it is 'A way of happening, a mouth'.⁴ Later in the century Seamus Heaney displays a similar confusion concerning his perceived responsibility to write for a Northern Irish, Catholic community. Heaney's angry response to an IRA man he meets on the train, recorded in 'The Flight Path' (1996), seems in direct contrast to the great political poems of *Wintering Out* (1972) and *North* (1975):

> 'When, for fuck's sake, are you going to write
> Something for us?' 'If I do write something,
> Whatever it is, I'll be writing for myself.'⁵

But what Heaney's statement tells us is that even when poets choose to write political poems, they are still essentially writing for themselves: hence Heaney's famous 'bog' poems reflect his own reading of the Northern Irish Troubles, through his use of what Helen Vendler calls 'the archaeology of bodies' to retrieve from the bog 'a series of murdered bodies, serving as emblems of cultural predisposition to tribal sacrifice'.[6] Similarly, Yeats's 'Easter 1916' reflects the poet's attempt to rewrite and shape political events according to his own desires for his monument of verse. The 'terrible beauty' that Yeats identifies as the unfortunate progeny of the Easter Rising signals a rebirth of poetic expression, beyond the violence and change that political events have engendered, that brings the dual modes of enchantment and disenchantment to the fore. This chapter will assess the extent of enchantment and disenchantment with Ireland in political poems by Americans Lola Ridge and Marianne Moore during a troubled period of history. And, in using 'Easter 1916' as a model, it will also ask to what extent a poet, even when writing a political poem, is always writing for herself.

Responses to the Easter Rising

'In April 1916, the Irish Volunteers of the I. R. B., ... after a conference in Liberty Hall, Dublin, planned a rising in Dublin which, as an immediate objective, would involve the seizure of a number of positions dominating the city, to enable the Volunteers from the country to ambush, harass and resist all British reinforcements'.[7] In his summary of the events of the Easter Rising, Edward Malins notes that despite a rather inauspicious start – during which the average Dubliner was less than enthusiastic, and instead disapproved of the looting that ensued – the insurrection of the Irish Volunteers inevitably won some support: as 'Heroism of the few against the many, almost whatever the cause, is bound to arouse sympathy'. This sympathy, of course, only increased when the leaders of the Rising were rounded up, imprisoned, and – with some exceptions – executed, on the orders of the British government. But pertinent to this study is the undercurrent of American support that ran throughout.[8] Malins notes, for example, that the Rising was ultimately a failure 'despite American dollars and some preparation'; these 'American dollars' had funded the Volunteers' efforts against a background of indifference within Ireland – as 'popular feeling in Dublin and the provinces had not backed it'.[9] Meanwhile the now notorious 'Easter Proclamation' of the Irish Republic, which Pádraic Pearse read out on the steps of the General Post Office, referred to the support of 'Ireland's exiled children in America'.[10] As Patrick Ward puts it, the declaration, 'like most foundational texts, elevates unquestioned premises into a universal and timeless scheme': thus Irish America was inscribed, unquestioningly, into the rhetoric of the Rising before it had even begun.[11]

In the weeks following the Rising – and with daily news of imprisonments, unfair trials and firing-squad executions – America was naturally brought further into the debate. The problem was that, as Malins puts it, 'within a month the British Government had lit a flame of martyrdom around the leaders, that turned the revolt into a triumphant success, providing an emotional stimulus for the birth of a nation'.[12] Thus while the cause of Irish independence could be stepped up, so too might anti-British feeling: creating a potent concoction for Irish-American nationalists. As Alan J. Ward points out, Irish Americans could capitalise on the situation to argue that '[t]he principles of American democracy ... were the principles for which Ireland was fighting. Ireland's struggle for freedom from English tyranny was therefore America's struggle too and the enemy was a shared one'.[13]

When we consider the number of Americans of Irish descent who lived in America during this period, their political influence becomes less surprising. As F. M. Carroll concedes, 'Americans of Irish descent may have represented nearly nineteen per cent of the entire population by 1920', and 'were a very remarkable and powerful element of American society': indeed, Irish Americans played hugely important roles in government, the police and the press.[14] Following the British government's mishandling of the Rising, *The Washington Post* carried biographical sketches of some of the known leaders and an analysis of the rebellion by New York resident Pádraic Colum. Colum and his wife, Mary, would assemble these sketches into a book, *The Irish Rebellion of 1916 and its Martyrs: Erin's Tragic Easter*.[15] Meanwhile, Eleanor Cox arranged a meeting of New York poets to express sympathy for the insurgents, and the recently established Friends of Irish Freedom (FOIF) collaborated with Clan na Gael to set up an 'Irish

Bazaar' to welcome Irish refugees like Nora Connolly, daughter of the executed rebel James Connolly. During this time, as Carroll notes, American opinion as a whole turned towards Irish nationalist causes, thanks mainly to Britain's mishandling of matters: 'although there were exceptions, native American opinion was predictable enough: it disliked the rebellion but tended to be shocked by the subsequent executions and disgusted with the British government's blunderings with Home Rule, [Roger] Casement's execution and the Irish-American relief efforts'.[16] In the meantime, the mainstream American press continued to debate Irish political matters: indeed, Carroll points out that even 'more sceptical' newspapers such as *The Literary Digest* had been discussing the question of Home Rule in Ireland as early as 1910.[17] 'The result was that opinion on the Irish question had reached such intensity that it could no longer be ignored or forgotten'.[18]

Ideological enchantment: Lola Ridge's 'Irish' poems

New York in the 1910s and 1920s was teeming with Irish-American writers and artists (and Irish-born expatriates) including Francis Hackett, literary editor of the New York journal *The New Republic*; artist, and wife of Alfred Stieglitz, Georgia O'Keeffe; Enniskillen-born poet Eleanor Cox; writers and critics Kay Boyle and Horace Gregory; and Irish-born writers Pádraic and Mary Colum and Joseph Campbell.[19] Hackett published his first full-length work in New York, *Ireland: A Study in Nationalism* in 1918, which blamed British treatment of the Irish for the Easter Rising and decided that Home Rule should be sought for Ireland. The book put forward Ireland's case as a 'depleted country' left 'retarded, handicapped, distrusted' by the actions of the 'British empire'.[20] Poet and editor Lola Ridge was part of the same intellectual scene.[21] Appointed American editor of *Broom* in February 1922, as part of her position Ridge was required to host a weekly literary salon on Thursday afternoons. All the new and upcoming writers and thinkers attended – including Hart Crane and William Carlos Williams – and Moore records visits to Broom's salon in her diaries.[22]

Dublin-born Ridge felt a life-long affiliation to Ireland, but in her 'Irish' poems Ireland was associated with her socialist politics.

Though this personal take reveals parallels with Yeats's self-concern to write himself into verse in 'Easter 1916' and with Heaney's claim to 'write for himself' in 'The Flight Path', Ridge's enchantment with Irish nationalism following the Rising is intricately connected with political ideology. Ridge's most direct response to political events in Ireland was her poem 'Tidings (Easter, 1916)', published in her first collection *The Ghetto and Other Poems* in 1918. Interestingly, though its subtitle appears to echo Yeats's poem, the fact that Yeats chose to delay publishing 'Easter 1916' until 1920 tells us that it is unlikely that Ridge would have seen a version of the poem.[23] It is more likely that her subtitle 'Easter, 1916' refers to the same mythology surrounding the date that Yeats would have tapped into for his poem. Daniel Tobin contends that Ridge's work 'comes to echo the spiritual radicalism of Padraic [sic] Pearse',[24] thus emphasising her association with the ideological rhetoric of the leaders of the Rising before and during the events of Easter 1916 rather than with Yeats's reluctant acquiescence to the cause after the rebels had been executed.

As if to support this reading of Ridge as an ally of the Rising, the poem uses the present continuous tense to emphasise the poet/speaker's desire to be part of the action – the concluding lines opining, 'They are fighting tonight in Sackville street / And I am not there'. But the opening lines contain axiomatic statements that are concerned with truth, liberty and freedom of expression, as if for Ridge the Irish rebels' execution is just one example of a much wider problem:

> Censored lies that mimic truth …
> Censored truth as pale as fear …
> My heart is like a rousing bell –
> And but the dead to hear …[25]

Ridge's contemporary Horace Gregory noted that she 'was possessed of a Celtic imagination whose insights gave life and colour to her convictions',[26] but here, in the poem's generalised opening, we can see how Irish events are rendered symbolic under Ridge's political gaze. What concerns Ridge here is the widespread problem of censorship, which is marked by the hypocrisy that lies in the British government's response to the rebels' demands; indeed, the trochaic metre of the opening couplet, and its personification of 'truth' as 'pale as fear', recall Shelley's 'The Mask of Anarchy' (1819), itself a protest against an execution – the British Government's massacre at Peterloo, Manchester.[27] This echo of Shelley's poem gives 'Tidings' a curiously archaic feel, while identifying itself as (romantic) polemic. Stirred up, here, is Ridge's desire to clamour in response to the silencing of the rebels' demands at the hands of the British, and to clang a 'rousing bell' to make this injustice known.

This symbolising of events, at a distance from them, is even clearer in Ridge's poem 'Incompatibility', published in her aptly titled third collection *Red Flag*:

> Bull's-hide whit under red wrath
> And a curt tone of blue …
> By a gold harp on a green cloth –
> How should they blend, these two?[28]

Daniel Tobin notes: 'though long departed from Ireland, Ridge's poem places her concern with the country of her birth and its continued dominance by John Bull's Union Jack in a volume that promotes its leftist sensibility in its title'.[29] The 'Incompatibility' that the poem despairs of – that between the 'Bull's-hide' of Britain and the 'harp' of Ireland, and of the red and blue crossed with green and gold – is, according to the poem, culturally and historically enduring. Yet the publication date of the collection, 1927, comes some years after the Anglo-Irish Treaty of December 1921. The poet's continued use of national stereotypes hints at an evasion of the present moment. For example, she does not address the more subtle complications and internal struggles that the division of Ireland, and the ensuing civil war, have caused; while the enduring portrayal of colonised and coloniser seems curiously outmoded. Instead, by discussing again the 'incompatibility' of Britain and Ireland, Ridge continues to revisit old arguments: and unlike Yeats's denunciation in 'Easter 1916' of the kind of sectarian divisions encouraged 'wherever green is worn',[30] Ridge's poem continues to use the cliché of 'national' colours (red, blue, green and gold) to rehearse old resentments.

Ridge's distance from events in Ireland allows her, then, to romanticise Irish culture and evade the troubled uncertainties of contemporary events. But the stereotyping of political heroism in Ridge's 'Irish' poems is reflective of a wider trend. John Harrington has revealed the extent to which New York critics such as Louise Bryant, Emma Goldman and H. L. Mencken romanticised events in Ireland in a display of uncharacteristic sentimentality and cultural bandwagonning. Harrington argues that these critics were influenced by the endeavours of three figures involved in Irish drama: the actor Whitford Kane, the playwright Lord Dunsany, and the critic Ernest Boyd, author of *Ireland's Literary Renaissance* (1916). As Harrington puts it, '[w]ithout evident pressure, Kane, Dunsany, and Boyd came to America and in a brief span of years around 1916 helped inspire in Manhattan a novel idea of "Ireland" that was eagerly embraced by their reviewers, Goldman, Bryant, and Mencken'. For example Goldman, known as 'Red Emma' for her anarchistic views, 'seem[ed] suddenly to suspend the power of critique' when she came to discuss Irish drama.[31] In her study *The Social Significance of Modern Drama* (1914), Goldman notes wistfully that: 'Only a people unspoiled by the dulling hand of civilisation and free from artifice can retain such simplicity of faith and remain so imaginative, so full of fancy and dreams, wild and fiery, which have kindled a spark in the Irish dramatists of our time'.[32] Meanwhile the social critic Louise Bryant, usually hard-headed and balanced in her commentaries, describes the Easter Rising as 'a splendid revolt ... led by poets and scholars ... fighting with the fervour of saints with a copy of Sophocles in one hand and a rifle in the other'.[33] Lastly, the 'hardest-nosed newspaperman of them all', H. L. Mencken, appears to lose all sense while reviewing Ernest Boyd's *Ireland's Literary Renaissance* for *Smart Set*: the Irish, he claims, 'face a firing-squad with sheaves of sonnets under their arms'.[34] As Harrington notes, 'Thus does the idea of "Ireland" transform capable, ambitious and activist thinkers into sentimental fools'.[35]

Though Harrington's claims are strong, and perhaps unfair given the strong current of popular sympathy for those executed, they do underline the extent to which certain New York critics and poets, Ridge included, became enchanted by Irish nationalist politics in the aftermath of the Rising. Their distance from events allowed them to become wrapped up in the myth of the poet-warrior and to avert their gaze from the political consequences of Easter 1916 and the ensuing decades of civil uncertainty and unrest.

Enchantment and disenchantment: Marianne Moore's 'Irish' poems

The 'idea of "Ireland"' clearly held a certain mystique for a relatively inexperienced poet, Marianne Moore, as she tried to make her way onto the New York social scene in the years preceding and following the Rising. In December 1915 Moore made her first extended trip to New York, an experience she described in letters to her brother, John Warner Moore, as her 'sojourn in the whale'; of the four-part sequence of letters sent to Warner, the last two carry this title.[36] This trip to New York signalled Moore's emergence as an established poet – and 'marked the end of her apprenticeship', as Linda Leavell puts it.[37] Moore's letters describing her trip to New York recount visiting Alfred Stieglitz's gallery '291', dining with poet and editor Alfred Kreymborg, meeting the poet and artist Adolf Wolff, and discussing poets Amy Lowell, Ezra Pound, Richard Aldington and H. D.[38] Yet the poem that Moore composed in the period following the Easter Rising – her first 'Irish' poem – was given the same name as her trip to New York: 'Sojourn in the Whale'. Proud of the sentiments expressed in the poem, Moore enclosed a copy of 'Sojourn in the Whale' in one of her first letters to Lola Ridge in April 1919.[39] This dual naming of personal experience and political poem underlines Moore's individualised response to the Rising, which sees her, like Yeats in 'Easter 1916' and Ridge in 'Tidings (Easter, 1916)', writing herself into the story.

The highly personalised link between 'Sojourn in the Whale' and Moore's own experiences, and its quixotic poeticising of the Easter Rising, appear to emphasise an individual's basic right to experience within a national context. After all, throughout the poem, Ireland (the female speaker) is addressed as an individual:

> Trying to open locked doors with a sword, threading
>   the points of needles, planting shade trees
>   upside down; swallowed by the opaqueness of one whom the seas
> love better than they loved you, Ireland –
>
> you have lived and lived on every kind of shortage.
>   You have been compelled by hags to spin

> gold thread from straw and have heard men say:
> 'There is a feminine temperament in direct contrast to ours,
>
> which makes her do these things. Circumscribed by a
>   heritage of blindness and native
>   incompetence, she will become wise and will be forced to give in.
> Compelled by experience, she will turn back;
>
> water seeks its own level';
>   and you have smiled. 'Water in motion is far
>   from level.' You have seen it, when obstacles happened to bar
> the path, rise automatically.[40]

In the poem's opening lines, Moore offers variations upon a theme – hinting at the futility of opening 'locked doors with a sword' (l. 1), the impossibility of 'threading/ the points of needles' (ll. 1–2), and the pointlessness of 'planting shade trees/ upside down' (ll. 2–3) – in order to envisage the confusion and frustration that could ensue should anyone whose imagination is naturally free and 'incapable of the shut door' encounter only 'locked doors'. Hence those who are guilty of locking those doors – the British government, which is not allowing Ireland the freedom it requires – are accused of representing an 'opaqueness', which 'swallows' Ireland, and its imaginative potential, whole. 'Opaqueness' (l. 3), a perverse onomatopoeia in that it inhabits and conveys an impression of nothing, and is rhythmically flat, represents for Moore the antithesis of the Irish imagination and the American spirit.

Throughout 'Sojourn in the Whale', the colonial occupier enforces an 'opaqueness' that requires the Irish to perform apparently impossible feats in order to realise their imaginative potential. In the second stanza, for example, the Irish are 'compelled' to perform alchemy in order to survive. They are forced to 'spin/ gold thread from straw' (ll. 6–7) because the different kinds of 'shortage' they face, as a result of the British occupation, are both economic and artistic. Whereas 'every kind of shortage' (l. 5) recalls the Great Famine of 1845–49, and the weaving metaphor in the following lines suggests industrial or economic deprivation, the imaginative shortage suggested by the alchemical idea is just as threatening. A lack of experience emerges as a further 'kind of shortage' described in the poem. In Moore's 1921 poem 'New York', experience – found in the last line's Jamesian expression '"accessibility to experience"' – represents new and exciting opportunities.[41] In 'Sojourn in the Whale', however, Ireland's experience is limited and limiting, while the activities described are as futile as they are physically and mentally stultifying. Moreover, 'experience' exercises its own restraint upon the Irish – '"Compelled by experience, she will turn back"' (l. 12) – as it reminds them of past failed rebellions and past suffering. This stands in stark contrast to the forward-looking notion of 'experience' offered by Moore's 'New York'.

What is particularly interesting here is how Moore's depictions of 'shortage' can be traced to her personal family background. The weaving motif recalls the Scotch-Irish settlers in New England who, according to the historian Maldwyn A. Jones, brought their skills with them to America: 'The Scotch-Irish ... introduced the combined farming-weaving economy based on flax growing and the spinning and weaving of fine linen cloth'.[42] A subtle irony implicit in Moore's poem, then, is that although the Irish were 'compelled' to 'spin/ gold thread from straw' (ll. 6–7), Scotch-Irish immigrants to North America could put into practice, through skills acquired during periods of 'shortage', a dual economy derived from 'straw' ('flax') and 'gold thread' ('fine linen cloth'). Its implication that spinning gold thread from straw is not as impossible as it might first seem offers hope that a similar change of fortunes is possible: one, indeed, on which both the native Irish and Americans of Irish descent may be able to capitalise.

When the British (presumably male) speaker takes over in line 8, we see him dismissing the feminised Ireland with tired clichés and psychological restraint, both intended to limit the country's 'accessibility to experience'. The Irish become trapped not only by the British occupiers' actions but also by the language that contains and controls them. The use of the passive in 'Circumscribed' (l. 9), 'be forced' (l. 11) and 'Compelled' (l. 12) implies that the Irish are shackled by their own self-restraint. This idea is enforced by the British speaker's implication that the Irish are either too misguided or too ignorant – thanks to their 'blindness' and 'native/incompetence' (ll. 10–11) – to change their situation. In this context, 'water seeks its own level' (l. 13) becomes as much a comment on the intelligence of the Irish as a complacent assurance that each nation knows its own natural limits. Moreover, underlying the whole stanza, and carried through into the next, is the sense of physical boundaries, suggested by 'Circumscribed' – meaning literally 'to draw a line round, encompass, limit, confine' – by 'turn back', and by 'its own level':[43] all are metaphors of physical containment, and are oddly prescient considering how Ireland would be divided geographically less than five years after the poem was written.

But 'Sojourn in the Whale' offers an alternative: it suggests that Ireland, through harnessing the political and imaginative potential of the Easter Rising, might create new conditions for 'experience' and rediscover its natural expression. By forging a link between the actual Rising and the metaphorical 'rising' of Irish culture, Moore is able to reinstate the importance of Ireland politically and poetically. Thus Ireland's reply to the British, coming at the end of the poem, is an assertion of nature over nurture:

> and you have smiled. 'Water in motion is far
> from level.' You have seen it, when obstacles happened to bar
> the path, rise automatically. (ll. 14–16)

Moore embraces 'Water' as the most natural of subjects, and uses the sea's natural rhythms to explain the Rising and the 'automatic' resurgence of Ireland and Irish culture.

Yet Moore's thesis of natural renaissance necessitates a simplification of the harsh realities surrounding the Easter Rising. In 'Sojourn in the Whale' Moore prioritises her metaphorical reading of the Rising in order to harness its poetic potential – and to inspire her as a novice female poet and as a writer of assumed Irish heritage. On the one hand the simplification of the Rising as political metaphor appears to empower the Irish speaker in her 'sojourn in the whale'. Fiona Green argues that in the poem 'the Easter Rising can be imagined as a kind of dyspepsia', where 'the colonising country' is 'unable to stomach its resistant movements. Its regurgitation is the inevitable consequence'.[44] In the 'Notes' to 'Sojourn in the Whale', Moore reveals that the Irish speaker's response, 'Water in motion is far/ from level', is taken from *The Literary Digest*;[45] the irony, both poetic and political, is that Moore uses the quotation in a stanza about indigestion, so that, in Green's words, 'the very form of the poetry poses the digestive difficulties that trouble the colonial project'.[46]

On the other hand, however, while the form of the poetry in the last stanza troubles the colonial framework assumed by the British speaker in the earlier part of the poem, and Britain itself is imagined throughout as a whale 'unable to stomach' its troublesome 'resistant movements', in the final section of the poem the Irish contingent arguably remains oddly inert. The Irish speaker's drawn-out smile, emphasised by the use of the present perfect in 'you have smiled', which is followed by a statement of fact in 'Water in motion is far/ from level', suggests a lack of involvement or personal agency, which is confirmed by Moore's conclusion that water 'rise[s] automatically'.[47] When contrasted with the British speaker's condescending axiom that '"water seeks its own level"' (l. 13), this sense of water rising automatically is disappointingly passive; one might have expected a more proactive riposte, especially considering the political impact of the Rising that occasioned the poem. Instead, Ireland is imagined on the one hand as Jonah regurgitated by the whale, suggesting a lack of agency on its part, and on the other as a body of water constantly in motion, but without a mind of its own, responding only in reaction to 'obstacles' which 'bar/ the path' (ll. 15–16). The poem's metaphorical reading of the Rising renders problematic critical readings of the poem as ostensibly political or nationalistic. While such concerns are present, in practice they merely form the backdrop to a poem that is more interested in what happens when natural expression, imagination and creativity are released following a long period of restraint.

George Bornstein gives 'Sojourn in the Whale' considerable attention, drawing parallels between Moore's feminising of Ireland and the representations of women in Irish nationalist tradition:

> Ireland speaks in its own voice at the end of the poem, asserting the counter-truth that water in motion is far from level. In that way the poem follows the iconography of Irish nationalist rhetoric, including that of the Easter Rising, which persistently portrays Ireland as a woman, whether the Shan Van Vog[h]t, Granuaile, or Cathleen ni Houlihan.[48]

But the female Irish voice that speaks at the end of 'Sojourn in the Whale' is ultimately unconvincing as an embodiment of Irish nationalist rhetoric, not least because its smiling hint '"Water in motion is far/ from level'" seems complacent rather than concerned, insouciant rather than inspiring.[49] The poem, written some months after the Easter Rising, reimagines the Rising as an inevitable occurrence, as natural as water in motion, rather than as a task undertaken by 'male warriors' inspired by a powerful Irish female voice. Moore reflects upon the Rising as a symbol of natural potentiality realised, rather than as an inspired act of nationalism – and in so doing, makes it pertinent to her own experiences instead.

The poem becomes, then, like the criticism of Bryant, Goldman and Mencken, a statement of cultural bandwaggoning, whereby what appears to be a celebration of Ireland's spirited nationalism becomes ultimately a poem about a young female poet trying to realise her natural potential: Moore has taken from the Rising what interests her most, and dispensed with uncomfortable realities. As she is distanced emotionally and geographically from the political moment, Moore is able to take from the events in Ireland those elements that inspire her – and instead ponder on what Irish politics can tell her about herself, as an American, a woman and a poet. By uniting in one title – 'Sojourn in the Whale' – her first experiences as a poet in New York and Ireland's experiences in Leviathan Britain, Moore is displaying her 'American view of the world' by writing herself into Ireland's political narrative just as she shapes it according to her own aims.[50] Like Yeats, and Heaney, Moore writes herself into the story – and like them, she too is ultimately writing for herself.

★

Moore's second 'Irish' poem, 'Spenser's Ireland', provides a fitting representation of the confused relationship between America and Ireland in the years 1940–41, when the countries were moving in different directions politically due to the Irish government's policy of neutrality during World War Two.[51] Eugene O'Neill had expressed his own confusions concerning this delicate situation. In response to being asked to sign an open letter to de Valera, urging him to enter Ireland into the war, O'Neill had written: 'I have fought it out with myself and I find I cannot sign it. My final conviction is that we Irish Americans owe it to the Irish people not to attempt to influence their decision by any means whatsoever'.[52]

Moore's uncertain stance in 'Spenser's Ireland' takes on a different hue, however. Alternately a celebration of Ireland's cultural heritage and a critique of Irish stubbornness and isolationism, the poem has generated critical disagreement concerning the extent of its enchantment and disenchantment with Ireland. Moore commented on this fact herself, as Elizabeth Bishop recalls: 'She said her poem "Spenser's Ireland" was not about *loving* Ireland, as people seemed to think, but about *disapproving* of it'.[53] Moore's earlier idealisation of Ireland, as clear in 'Sojourn in the Whale', was rendered problematic as she now found her allegiances tested, and her loyalties divided. Indeed, while the ultimate poem expresses the poet's uncertainties concerning her self-identification as 'troubled', 'dissatisfied' and 'Irish',[54] the draft notes to 'Spenser's Ireland' help clarify Moore's political viewpoint. They are far more aggressive, bespeaking a poetic voice that is 'less & [sic] less in love with Ireland', and which despairs that 'Ireland never took my fancy less than now'.[55]

Fiona Green suggests that 'Spenser's Ireland' emerges as a commentary on the 'delicately poised' relations between Britain, Ireland and America in the early 1940s, as Ireland's isolationism – and particularly its neutral stance during World War Two – led Moore to question America's 'own position in relation to the war'.[56] The timing was certainly apposite. Moore sent the poem for publication in *Furioso* in response to a letter from James Angleton, a Yale undergraduate who set up the magazine with his friend and roommate Edward Reed Whittemore in the spring of 1941; 'Spenser's Ireland' appeared in the first edition. *Furioso* was not an ostensibly political magazine, and neither is 'Spenser's Ireland' an ostensibly political poem. In fact, Moore famously declined to write poems as a direct response to the war until 1943, when she wrote 'In Distrust of Merits' to reflect her 'sense of the poet's need to take public stock of what was happening in the world at large'.[57]

Nevertheless, the very title of Edmund Spenser's *View of the Present State of Ireland* (c. 1598) casts its shadow over the whole of 'Spenser's Ireland', as the poet aims both to summarise where Ireland stands in the world at the time of writing and to suggest where it might stand in future. Moore's stance in relation to Spenser's text is two-sided – and intentionally so. On the one hand she wishes, like Spenser, to summarise the present situation in Ireland and in so doing displays frustration with the Irish for their obstinacy and persistence. On the other, she satirises the disingenuous opinions of those for whom, like Spenser, Ireland 'has not altered' and is 'a place as kind as it is green':[58] as if through such patronising dismissals they will – like Moore's wide-eyed narrator – be in for a shock. The draft notes to 'Spenser's Ireland' help us to unravel some of the complexities of the poem, by illustrating Moore's anxiety about Ireland's relationship with the outside world. As the metaphors of the draft notes to the poem suggest – Moore describes Ireland as, variously, a 'hedgehog', a country full of 'snakes', and a place stagnating in its own 'bog'[59] – a more positive future for Ireland seems only possible should the Irish embrace the potential for change. The Ireland of 'Spenser's Ireland', and particularly of its draft notes, is a country mired in stubbornness, in its inability to acknowledge the realities of a changing world.

In the draft notes to 'Spenser's Ireland', Moore criticises Ireland's 'distrust' of others, portraying 'Distrust' as 'sure defeat / in which no boat can land'.[60] This may be a commentary on President de Valera's refusal to hand Irish ports over to Britain that were thought to be crucial to British defences. Indeed, both the notes to 'Spenser's Ireland' and the eventual poem link 'Eire' with 'air' and employ metaphors for water and sea travel to imply ideological opposition to Ireland's neutral stance. But the notes to the poem, in their despair for the increasingly isolationist role that Ireland is adopting, also share similarities with Louis MacNeice's 1942 poem 'Neutrality', which portrays Ireland as 'The neutral island in the heart of man' while attacking the false 'heart' of poetic Ireland, in which one might 'find a County Sligo, / A Knocknarea with for navel a cairn of stones'.[61]

Scribbled on the back of an envelope dating from December 1940, the first (incomplete) stanza of notes for 'Spenser's Ireland', with extra notes added at the side, sees the 'I' of the narrator speaking freely about her opinions on Ireland. What is prevalent here, as in MacNeice's poem, is the idea that the time for imaginative fancy has passed:

> I'm less & less in love with
>   Ireland
> It takes my fancy   I used to hear them
> Blood is thicker than water   they used to say
> ~~and it~~ It is but not in ~~just~~ the way
> in which they meant it

> The serpents ~~has the best~~ of
> receiving noble food, purveying poison   Ireland never
>   took my fancy
>   less than now[62]

In the draft notes to 'Spenser's Ireland', then, Moore's 'fancy' – her romantic attachment to Ireland – has been destroyed, or 'poisoned', by the inability of Ireland to live up to her expectations. Ireland is the 'serpent' who, like Milton's Satan, seduces then abandons; promises then fails to deliver.

'Blood is thicker than water/ It is but not in the way/ in which they meant it' (notes, ll. 3–5) is, initially, a surprising commentary. Yet it is possible that 'thicker' carries an undercurrent that implies that the Irish are stubborn, and perhaps even foolish, for maintaining their concern for familial bloodlines and cultural self-protection despite the severity of the political climate. In this atmosphere, their reliance on an aphorism, 'blood is thicker than water', appears to defy logic and sense. This accusation runs throughout the draft notes and filters into the eventual poem, where Moore mocks her great-great-grandmother's refusal of a marital match on the grounds that the suitor 'is not / Irish'.[63] In the draft notes, Moore regrets her own stubbornness regarding a professed attachment to, and a familial relationship with, a country that has disappointed her poetic expectations: 'Ireland never took my fancy less than now' (notes, l. 7). In the eventual poem, a similar disappointment finds its expression in the concluding line: 'I am troubled, I'm dissatisfied, I'm Irish' (l. 67).

Notes for a possible second stanza to 'Spenser's Ireland' suggest that Moore is not only angered by Ireland's promises but also frustrated by its tired metaphors – note the ironic 'rusted' in the comments:

> Ireland like a hedgehog   everyone's
>   I'm a bog   everyone   distrustful
> Back to your bog   untrusting
>   Betray confidence with ~~dearly~~
>   deafness
>
> St. Patrick would find   rusted
>   snakes in Ireland   distrusted
>   ~~rust~~ not trusty

> con cord v <u>discord</u>
> and trusty distrustful (ll. 11–17)

Here, Moore explores various possibilities suggested by the main root 'trust' and the prefix-noun combinations generated by 'con cord' and 'discord'. The proliferation of negatives recalls Clair Wills's description of the tendency of those outside Ireland to view its neutral stance as entirely 'negative' – as 'defensive, distrustful and inward-looking' rather than 'active, sovereign and independent'.[64] Moreover, this section of the notes reveals the foundations of an argument explored in 'Spenser's Ireland': that Irish stubbornness, the Irish people's refusal to seek a resolution to their 'Troubles', is thanks to their 'native genius for / disunion' (ll. 27–8). For Moore, as these notes reveal, the implication of 'native genius for / disunion' in 'Spenser's Ireland' is savagely ironic, as if the Irish are delusional, existing in a state of denial generated by their deliberate 'deafness' which enables them to ignore pleas, and to 'betray confidence' in their country and its culture. If Ireland is, as the notes suggest, 'like a hedgehog' (notes, l. 11), then it is prickly and defensive, while 'Back to your bog' (l. 13) displays Moore's personal concerns, and accompanying anger, that Irish culture may stagnate if the Irish continue to avoid taking action.

In the concluding lines of her draft notes to 'Spenser's Ireland', Moore refigures the Irish people's negative qualities in axiomatic statements of hope and repair:

> Distrust is sure defeat
>   in which no boat can land
> Over belief is better than than [sic] not to believe enough …
>
> One must ~~learn~~ know how to be patient with
>   impatience
>   succeed in
> What is liberty? To ~~seek~~ to be captive to the
>   right kind of captivity[65]

Here Moore, somewhat idealistically, uses a metaphor of occupation to suggest the possibility of political harmony: she implies that if the Irish dismiss their 'Distrust' in others – and with it, their protective attitude over their ports ('in which no boat can land') – their self-imposed 'captivity' will be refigured as 'liberty', and their culture will 'succeed'. But feelings of dissatisfaction are resolved internally rather than externally by embracing the somewhat abstract, and perhaps dubious, benefit of 'the/ right kind of captivity' (ll. 33–4).

In the published version of 'Spenser's Ireland', the negative and somewhat officious tone established at draft stage is undermined by a glimmer of hope sparked by Moore's lively use of literary sources. It seems that Moore, through reading an eclectic range of literature by Irish writers, was inspired to abandon some of her frustrations, falling under the spell of Ireland despite herself, and creating a poem whose attitude towards Ireland is apparently contradictory. Taffy Martin contends that despite its apparently hopeless conclusion ('I am troubled, I'm dissatisfied, I'm Irish'), 'Spenser's Ireland' 'has already offered a solution to the alleged dissatisfaction by portraying freedom and success as state of mind rather than as action', while 'show[ing] that imagination offers escape' from 'discouragement'.[66] Similar advice is given in the draft notes concerning 'captivity', above, but the narrative strand of the published poem also offers a 'solution'. Here, Moore harnesses her own imaginative power to offer a model by which the Irish might find for themselves a 'means of escape' from both political and ideological 'dissatisfaction'. Her method is to enact a recollection of Irish cultural strands which might reaffirm the enchanting potential of Ireland to itself: an ambitious project perhaps, and certainly an idealistic one, considering the political complexities of the present situation in Ireland. She uses an eclectic range of sources for the poem, ranging from Spenser to Maria Edgeworth and Donn Byrne,[67] in an attempt to weave together disparate threads of Ireland's cultural heritage into a tapestry of association that aims to counteract, or even rise above, the troubled actualities of Ireland's present.

In the second stanza of the published poem, Moore uses Pádraic Colum's tales of magic to illustrate her hopes for the imaginative future of Ireland:

> If in Ireland
>   they play the harp backward at need,
>   and gather at midday the seed
> of the fern, eluding

> their 'giants all covered with iron', might
>   there be fern-seed for unlearn-
> ing obduracy and for reinstating
> the enchantment? (ll. 13–20)

In an earlier draft of these lines, Moore adds the note 'secret sly hint' in the margin, next to 'enchantment'.[68] Moore's wish for Ireland, then, is as simple as it is idealistic: that the stubborn Irish learn to move on by 'unlearn-/ing' their traditionally 'obdurate' ways and embracing instead another aspect of their culture – the magic of their folklore and traditions. This idea is emphasised in Moore's notes to Colum's lecture, in which she circles with red crayon the note 'If you want to be musical, find the seed of the fern'.[69] Yet Moore's plea comes with a warning: as the draft notes to 'Spenser's Ireland' indicate, reinstatement means more to her than simply restating the past. Moore's method aims to elevate Ireland's 'enchantment' to a higher position on the cultural hierarchy.

The poem also uses Colum's lecture on Irish storytelling to suggest the potential for metamorphosis in Ireland's cultural tapestry. Ireland's tired metaphors, Moore suggests, can be turned into something entirely new by re-engaging with its storytellers' long-held abilities to enchant. Discussing whether poetic archaisms depicting Ireland/ 'Eire' 'bespeak relentlessness', the speaker comments:

> they are to me
>   like Earl Gerald who
>   changed himself into a stag, into
> great green-eyed cat of
> the mountain. Discommodity makes
>
>   them invisible; they've dis-
> appeared.[70]

Moore's notes to Colum's lecture reveal that she borrowed all of the above lines from Colum.[71] Here, then, Moore exploits the imaginative potential of Irish folklore to give life to her poem, while hinting at wider possibilities for regrowth and renewal. Yet such idealism is tempered by the concern that thanks to the 'Discommodity' of the

Irish people – their dislike of change – the cultural heritage of Ireland may become invisible, and even disappear completely. This section actually references Spenser's text, where the two speakers – Iren and Eudox – debate the tendency for the Irish to wear mantles, a type of cloak that they use, 'by reason of the raw cold climate', for 'housing, bedding, and clothing'.[72] Iren suggests that he 'would think it meet to forbid all mantles' in Ireland as they have come to be used for deception: so that when a 'thief', or a 'rebel', has carried out his misdeeds 'he can, in his mantle, pass through any town or company, being close hooded over his head' – he has been rendered invisible. Thus Iren surmises that, despite the usefulness of the mantles to the Irish people, 'the commodity does not countervail the discommodity'.[73]

Where Moore's speaker worries of the Irish that 'Discommodity makes // them invisible; they've dis- / appeared', she converts Spenser's 'mantle' into a metaphor for Irish discommodity, suggesting that through stubbornly clinging to their rebellious principles, they are merely hiding – and rendering themselves ultimately invisible. Moore's speaker implies, then, that the 'commodity' to the Irish of staying steadfast does not 'countervail' the discommodity to others of their non-cooperative stance; but it does the Irish no favours either, as in such as a relentless circle of cultural self-promotion and global self-denial they are in danger of losing the same identity that they hold so dear.

The poem does offer an alternative, however: that the Irish might instead embrace change and use it as a powerful tool, exploiting the imaginative potentialities of their magical inheritance to enact their own cultural metamorphosis. Perhaps, Moore suggests, Ireland's negative associations – with 'serpents' 'purveying poison', or with 'distrust' or stagnation – as expressed in the draft notes to the poem, might be transformed into something magnificent, like Colum's 'great green-eyed cat of / the mountain':[74] a Celtic Tiger indeed.

★

In certain responses to events in Ireland following Easter 1916, we find extremes of political affiliation: in critics like Bryant, Goldman and Mencken expressing a romanticised sympathy with the Irish nationalist cause, or in Lola Ridge's claim in 'Tidings' that she wished she had played an active role in the Rising itself.[75] Yet our assessment of such extremes of political enchantment is necessarily tempered by an acknowledgement of the tendency for Americans to prioritise their American affiliations over their Irish sympathies. This tendency extended even to Irish-American supporters. Summing up de Valera's visit to the USA in 1919–20, Alan J. Ward notes: 'one lesson of de Valera's mission [was] that no matter how right or wrong in their attitudes towards Ireland, the leaders of the Irish in America were independent Americans with their own American view of the world'. This is highlighted by the fact that, as Ward points out, once the Anglo-Irish Treaty of December 1921 had been passed, so far as many Americans were concerned, 'Ireland now had home rule, or independence, or whatever one chose to call the constitutional manifestation of its freedom'.[76] As Ireland descended into civil war, Irish America was plunged into confusion.

Even the literature produced in apparent response to the Rising appears, on closer inspection, to be dominated by its authors' 'American view of the world'. Ridge, as an Irish-American poet, looked towards Ireland while simultaneously promoting her left-wing ideologies, and exploring other facets of her identity as a New York writer. The collection in which 'Tidings' is found, *The Ghetto and Other Poems*, contains poems about Jewish-American life (the subject of the 'ghetto' of the title), and begins with the poem 'To the American People'. For Ridge, Ireland merely makes up part of this story, contributing to Ridge's identity as a New York (Irish) American who has also lived in a Jewish-American area and has socialist leanings. As Tobin points out, discussing *The Ghetto and Other Poems*, 'It is a volume at once conscious of its desired place in the tradition of American poetry, of its author's drive to innovate upon that tradition, and of its own historical and social moment'.[77] In this context, it is perhaps unsurprising that in Ridge's 'Tidings' and her later poem 'Incompatibility', the political message ultimately functions symbolically, so that Ireland's quest for self-government represents the poet's promotion of national self-expression at a time when she is trying to forge her own place within American literary history. Likewise, Moore's poem 'Sojourn in the Whale' uses the Easter Rising metaphorically to celebrate an organic cultural 'uprising' that reflects in turn Moore's self-assertion as a female poet on the New York scene, as she emerges from her own period of 'sojourn' in the city. Through Moore's highly individualised reading of events in Ireland in 1916, 'Sojourn in the Whale' comes to represent an instance of personal experience grafted onto a symbolic (and actively symbolised) political moment.

Moore's sympathetic stance becomes more difficult, however, once 'American' and 'Irish' ideals are brought into ideological opposition in 1941. Hence in Moore's poem 'Spenser's Ireland' (1941) – and particularly in the draft notes of the poem – we watch as the poet tries to extract herself from her earlier pact with Ireland, a country whose stubbornness she sees as potentially threatening to America's security. We are reminded of Louis MacNeice's portrayal of Ireland's hypocrisy in *Autumn Journal*, which, although composed in 1938, appears to anticipate his country's stance during the war:

> Why should I want to go back
>   To you Ireland, my Ireland?
> The blots on the page are so black
>   That they cannot be covered with shamrock.
> I hate your grandiose airs,
>   Your sob-stuff, your laugh and your swagger,
> The assumption that everyone cares
>   Who is the king of your castle.
> Castles are out of date [.][78]

Moore's 'Spenser's Ireland' implies, similarly, that idealistic representations of Ireland – its 'shamrock' and its 'castles' – are 'out of date' in a country whose government refuses to accept the dark realities of the Second World War. Yet at the same time, a counter argument runs through 'Spenser's Ireland' to imply that Moore finds solace in the very culture that she appears to dismiss. Here the poet/speaker suggests that by rediscovering its mythic inheritance, Ireland might find a means of 'reinstating/ the enchantment'[79] – which might provide a solution to its cultural and political malaise.

In 'Easter 1916' Yeats provides a model for a politics of (dis)enchantment – one that finds echoes in the political poems of Ridge and Moore, as they negotiate their personal and public roles and responsibilities. But several questions remain. Is it possible for American writers like Moore to disaffiliate themselves politically from Ireland while remaining affiliated to its culture? Does a poet have a responsibility to their public, and if so, what (in the case of Ridge and Moore) is their responsibility to their immediate public as well as to the public, over the Atlantic, to which they have previously declared an affiliation? And finally, is it all that we can expect of a poet, ultimately, to write for herself – even as she writes political verse? In her review of Yeats's *Collected Poems* for the *New Yorker* in 1934, Louise Bogan remarked that the volume contained 'the greatest political poems (although they denounce politics) of our time'.[80] In this apparent paradox we might find some answers: for while Yeats claims that he has 'no gift to set a statesman right', his poetry bypasses state politics and speaks straight to the public – to 'young girl' and 'old man' – through its own denunciations.[81] Thus we find in poems such as 'On Being Asked for a War Poem' and 'Easter 1916' a model for the kind of poetry that declares as it holds back from declaring, that universalises as it individualises, that enchants as it disenchants – and in so doing, marks itself out as exactly of, and for, its time.

Notes

1. W. B. Yeats, 'Easter 1916', *The Variorum Edition of the Poems of W. B. Yeats*, ed. Peter Allt and Russell K. Alspach. New York: Macmillan, 1966, pp. 391–4, ll. 74–80.
2. W. B. Yeats, 'On Being Asked for a War Poem' (initially entitled 'A Reason for Keeping Silent'), *Variorum Edition*, p. 359, whole poem.
3. Yeats, 'Easter 1916', l. 74.
4. W. H. Auden, 'In Memory of W. B. Yeats', *Selected Poems*, ed. Edward Mendelson. London: Faber, 1979, pp. 80–3, ll. 34, 41 (and see further discussions in Chapter 5).
5. Seamus Heaney, 'The Flight Path', IV, ll. 28–31, *Opened Ground: Poems 1966–1996*. London: Faber, 1998, pp. 412–13.
6. Helen Vendler, *Seamus Heaney*. London: HarperCollins, 1998, pp. 42, 39. Vendler discusses how Heaney took inspiration from P. V. Glob's *The Bog People: Iron Age Man Preserved* (1969) to find suitable symbols for describing the ritualistic violence of the Troubles; see especially the following poems from *Opened Ground*: 'Bogland' (pp. 41–2), 'The Tollund Man' (pp. 64–5), 'Bog Queen' (pp. 112–14), 'The Grauballe Man' (pp. 115–16), 'Punishment' (pp. 117–18), and 'Strange Fruit' (p. 119).

7 Edward Malins, 'Yeats and the Easter Rising', *Dolmen Press Yeats Centenary Papers*, ed. Liam Miller. Dublin: Dolmen Press, 1968, I, pp. 1–28 (5). The I. R. B. was the Irish Republican Brotherhood, founded on St Patrick's Day (17 March) 1858.
8 Of course, Irish-American support for Irish nationalism has a long and enduring history. There is insufficient space to discuss this here, but see Thomas Brown, *Irish-American Nationalism 1870–1890* (New York: Lippincott, 1966), and Charles Callan, *America and the Fight for Irish Freedom, 1866–1922* (New York: Devon Adair, 1957) for extended discussions of nineteenth and early twentieth-century responses to Irish nationalism within Irish-American and American circles.
9 Malins, 'Yeats and the Easter Rising', pp. 8, 9.
10 The 'Proclamation of the Irish Republic' can be accessed online as part of the National Library of Ireland's online exhibition, 'The 1916 Rising: Personalities and Perspectives': see www.nli.ie/1916/1916_main.html.
11 Patrick Ward, *Exile, Emigration and Irish Writing*. Dublin and Portland, Oregon: Irish Academic Press, 2002, pp. 232–3.
12 Malins, 'Yeats and the Easter Rising', p. 10.
13 Alan J. Ward, *Ireland and Anglo-American Relations, 1899–1921*. London: LSE / Weidenfeld and Nicolson, 1969, p. 3.
14 F. M. Carroll, *American Opinion and the Irish Question 1910–1923*. Dublin and New York: Gill and Macmillan and St Martin's Press, 1978, p. 3.
15 See Pádraic and Mary Colum, *The Irish Rebellion of 1916 and its Martyrs: Erin's Tragic Easter*, ed. Maurice Joy. New York: Devin-Adair Co., 1916.
16 Carroll, *American Opinion and the Irish Question*, p. 55. Roger Casement (1864–1916) was executed by the British for treason on 3 August 1916. However, the trial was highly controversial as the prosecutors could not prove that Casement had committed treason, through collusion with the Germans, on British soil. Casement had not been involved in the Rising, as he had been too weak to travel from Kerry, where he had landed after leaving Germany. Several high-profile public figures, including Yeats and Bernard Shaw, appealed (unsuccessfully) to the government for clemency.
17 Ibid., p. 15: Carroll uses as examples Volumes Xl, No. 3 (15 January 1910) and XL, No. 8 (19 February 1910).
18 Ibid., p. 55.
19 Paul Giles discusses the intellectual circle surrounding Alfred Stieglitz in *Virtual Americas: Transnational Fictions and the Transatlantic Imaginary*. Durham and London: Duke University Press, 2002; see especially p. 88.
20 Francis Hackett, *Ireland: A Study in Nationalism*. New York: B. W. Huebsch, 1918, p. 7.

21 Lola Ridge (1873–1941) was born Rose Emily Ridge in Dublin, and emigrated to the USA following the death of her mother in 1907. For more biographical information, see Daniel Tobin, 'Modernism, leftism and the spirit: the poetry of Lola Ridge', in *Awake in America: On Irish American Poetry*. Notre Dame, Indiana: University of Notre Dame Press, 2011, pp. 61–86 (61).

22 Moore began attending parties at Ridge's apartment from 1919. Her 'Daily Diary' for 1920 records frequent visits: the first of these entries reads 'Jan 31st 7 E 14th St Lola Ridge/ 8pm', suggesting that this was probably Moore's first visit. See RML VIII:01:01, 'Daily Diary', 1920.

23 'Easter 1916' was first published in *The New Statesman* (23 October 1920) and then in *The Dial* (November 1920); it was collected in *Michael Robartes and the Dancer* in 1921. See *Variorum Edition*, note, p. 391.

24 Tobin, 'Modernism, leftism and the spirit', p. 64.

25 Lola Ridge, 'Tidings (Easter, 1916)', *The Ghetto and Other Poems*. New York: B. W. Huebsch, 1918, p. 101, ll. 11–12; ll. 1–4. Ellipses are the poet's own.

26 Horace Gregory, in Gregory and Marya Zaturenska, *A History of American Poetry, 1900–1940*. First published 1942; New York: Gordian Press, 1969, p. 444.

27 Shelley's poem also uses a trochaic trimeter/tetrameter pattern, and personifies 'Murder', 'Fraud' and 'Anarchy' as Ridge personifies 'truth': see Percy Bysshe Shelley, 'The Mask of Anarchy. Written on the Occasion of the Massacre at Manchester', *Romanticism: An Anthology*, ed. Duncan Wu. Oxford: Blackwell, 1998, pp. 930–40, and especially opening stanzas and ll. 5, 14, 30.

28 Ridge, 'Incompatibility', *Red Flag*. New York: The Viking Press, 1927, p. 73. Ellipses are the poet's own.

29 Tobin, 'Modernism, leftism and the spirit', p. 64.

30 Yeats, 'Easter 1916', l. 78.

31 John P. Harrington, 'Transatlantic transactions: Irish players and American reviewers', *Ireland and Transatlantic Poetics*, ed. Brian G. Caraher and Robert Mahony. New Jersey: Rosemont, 2007, pp. 168–78 (170, 171).

32 Emma Goldman, *The Social Significance of [the] Modern Drama*. First published 1914; New York: Applause Books, 1987; cited in Harrington, 'Transatlantic transactions', p. 171.

33 Louise Bryant, 'The poets' revolution', *The Masses* (July 1916), 29; cited in Harrington, 'Transatlantic transactions', p. 173.

34 Harrington, 'Transatlantic transactions', p. 175; H. L. Mencken, 'The Irish Renaissance', *Smart Set* (March 1917), reprinted in *H. L. Mencken's*

Smart Set Criticism, ed. William H. Nolte. Ithaca, New York: Cornell University Press, 1968. p. 309.
35 Harrington, 'Transatlantic transactions', p. 171.
36 See especially letter from Moore to Warner dated 19 December 1915, *The Selected Letters of Marianne Moore*, ed. Bonnie Costello, Celeste Goodridge and Cristanne Miller. London: Faber, 1998, pp. 107–12.
37 Linda Leavell, *Marianne Moore and the Visual Arts*. Baton Rouge and London: Louisiana State University Press, 1995, pp. 10–11.
38 See Moore, *Selected Letters*, pp. 103–12.
39 RML V:53:16, Correspondence between Moore and Lola Ridge, MM to LR, 19 April [1919].
40 Marianne Moore, 'Sojourn in the Whale' (whole poem), *Complete Poems*, ed. Clive Driver. London: Faber, 1984, p. 90.
41 Moore, 'New York', *Complete Poems*, p. 54, l. 25 (counting title as first line, as was Moore's practice). I use the term 'Jamesian expression' deliberately loosely, as although Moore claims in the 'Note' to the poem that the quotation is taken from Henry James (see *Complete Poems*, p. 269), I have not been able to locate the exact phrase 'accessibility to experience' in any of James's texts. However 'accessibility' and, particularly, 'experience' are commonly used terms in James's corpus.
42 Maldwyn A. Jones, 'The Scotch-Irish of British America', in *Strangers within the Realm: Cultural Margins of the First British Empire*, ed. Bernard Bailyn and Philip D. Morgan. Chapel Hill and London: University of North Carolina Press, 1991, pp. 284–313 (299).
43 *Oxford English Dictionary* online (www.oed.com), 'circumscribed'.
44 Fiona Green, '"Your trouble is their trouble": Marianne Moore, Maria Edgeworth and Ireland', *Symbiosis: A Journal of Anglo-American Literary Relations*, 1.2 (October 1997), 173–85 (175).
45 Moore, 'Sojourn in the Whale', ll. 15–16; 'Notes' to 'Sojourn in the Whale', *Complete Poems*, p. 276.
46 Green, '"Your trouble is their trouble"', p. 175.
47 Moore, 'Sojourn in the Whale', ll. 14–16.
48 George Bornstein, *Material Modernism: The Politics of the Page*. Cambridge: Cambridge University Press, 2001, p. 105.
49 Moore, 'Sojourn in the Whale', ll. 14–15.
50 Ward, *Ireland and Anglo-American Relations*, p. 233.
51 A fuller treatment of the ways in which Moore developed the draft notes into the ultimate poem can be found in: Tara Stubbs, 'New readings of Marianne Moore's "Spenser's Ireland"', *Peer English: A Journal of New Critical Thinking*, 2 (December 2007), 32–44.

52 Eugene O'Neill to William Agar, 5 February 1941, *Selected Letters of Eugene O'Neill*, ed. Travis Bogard and Jackson R. Bryer. New Haven and London: Yale University Press, p. 515.
53 Elizabeth Bishop, 'Efforts of affection: A Memoir of Marianne Moore', *Bishop: Poems, Prose, and Letters*. New York: Library of America, 2008, pp. 471–99 (481).
54 Moore, 'Spenser's Ireland', *Complete Poems*, pp. 112–14, l. 67 (concluding line).
55 Moore, Draft notes to 'Spenser's Ireland', RML I:04:21.
56 Fiona Green, '"Your trouble is their trouble"', p. 177.
57 Bonnie Costello, in *Selected Letters of Marianne Moore*, p. 338.
58 Moore, 'Spenser's Ireland', ll. 2, 3 (counting title as first line, as was Moore's practice).
59 Moore, Draft notes to 'Spenser's Ireland', RML I:04:21.
60 Draft notes, RML I:04:21.
61 Louis MacNeice, 'Neutrality (*September, 1942*)', first published in *Springboard* in 1944, reprinted in *Collected Poems*, ed. E. R. Dodd. London: Faber, 1966, pp. 202–3, ll. 2, 6–7.
62 RML I:04:21, draft notes, ll. 1–7: line numbers are my own, for ease of reference.
63 Moore, 'Spenser's Ireland', ll. 30–1.
64 Clair Wills, *That Neutral Island: A Cultural History of Ireland During the Second World War*. London: Faber, 2007, p. 5.
65 RML I:04:21, draft notes, ll. 27–9, 32–4. The last line is set on a right angle from the rest of the text and reads, in full, 'right ~~thing to [?]~~ kind of / ~~succeed the~~ captivity'.
66 Moore, 'Spenser's Ireland', l. 67; Taffy Martin, *Marianne Moore: Subversive Modernist*. Austin, Texas: University of Texas Press, 1986, pp. 123, 124.
67 The sources are *Ireland: The Rock Whence I Was Hewn* (1927), a little-known piece of travel writing by Donn Byrne (discussed in Chapter 2); Edmund Spenser's *A View of the Present State of Ireland* (c. 1598); Maria Edgeworth's balanced but ultimately pro-Union novels *Castle Rackrent* (1800) and *The Absentee* (1812); the Cork poet Denis O'Sullivan's parochial lines from the little-known volume *Happy Memories of Glengarriff* (1930); and the pro-republican Irish poet and storyteller Pádraic Colum's tales of enchantment from a lecture entitled 'Story-telling to the Young and Ever Young' given in 1937 (discussed in Chapter 2).
68 RML I:04:21, draft 1, l. 21.
69 RML VII:06:03, 'Story-telling to the Young and Ever Young'.
70 Moore, 'Spenser's Ireland', ll. 57–63.

71 RML VII:06:03, 'Story-telling to the Young and Ever Young': Moore records here how Colum describes a 'great big stag … a cat of the mountain w[ith] great green eyes'.
72 An earlier phrase in 'Spenser's Ireland' has discussed 'Venus' / mantle lined with stars' (ll. 10–11), and Moore has added in a 'Note': 'Lines 10–11: *Venus' mantle*. Footnote, *Castle Rackrent*: "The cloak, or mantle, as described by Thady is of high antiquity. See Spenser's 'View of the State of Ireland'"' (*Complete Poems*, p. 280). Moore refers to Maria Edgeworth's 1800 novel *Castle Rackrent*. In the opening pages to the story, narrated by Thady Quirk, Edgeworth includes an extended reference to Spenser's description of the history of the mantle in *A View of the Present State of Ireland* (including the section on its 'discommodity'): it is possible, then, that Moore first encountered Spenser's text through Edgeworth. See Maria Edgeworth, *Castle Rackrent*, ed. George Watson. Oxford: Oxford University Press, 1999, pp. 7–8.
73 Edmund Spenser, *A View of the Present State of Ireland* (first published c. 1598), ed. W. L. Renwick. Oxford: Clarendon Press, 1970, pp. 51–3.
74 Moore, 'Spenser's Ireland', ll. 60–1.
75 Ridge, 'Tidings', ll. 11–12.
76 Ward, *Ireland and Anglo-American Relations*, pp. 233, 267.
77 Tobin, 'Modernism, leftism and the spirit', p. 69.
78 Louis MacNeice, *Autumn Journal*, XVI, *Collected Poems*, pp. 131–4, ll. 105–13.
79 Moore, 'Spenser's Ireland', ll. 19–20.
80 Louise Bogan, review of Yeats's *Collected Poems*, *The New Yorker* (7 April 1934), collected in *A Poet's Prose: Selected Writings of Louise Bogan*, ed. Mary Kinzie. Athens, Ohio: Swallow Press, Ohio University Press, 2005, pp. 200–1 (200).
81 Yeats, 'On Being Asked for a War Poem', ll. 5, 6.

Chapter 5
The legacy of Yeats's poetic conviction

> America and its poets have stimulated Irish poetry in many ways. Perhaps one of the things that Irish poetry offers in return is ... its conviction – whether well-founded or not – that poetry matters.[1]

For Edna Longley, the contribution that Irish poetry can make to American verse is founded on the idea that poetry not only 'matters', but that it should matter, in the emotional and the material sense. In the modernist period, the Irish poet whose conviction seems to inspire American writers most significantly is W. B. Yeats. For Terence Diggory, '[t]his conviction of the power of language is one of the points of agreement between the tradition of the self as developed by Yeats and the second principal source of that tradition: the American poetry that regards the poet as another Adam who hails the world anew'.[2] This 'Adamic' description of American poetry clearly evokes Whitman, whom Diggory allies with Yeats thanks to each poet's tendency to self-romanticise in their quest to find a national poetic identity: as 'America or Ireland existed for each poet more as an ideal than as a reality, for each created his nationality out of himself' (p. 22). Diggory sees American poets' turn towards Yeats as a turn away from English tradition, noting Yeats's role as imitator (and imitated) in this process: 'The Americans had succeeded in declaring aesthetic independence from England. Yeats wanted the Irish to follow the American lead' (p.4). Diggory's claim of mutual inspiration, in which Yeats turns to America just as American writers turn to Yeats, reveals something of the complex nature of influence between Yeats and American writers during the first half of the twentieth century. Meanwhile the distinction that Diggory sets up, between Yeats as individual poet and national cultural symbol, is crucial to an analysis of Yeats's influence during this period.

In recent years, critics have tended to view Yeats's influence on American poetry as complex, subtle and shifting, as they unearth individual cases of interaction and imitation. For example Philip Coleman, in a 2003 essay on the influence of Yeats on a young John Berryman, argues that Berryman's 'early turn towards Yeats signalled his rejection of mainstream American authority' and his 'recognition of the Anglo-Irish poet's rejection of narrow cultural genealogies in favour of a more open and international form of cultural self-positioning'.[3] This instance of influence, then, shows an American poet turning towards a transnational, trans-cultural – rather than an 'Irish' – Yeats for inspiration. Meanwhile in a 2007 essay on 'Duppy poetics', Michael Malouf considers an 'instance in the varied afterlife' of 'The Lake Isle of Innisfree' by assessing Lorna Goodison's 1999 work 'Country, Sligoville', a reworking of Yeats's poem in a Jamaican location. Here, Goodison's poem becomes an exercise in 'circum-Atlantic performance', where the poet is: 'reconsidering tradition in spatial terms – the contract of three places in Innisfree, Sligo, and Sligoville – as conveyed through names that not only evoke the legacy of slavery and freedom that marks the landscape of Jamaica, but also express the repressed history of a transatlantic Irish culture with its ambiguous legacy of ownership, servitude, and struggle'.[4] Thus Yeats's poem, scrutinised against a millennial, transatlantic background, is reread as part of a larger struggle for national – or, indeed, transatlantic – self-expression, and is excised from its original, local and localised, setting.

In another example of textual revision as poetic criticism, Sharon Olds's 2007 poem 'Easter, 1960' makes use of the portentousness of Yeats's 'Easter 1916' to ascribe similar significance to her chosen date. Although Olds's poem, a commentary on a private grief that desires some sort of public outlet, is apparently far removed politically from Yeats's original, the allusive title allows the speaker's loss of her lover to become as pregnant with symbolism as Yeats's memorial to the executed rebels of 1916. Thus when the poem's grieving lover returns to her room, she reads the world as poised upon a moment of terrible change:

> I sat on the floor with a *Sunday Times*
> and read the columns of the first page down,

and then the next, and then the next,
I can still see how every 'a' looked eager – it hadn't heard, yet, that its
boy was gone – and every 'f' hung down its head on its broken neck,
its little arms held out, as if to
say, *You see me, this is what I am.* [5]

Understanding the inscribed textual history of the poem allows the speaker's desire for public recognition of her private sorrow to resonate further. In 'Easter 1916' the poetic (and political) moment is hinged on the present tense, as 'A terrible beauty is born';[6] while here the speaker forces upon the black and white neutrality of the printed page an emotional response to her private grief, so that the present tense statement '*You see me, this is what I am*' urges that moment of suspense before change. The speaker hopes that, as in Yeats's poem, everything will subsequently 'change utterly', both in terms of the things that will happen, and the language that will describe these happenings.[7] Yet the tragedy of 'Easter, 1960' lies in the fact that whereas for Yeats 'Easter 1916' represents a public event reimagined in personal terms, for Olds's speaker the private event cannot be reimagined publically as hers is a private sorrow. 'Easter, 1960' may mean something to her, but it may not to others; the title, then, underlines and magnifies a personal grief at the same moment that we, as readers, realise – and are thankful for – its lack of significance for ourselves.

The first publication of Olds's poem in *The New Yorker* tells us something of the poet's expectations for her largely American readership: that they will appreciate and understand the complexities of her poem in relation to its 'urtext', Yeats's 'Easter 1916'. Through alluding to Yeats within an American context, Olds illustrates how Yeats's poems – or, at least, their more memorable lines and titles – have been absorbed into American culture. This tradition has continued into recent years: for example, Cormac McCarthy's novel *No Country for Old Men* (2005) – its title a direct steal from the opening line of Yeats's 'Sailing to Byzantium' – was adapted into an Oscar-winning Coen brothers film in 2007; while the Seattle folk band Fleet Foxes produced an album, *Helplessness Blues* (2011), based on Yeats's early lyrics, and particularly 'The Lake Isle of Innisfree'.[8]

But this looseness of reference only serves to complicate the relationship between Yeats and American writers. In the modernist period, the ways in which writers make use of Yeats differ from individual to individual, reflecting their own personal readings and desires. Therefore, in order to assess the extent of his influence upon American modernist writing, and so gain a sense of his legacy within twentieth (and twenty-first) century American culture, we need to consider Yeats as an Irish writer and a European, as an individualist and a cultural nationalist. Such readings are pertinent to Yeats, as a poet of multiple identities who (as Diggory puts it) 'created his nationality out of himself'.[9]

Taking into account some of these multiple identities, this chapter takes as its focus poets and critics who engaged directly with Yeats as man and poet. It considers, through Marianne Moore, the 1910s to early 1930s when his star was in the ascendant in America; through John Berryman and Louise Bogan, the mid to late 1930s when Yeats and others were contemplating his legacy; and through Babette Deutsch, the decades immediately following his death. This biographical and critical framework allows for an assessment of 'the politics of praise' that views influence as both direct and active – in the physical presence of the living (or recently dead) poet – and poetic and allusive, in the shadowing of the poet's works in the works of the poets who proceed after him. But the story begins with the moment(s) that Yeats's writings were first introduced to his American readers.

Yeats's introduction to America: Pound, pirates and promoters

For some, it was Ezra Pound who successfully introduced American readers to Yeats's work; for example, Diggory calls Pound '[t]he man most responsible for transmitting Yeats's influence to America', and discusses what he terms 'the indiscriminate nature of Pound's early admiration for Yeats'.[10] It is well known that Pound, following a request made by Harriet Monroe in 1912, sent to Monroe selections of Yeats's poetry for inclusion in her new Chicago-based magazine *Poetry: A Magazine of New Verse*; indeed, Diggory suggests that Pound published five of Yeats's poems in *Poetry* in December 1912 in order to advocate a renaissance in American poetry, as 'Yeats's experience in Ireland had made him, as Pound had acknowledged him in 1911, a "specialist in renaissances"'.[11] According to James Longenbach, Pound's comment stemmed from a belief that 'America was the only place that a second Renaissance could take place'.[12] The Irish-born poet Pádraic Colum seconded this opinion with a review, 'Mr. Yeats's *Selected Poems*', in *The Dial* in October 1921, in which he 'declared Yeats to be the forerunner of the poets who rallied around *Poetry*'.[13]

Yeats's impact on the founders of *Poetry* extended beyond verse, however; as Diggory comments:

> In notes for a lecture, *Poetry's* founder, Harriet Monroe, suggested a similarity between *Poetry* and the Irish National Theatre, and in no respect is there greater similarity between the two projects than in their emphasis on locality. On their first American tour in 1912 the Abbey players stimulated interest in the regional theatre in Chicago. An immediate result was the founding of Maurice Brown's Little Theatre, which headed its repertory with works by Synge and Yeats.

The connection between Yeats and *Poetry* extended further into the decade, with Yeats speaking at a banquet in Chicago organised in his honour, by *Poetry*, in 1914. The speech led to critical debate. Vachel Lindsay argued that the Abbey Theatre might provide a model for regional film companies in the USA, while poet Alice Corbin Henderson, assistant editor of *Poetry*, argued how difficult the task would be for an American poet to stimulate a poetic 'renaissance', and declaimed Yeats's suggestion that Americans should look to Paris for models; instead, she asserted, they should look to their own, indigenous culture.[14]

Pound's promotion of Yeats must be contextualised, however. Along with work by Yeats, he also sent to *Poetry* selections by Rabindranath Tagore, Richard Aldington, H. D. (Hilda Doolitle) and T. S. Eliot, together with his own offerings.[15] His admiration for Yeats should also be considered alongside the fact that, despite a later admission to having been 'drunk with "Celticism"' in the early part of the twentieth century,[16] by 1917 Pound was already complaining that 'the Celtic twilight has been eked out'.[17] For Pound, Yeats certainly represented a poet of extraordinary talent. Referring to a selection of poems about to be published in the *Little Review* in June 1917, Pound notes to Margaret Anderson that '[t]he Yeats' [sic] poems are ripping. No one else could have turned out such a bunch'.[18] Hence it is perhaps more accurate to see Pound's support of Yeats in the long term as the promotion of an individual talent rather than a national icon – even though Yeats's role in the Irish Renaissance had been difficult to resist. And it is important to note that Pound's selections for *Poetry* in 1912 represented his current promotion of imagist poetry and its adherents.[19]

From a more commercial point of view, key publishing figures and patrons played a significant role in promoting Yeats's work in the USA. Robert Keating O'Neill describes how the American publisher Thomas Bird Mosher 'did much to further awareness in America of the Irish Literary Renaissance' by publishing (usually) pirated editions of works by George Meredith, Æ (George Russell), Katharine Tynan Hinkson and Oscar Wilde; indeed, Yeats gave Mosher permission to publish *The Land of Heart's Desire* in 1903, and was pleased to hear that the second edition had sold out within a few months.[20] But Yeats was soon worrying that Mosher might publish his work without permission, and instead sought the legal advice of his patron and friend, the Irish-American New York-based lawyer John Quinn, on how to proceed with publishing subsequent works in the USA.

As Keating O'Neill illustrates, Quinn made considerable efforts to publicise Yeats's drama, poetry and ideas in the United States:

> [I]n September 1902, Quinn performed what was to become the first of many services he would render to his new-found Irish literary and artistic friends. He copyrighted in America for W. B. Yeats the play *Where There is Nothing* by arranging an edition through the firm of John Lane. In that same year he helped form the short-lived New York branch of the Irish Literary Society, modelled after local societies formed in Ireland by W. B. Yeats and his friends. In the summer of 1903 Quinn returned to Ireland and became a patron of Dun Emer (later Cuala), crafts and subscribed to multiple copies of their hand-printed volumes. He also arranged for W. B. Yeats to give a speaking tour in the United States in the fall and winter of 1903–4. Quinn organised more than thirty lectures for Yeats and hosted him at his apartment in New York City before and after his tour. (p. 426)

Few culturally inclined Americans could have missed Quinn's multi-pronged attack as he launched Yeats upon the literary scene. The attack was so successful, indeed, that Yeats secured a publishing contract with Macmillan New York; Macmillan published *When There is Nothing:*

Being Volume I of Plays for an Irish Theatre (1903), *In the Seven Woods* (1903), and a second volume of plays, *The Hour-Glass and Other Plays* (1904). Warwick Gould notes that it was only after 'protracted negotiations' that Yeats, 'with considerable reluctance, granted an exclusive licence to the Macmillan Company of New York to produce collected editions of his works in that market for the lifetime of his copyright'; thus was published *The Poetical Works of William B. Yeats* in 2 volumes in 1906–7, 'even giving the author a recognisably American name'.[21]

Quinn's support and promotion of Yeats would peak once again in 1911, when he agreed to help with the Abbey Theatre's American tour. Serving as the Abbey's attorney in the USA, he got the charges dropped against Lady Gregory and her company following their arrest in Philadelphia over their performance of Synge's *The Playboy of the Western World*. It is perhaps unsurprising, then, that Keating O'Neill claims that '[i]f any individual deserves to be singled out for promoting early twentieth century Irish writers and their works in America', it is John Quinn (p. 425).[22] Modernist American writers' responses to the work of Yeats, in particular, reveal the extent of this successful promotion.

Yeats as a contemporary: Marianne Moore

For Marianne Moore, Yeats represented several things: a literary forebear whose impressive legacy was impossible to ignore; a poet whose aesthetic she aimed to imitate; and a larger-than-life figure whose personal life, and interests in spiritualism, she disapproved of. Moore's first significant poems were published in 1915, three years after Yeats's work was first published in *Poetry*. Hence the issue of poetic praise was complicated for Moore by the trajectory of her own career. As Moore began her writing career, Yeats entered the prime of his; while as Yeats's reputation dwindled towards the end of his life Moore entered the prime of her writing life, winning the Helen Haire Levinson Prize, from *Poetry*, in 1933.

As a (relatively) young poet, Moore composed a poem addressed to Yeats – 'To William Butler Yeats on Tagore' (1915) – that was published alongside other similar poems addressed to various literary and cultural figures. These included Gordon Craig, Disraeli, Robert Browning, Bernard Shaw, Blake, and George Moore. This series of poems marked, in Robin Schulze's words, the first year of Moore's life as an 'internationally published poet'.[23] In each of these poems Moore establishes what Charles Molesworth describes as a 'balance of praise and blame' in response to each addressee. Indeed, with the exception of Blake, the English and Irish figures 'addressed' in these poems are, in Moore's mind at least, as notorious for their personal failings, whether of conduct or character, as for their public achievements. As Molesworth puts it, Moore 'may be the one artist who most questions the value and effectiveness of an assertive artistic ego'.[24] In virtually every case, the young poet finds inspiration from the more mature, pointedly male, figure she addresses, while discriminating between what she perceives as the strengths, and what she views as the weaknesses, of each of her subjects. For example 'To a Strategist', addressed to Benjamin Disraeli (1804–1881) and published in *Lantern*, simultaneously praises Disraeli's achievements at overcoming prejudice and employing 'sound sense' to establish lasting conservatism in Britain, and criticises his slipperiness and political manoeuvring.[25]

Similarly in 'George Moore', published in *Others* in December 1915, the poet's praise of the Irish novelist is complicated by the younger Moore's ironic commentaries on George Moore's misguided arrogance and dubious morals. Moore mocks the 'murky' qualities of George Moore's autobiographical style, and wonders if he has 'known beauty other than that of stys [sic] / on which to fix your admiration'.[26] Nevertheless the poem almost betrays itself through its respect for George Moore's aesthetic achievements. The complicated syllabic structure reveals an admiration for George Moore's stylised prose just as it tries to ridicule it. As Linda Leavell puts it, 'while Moore ridicules George Moore's self-conscious aestheticism (comparable with the poem's contrived symmetry), she praises his "spirit of narrative", which like the prose of her own poem, prevails despite the contrivance'.[27] A comparable paradox is established in Moore's poem addressed to Bernard Shaw, 'To a Prize Bird', in which the poet/speaker seems uncertain whether Shaw's pride in his abilities makes him a poetic 'Samson' or a strutting barnyard cock.

> You know to think, and what you speak
> With much of Samson's pride and bleak
> Finality; and none dare bid you stop [.]

Yet the speaker concludes, again almost despite herself, that 'Pride sits you well, so strut, colossal bird' – as 'Your brazen claws are staunch against defeat'.[28]

'To William Butler Yeats on Tagore', which appeared in the London periodical *The Egoist* in May 1915, also sees Moore attempting to assess her own relationship to an older poet and literary figure; but this time her chosen topic seems to be the issue of poetic praise itself. Schulze illustrates how *The Egoist* gave Moore, early on in her career, a 'literary outlet' that was 'attuned to her English and Irish subject matter'; but it also gave Moore a sounding board for her early forays into poetic criticism.[29] Indeed, Moore's poems 'To Browning' (later published as 'Injudicious Gardening') and 'To a Prize Bird' were published in *The Egoist* during the same period.[30] In 'To William Butler Yeats on Tagore', Schulze contends, 'Moore offers up a moment of double praise: she appreciates Yeats's appreciation of the Bengali poet Rabindranath Tagore'.[31] Mary Lago suggests why Moore's 'double praise' of Yeats may have been warranted: the 'zeal' of Yeats and Pound in publicising Tagore's work in Britain led to its first publication in America and 'the first genuinely critical appraisal of his work to appear in a Western journal'.[32] Moore described this episode in 1926, in an essay entitled '"New" poetry since 1912':

> In 1913, coincident with the translating into English of *Gitanjali*, Rabindranath Tagore visited the US, was termed by our press, 'The creator of a new age in literature', and W. B. Yeats wrote in *The Athenaeum*, 'A whole people, a whole civilisation, immeasurably strange to us, seems to have been taken up into this imagination; and yet we are not moved because of its strangeness, but because we have met our own image; as though we had walked in Rossetti's willow wood, or heard, perhaps for the first time in literature, our voice as in a dream'.[33]

Moore's use of quotations gives the impression that she is painting an unbiased picture of Tagore's visit. At the same time however, by combining Yeats's poetic praise of Tagore with the grandiose declaration of the American press, Moore subtly implies that their descriptions might be over-emphatic. As Roy Foster puts it, 'To connoisseurs of Yeats's enthusiasms', the note of praise for Tagore 'was familiar', but it was 'more extreme than anything since his endorsement of [Lady] Gregory's *Cuchulain*'.[34]

'To William Butler Yeats on Tagore', which also describes Tagore's visit and Yeats's praise of Tagore, initially reveals Moore as a 'connoisseur' of Yeats's 'enthusiasms'. The poem appears superficially to offer, as Schulze claims, a 'moment of double praise', but Moore draws our attention to the emphatic nature of praise, not only in Yeats's praise of Tagore, but also in the poem's praise of Yeats himself.

> It is made clear by the phrase,
> Even the mood – by virtue of which he says
>
> The thing he thinks – that it pays,
> To cut gems in these conscience-less days;
>
> But the jewel that always
> Outshines ordinary jewels, is your praise.[35]

On the one hand, the poem's praise of Yeats and, by implication, Tagore, appears genuine. For example, Moore's 'jewel'/'gem' metaphors appear to work as an emblem of her gift of praise to both poets and as a flattering imitation of the opalescent qualities of Yeats's early poems, such as the shell and pearl metaphors in 'The Song of the Happy Shepherd', or 'the enamelled sea' in 'The Indian to His Love'.[36] Moore's letters and reading practices certainly imply that she regarded herself as a connoisseur of Yeats's work. Her library contains the 1907 third edition of Yeats's *Ideas of Good and Evil*, which Molesworth claims Moore bought in 1915 along with *The Cutting of an Agate*, describing them as 'worth their weight in gold', and a limited signed edition of *The Winding Stair* from 1929.[37] Her copies of *Ideas of Good and Evil* and *The Winding Stair* are heavily annotated and underlined.

Yet 'To William Butler Yeats on Tagore' is not simply a 'moment of double praise'; in fact further analysis suggests that it is a somewhat confused work of praise and blame. Heuving argues that the poem 'praises Yeats for his staunchness', but a celebration of 'staunchness' seems somewhat limited.[38] Returning to the poem, it appears that Moore's 'praise' of Yeats relies on external qualities to illustrate his 'staunchness' of opinion: his words and manner – 'he says/ The thing he thinks' – and the value of speaking highly of another: 'it pays /To cut gems in these conscience-less days' (ll. 2–3/ l.4). This technique allows Moore to celebrate the sincerity of Yeats's expression of praise while subtly questioning the wisdom of the praise itself. Perhaps Moore wonders whether Yeats is simply following fashion by praising Tagore; after all, on his visits to the two countries in 1912–13, Tagore had been regarded by British and American polite society as an object from the East to be gazed at and admired. For example, Sturge Moore notes in a letter to [Robert Calverley] Trevelyan that 'The Poet himself is a sweet creature beautiful to the eye in a silk turban' who '[s]peaks very little, but looks beneficent and intelligent'.[39] Logically, then, the wide-eyed wonder of the poem might be insincere, mocking Yeats for being caught under Tagore's spell. The rhyme scheme of the poem appears especially disingenuous: although other poems Moore composed during this period, such as 'Appellate Jurisdiction' and 'The Wizard in Words',[40] employ rhyming couplets and triplets, the triple couplet structure of 'To William Butler Yeats on Tagore' is particularly, even deceptively, simplistic.

Perhaps Moore intends the AAAAAA rhyme to appear primitive: evoking chant and incantation, and recalling Yeats's interest in spiritualism, as well as his enchantment with Tagore. In a letter to her brother in 1915, the same year in which 'To William Butler Yeats in Tagore' was first published, Moore recorded that 'To my disgust I learn that Yeats has interested himself in spiritualism'.[41] Could it be that the 'double praise' of the poem rings as hollow as its rhymes? Yet Moore's 'disgust' at Yeats's spiritualist endeavours was not unusual, and other writers shared her suspicion with his methods. Elizabeth Bishop, for example, joked to Robert Lowell on reading Yeats's *A Vision*: 'The picture of Yeats going "Woof! – Woof!" in a lower berth, in the dark, in California, in order to wake up his wife who was dreaming she was a cat, is very pleasing, I think'.[42] In Bishop's mockery of Yeats's interests in dreams and visions we find a discomfort at the behaviour and proclivities of the man, which is dismissed through humour: but this reaction, despite the sincerity of Yeats's personal beliefs, risks damaging his reputation as a poet in the minds of his fellow writers.

In 'To William Butler Yeats on Tagore' Moore's appreciation of the older poet's expression of praise, in which she appears to detect sincere emotion, may be undermined by reservations about the wisdom of the praise itself and the strength of Yeats's character and judgements. Indeed, Moore seems unsure how far praise of another artist can help or hinder a poet. Yeats is perhaps an obvious choice for such an analysis: his early poems 'The Rose of Peace' (from *The Rose*, 1893), 'The Blessed', 'The Lover Pleads with his Friend for Old Friends' (both from *The Wind Among the Reeds*, 1899), 'Against Unworthy Praise' and 'To a Poet, who would have me Praise certain Bad Poets, Imitators of His and Mine' (both from *The Green Helmet and Other Poems*, 1910) all ask why and how one should offer praise.[43] In fact, the AAAAAA rhyme of 'To William Butler Yeats on Tagore' is both primitive and imitative, as its rhyming couplets recall similar rhymes found in Yeats's early poems. Indeed the rhyme 'Though you are in your shining days'/ 'And new friends busy with your praise' from 'The Lover Pleads with his Friend for Old Friends', appears to predict the 'days'/ 'praise' rhyme of Moore's poem.[44] Of course such rhymes are hardly unusual, but they do point to a possible level of imitation on Moore's part in employing such similar rhymes, and comparable line lengths, in her poem. This use of imitation enables poet and poem to act simultaneously as critic and connoisseur of Yeats's preoccupation with praise.

★

Moore's reviews of Yeats's poetry, published in 1918 and 1933, continue to develop the uneasy balance between explicit appreciation and implicit reservations that first emerges in 'To William Butler Yeats on Tagore'. The earlier review, 'Wild Swans', discussing Yeats's collection *The Wild Swans at Coole*, was published in *Poetry* in October 1918. On first reading, Moore appears to be in awe of the older poet: she admits that '[o]ne cannot but pay reverence to a poet' who 'can still be read with the same critical alertness that one would give the best of the younger poets'; and comments that Yeats 'hardly has to make poetry', as 'he just lets his heart talk'.[45] Yet Moore's disingenuous double negative 'One cannot but pay reverence', where 'reverence' is pointedly over-emphatic, reveals an implicit (self-)criticism of the dangers of praising a poet simply because he is older, or apparently more accomplished. Indeed, where Moore is most appreciative of Yeats's work in the review is where she feels he has spent time thinking about his craft: 'The weighing and measuring, the critical care evidently spent on this thin volume', Moore argues, 'save the reader most of his labour'.[46]

In fact, as Patricia Willis puts it, the review actually reveals Moore 'taking on' the 'major poet', mocking his 'ivory tower' status and his advanced years (he was fifty-three).⁴⁷ But beyond this Moore undermines Yeats's apparent sincerity, noting that he 'just lets his heart talk', commenting that 'Yeats makes poetry out of the fact that he is a proud, sensitive, cultivated Irishman', and claiming that the 'longer poems' might 'seem' 'somewhat old-fashioned' to a reviewer. Moore implies that Yeats is relying on his poetic conviction to charm his established and trusting readership. Indeed, where Moore apparently celebrates the ease with which Yeats writes poetry, she also includes an implicit criticism of his more traditional attitude to prosody: 'He hardly has to make poetry – except the rhymes, which don't matter'. Additionally, Moore describes Yeats's poetry as material that 'can still be read with the same critical alertness that one would give the best of the younger poets'. Her comment implies that while younger poets might be able to read Yeats's poetry with 'critical alertness', his age and superiority might prevent him from returning the favour.⁴⁸

But while it might seem unfair to question Yeats's poetic and critical competence on the grounds of age, the review's further implicit criticisms reveal a more personal response to Yeats. For example, despite appearing to discuss Yeats's poetic technique, Moore employs thinly disguised sexual metaphors, which simultaneously ridicule and censure Yeats for his self-declaredly unsuccessful amorous pursuits: 'And if there is a drooping line here and there, the author is too proud, too able, and too conscientious to arouse misgivings that he will ever bank on his reputation' (p. 40). Here, 'drooping' is contrasted with 'arouse' to imply that Yeats's age has rendered him physically incapable of rising to the occasion, or of living up to the 'reputation' he has earned for his well-publicised love affairs. Yeats had finally married the year before, in the autumn of 1917, and was to have two children with his wife George Hyde-Lees, so Moore's innuendos are perhaps unfounded. Nevertheless, Moore insinuates that it is virtually impossible to disentangle Yeats's poetic and public reputations. Elsewhere in the review, she clarifies her opinion on Yeats's public persona by arguing that 'For a poet with such a personality as Yeats, it seems almost indecorous to bare it all before us' (p. 39).

However, the last section of 'Wild Swans' begins to explain why Moore might be so judgemental of Yeats's apparent self-exposure. As in 'To William Butler Yeats on Tagore', Moore marvels at Yeats's poetic attributes, but these attributes are clouded by inappropriate behaviour. It is unsurprising that Moore, as a staunch Presbyterian who valued her privacy, appears to have been anxious about her admiration of Yeats's work. His intense sexuality, extrovert manners and interest in spiritualism must have been far removed from her own moral codes. Therefore, in a long paragraph at the end of the review, Moore devises a means of appreciating the poet rather than the man himself: 'In "Ego Dominus Tuus", the beautiful poetic dialogue which appeared first in *Poetry* and is reprinted here in his latest prose volume, the poet would have us believe that great poems are the result of the poet's "opposite" image – an expression of what the poet is not. I think this opposite, and not his little everyday thoughts and actions, *is* the poet'.[49]

In Yeats's poem, the first speaker, *Hic*, desires that through his 'opposite', *Ille*, 'I would find myself and not an image', but *Ille* appears to doubt this possibility:

> That is our modern hope and by its light
> We have lit upon the gentle, sensitive mind
> And lost the old nonchalance of the hand;
> Whether we have chosen chisel, pen or brush,
> We are but critics, or but half create[.][50]

Yet Moore contends that one finds oneself and not an image through the very act of discovering one's opposite. *Ille* worries that 'modern hope' relies too heavily on deliberate thought rather than instinctive action – the 'sensitive mind' rather than 'the old nonchalance of the hand' – but Moore's 'modern' method foregrounds the creative process. Through the very act of making art, whether with 'chisel, pen, or brush', the work becomes its own entity, reflecting an impression of the poet but remaining distinct from the personality that created it. This distinction recalls 'To William Butler Yeats on Tagore', where Moore celebrates Yeats's poetic expression of praise while questioning the personal nature of the praise itself.

In her review, Moore plays upon the distinction between poet and personality to exonerate herself for admiring 'flawed' characters. Beginning with allusions to 'Ego Dominus Tuus' – where Yeats's speakers discuss 'The chief imagination of Christendom / Dante Alghieri', who is 'mocked' for his 'lecherous life'[51] – Moore comments that failures such as these 'are somewhat beside the mark, as their effects on the poet's soul are mainly those of health and sickness'. She continues:

> They are ethical and civil sins, but hardly poetic *sins*. Their scars on the poet are not of the same character as Turner's miserliness, or as malice, envy, etc. But even these, when present, are hardly more than the masks of the poet's soul – perhaps hardly more than the masks of any soul; it is in his poems that the real soul can be seen.[52]

Here, Moore appears to corroborate Yeats's theory of the mask, which as A. Norman Jeffares summarises is 'based upon antithesis in character, upon the differences between a natural and a chosen personality, upon contrariety';[53] yet at the same time she is careful to theorise that a poem cannot be seen as a mask. Rather than a 'trying on' of different identities, Moore claims, a poem is actually as truthful as a mirror: 'it is in his poems that the real soul can be seen'. This theory appears to rely on a Romantic view of the poet, or at least of a successful poet, as somehow imbued with a greatness that they must seek out.

Moore constructs a definition of poetry as a 'beautiful' creation reflecting the 'soul' of the poet; this 'soul' is necessarily distinct from the writer's (non-poetic) personality, the latter shaped by his 'little everyday thoughts and actions'. Through this definition, Moore is free to admire the work of artists whose 'ethical and civil sins' amount to no more than 'everyday thoughts and actions' and can be distinguished from 'poetic *sins*': it is neither sinful for such men to write poetry, nor is it sinful for Moore to admire their efforts. The antiquated, quasi-biblical language – 'lecherous', 'ethical and civil sins', 'miserliness', 'malice' – gives this last paragraph the tone of a parable, suggesting that these poets might have been, or might yet be, saved by their poetry. In 'Anima Hominis', a section of *Per Amica Silentia Lunae*, Yeats argues that 'We make' poetry 'out of the quarrel with ourselves', but Moore in fact sees a distinction in the poet between personal 'self' and poetic 'self' that makes this quarrel unnecessary.[54] As she puts it, as if in conclusion, 'Nor is indulgence due, as Yeats thinks, to the poet's desire to escape from himself; but rather, in so far as it is more than mere exhaustion, due to his desire to find himself. It is the disappointment with pleasure, and life's egging on'.[55] Moore suggests that the poet is critic and poet in one, taking pleasure in his/her work or the work of others while being anxious to create something that reflects his/her poetic self more accurately. In fact, Moore appears to ask how far poetry is itself a creation of selfhood. As if to corroborate her argument, on the back of her copy of Yeats's *Ideas of Good and Evil*, bought in 1915, she notes 'His imagination is the man himself'.[56]

Throughout her career, Moore would develop such ideas into a more consistent theory about the interconnectedness of aesthetics and morality. In an Editor's 'Comment' in *The Dial* in September 1926, for example, she would attest to the 'potent energy' of 'work which is aesthetically serious'.[57] Molesworth contends that Moore 'conceived of writing as a selection of one pure stylistic or moral alternative among others'; but where the 'moral alternative' was absent, it could be suggested by the 'stylistic' alternative presented.[58] As if to reflect this developing theory of the interrelation of the stylistic and the moral, Moore's later review of Yeats, published in *Poetry* in 1933, makes far fewer moral judgements. Of course Moore's own reputation, both as a poet and a critic, had been firmly established by this time; this probably contributed to her less combative critical style. In an article entitled 'Words for Music Perhaps', a review of Yeats's *The Winding Stair* and *Words for Music Perhaps and Other Poems* (1933), Moore argues that any of Yeats's 'failures' vanish among the intricacies of his poetic design: 'he is, for me, the one author whose failures – if they are that – subtract themselves as one comes to them and do not in memory remain to mar the fortunate cloak of invisibility'. Moore relies on visual metaphors and aesthetic analysis to judge the overall impression of the work itself, contending later in the review that 'there is no end to the beauties one might separate out from Mr Yeats' abundance'.[59]

William Carlos Williams argued, in a review of Moore in 1925, that separation was integral to Moore's own poetic method: 'Miss Moore undertakes in her work to separate the poetry from the subject entirely, like all the moderns. In this she has been rarely successful and this is important'.[60] In her reviews of Yeats, this technique has become a means by which Moore can separate the poetry of her subject from his personality, while separating her personal views as a Christian from her literary views as a critic, so avoiding the need to justify her appreciation of their work. It seems that in the intervening years between the two reviews, Moore had addressed some of the ambiguities of her earlier poetry and criticism to develop a more coherent, less morally judgemental style. But we should also bear in mind that by 1933 Moore had become a successful poet in her own right, and had also spent some four years as Editor of *The Dial* (1925–29); perhaps, then, the shadow of Yeats could finally be shaken off. As a poet and critic, Moore had to find a way to engage impartially with Yeats as a writer who, for over twenty years, was her contemporary: and for her, this meant cutting out the biography of the man himself.

Yeats as ageing poet: Berryman and Bogan

For John Berryman, Yeats the man was intrinsically connected to Yeats the poet. Berryman's early fascination with Yeats is well known, thanks to his claim in 1965 that he 'began work in verse-making as burning trivial disciple of the great Irish poet W. B. Yeats',[61] and to his famous address to Yeats in his 'Dream Song 312': 'majestic Shade, You whom I read so well/ so many years ago'.[62] These two oft-quoted statements are useful for underwriting the dual legacy of Yeats within Berryman's early work: as one who informed his 'verse-making' and shaped his reading of poetry. We might see Berryman's speaker, in his 'Dream Song 312', as one who learnt to read poetry through reading Yeats – the use of 'well' suggesting an earnest reading of Yeats which may, or may not, result in a 'good' reading of his works. It is not a surprise, then, that Berryman's narrator Henry asks of Yeats 'did I read your lesson right?'.[63] Both of these examples give the impression of a poet starting out against one who has achieved his goal: in the former, Yeats is as old as he is great; in the latter, he is a 'shade', long dead, who is always present, but has the potential to conceal as well as to protect. Borrowing from Coleman, then, we might read both statements as commentaries on the praise relations between the young American and the 'great Irish poet'.[64]

John Berryman was twenty-one when he arrived at Cambridge in September 1936, on a two-year Kellett Fellowship from Columbia University. Almost immediately, he set about trying to achieve his major aim while residing in Britain: meeting his idol, W. B. Yeats. Straightaway he wrote to Yeats, enclosing a selection of his own poems.

In a breathless letter to his mother, dated 11 November, Berryman recounts his pleasure at receiving a reply, from Yeats, to his letter of praise: 'I am still so excited that I want to rush in various contradictory directions. Coming in for breakfast today, I found on my table a letter from Ireland and lo – you are correct – it was from Yeats'.[65] In the same letter, Berryman transcribes the 'quite illegible and characterless scrawl' of Yeats's reply, managing to 'make the few lines out' after an hour. Yeats's reply, fittingly, is set out as verse:

> I thank you for it and the more because
> the poems you select for praise
> are those that I most approve.
> I thank you too for the eloquent
> compliment of your verse.[66]

The verbal encounter between Berryman and Yeats is poeticised by the older poet as a mutual appreciation – a two-way praise-giving framed by the poems of Yeats that Berryman has 'selected for praise' and the 'compliment of your verse' that Berryman has sent in turn. Berryman adds, in a note to the conclusion of the letter, that the poems he mentioned – and those that Yeats similarly 'most approves' of – were '"The Second Coming", the poems in "Words for Music Perhaps", "Sailing to Byzantium", "The Fisherman", and, I think, "In Memory of Major Robert Gregory" and several others'.[67]

It is interesting to identify imitations of some of these poems in Berryman's early poetry in praise of Yeats. For example, in one of the poems Berryman sent to Yeats, which begins 'A glory there is over Ireland now', the young poet combines an imitation of 'Sailing to Byzantium' (and echoes of 'The Fisherman' and 'Nineteen Hundred and Nineteen') with a self-conscious eulogy to the 'aged' Irish writer:

> An aged man there is in Ireland now
> Alone who is the honour of that praise.
> Craftsman intense and disciplined, a man
> Who set luxuriance aside and ran,
> A creature of bone & heat & rigid brow,
> The race that wears the rest, eternal ways,
> That solitary man.[68]

Though Berryman's attempts to reshape Yeats's familiar poetic motifs into a 'compliment of verse' – and, particularly, his forced iambics – are amusing in their naïvety, they do display an understanding of the poetic lexicon of Yeats's work at a time when he is beginning to collect his thoughts on this topic. Indeed, Berryman's 'bone & heat & rigid brow' actually predates by two years the 'foul rag-and-bone shop of the heart' conclusion of Yeats's 'The Circus Animals' Desertion'. First published in *The Atlantic Monthly* and *The London Mercury* in January 1939, 'The Circus Animals' Desertion' self-consciously edits the motifs and symbols of a long career like a greatest hits compilation.[69]

In his Cambridge letters, Berryman displays not just an admiration for Yeats, but a yearning to imitate him as closely as possible. This is particularly true of a stanza that he includes in a letter to his mother, of which he claims:

> I have written only four lines (and of them really only the second) that I would consider by (or in the same realm with) Yeats:
> Yet agony has outline, the flesh bone,
> Christ cried a formal anguish on the cross;
> Leaving the twelve and time he saw the loss
> Balanced with white hair but white hair alone.[70]

The second line, which Berryman identifies as the strongest, actually comes closest to iambic pentameter of the four – and arguably recalls the famous line 'What made us dream that he could comb grey hair?' from 'In Memory of Major Gregory' (another of the poems identified as Berryman and Yeats's mutual favourites), in its combination of alliterative 'c' sounds and consonantal patterns.[71] Yeats's question is clearly in mind here, as Berryman's fourth line – 'Balanced with white hair but white hair alone' – seems to be a thematic and tonal echo of Yeats's original with its commentary on Gregory's solitary, premature death. Here, however, it is Christ on the cross who will not live to comb his white hair. This curious, and confusing, imitation of Yeats sees the young Berryman trying to compose lines that sound as if one might consider them 'by (or in the same realm with) Yeats', revealing a self-conscious self-sacrifice of individual expression, which almost parodies the 'anxiety of influence' that Bloom argues 'governs relations between poets as poets'.[72]

Writing on the extent of Yeats's influence on American poetry, Diggory claims that 'A poet who admitted Yeats into his work found he had room for little else, including himself'.[73] Berryman's self-description as a 'disciple' of Yeats seems particularly apt, considering the spiritual overtones in the lines above, and the monastic approach with which he reads and studies everything to do with Yeats. To his mother, Berryman describes how, in preparation for a talk he is planning to give on Yeats at Clare College, he has discovered 'influences (mainly, in the development from Spenser, Shelley and Rossetti, French Symbolist and English Metaphysical influences, the hard vigor of Pound's versification, and tightening his stanza forms by comparison with good speech), and random details'. Add to this the seriousness with which he approaches the talk itself, and we are given a clear picture of the level of devotion Berryman commits to Yeats in his earliest years as a student and poet: 'I spent rather too much time on Yeats's life and various activities, reading occasionally from the *Autobiographies* and essays and philosophy, and read only some twenty poems, of which I discussed only a half-dozen. There is no compromise possible in these things'.[74]

Of course, such intense interest is only possible as Yeats nears what Berryman perceives as the end of his life (and career), and the beginning of Berryman's own; the young American poet, it seems, is planning to write Yeats's biography while he still can: 'Tremendous work would be necessary', he points out, 'but now is the time, before material has vanished and the man has died (although in no circumstances would I publish during his lifetime, for many and strong reasons)'.[75] In fact, Berryman's lines 'An aged man there is in Ireland now / Alone who is the honour of that praise', which he included in his letter to Yeats, prove ultimately prescient: as if Berryman's 'praise', which can only be meted out in his role of Yeatsian 'disciple', is linked entirely to Yeats's role as 'aged' poet. Berryman told his mother of his aims to sum up, in his talk at Clare, Yeats's 'achievement in the drama, in various kinds of prose, in moral philosophy, and in poetry'.[76] Thus the living Yeats has already become, for Berryman, a poetic and historical artefact, to be investigated, searched for, imitated, and recorded.

★

Although Louise Bogan was of a slightly older generation than Berryman, her responses to Yeats — recorded in her reviews of his poetry and achievements — might be seen similarly as attempts to position herself against an ageing poet and to summarise the extent of his poetic achievement in the years before his death.[77] Bogan was a frequent — and somewhat superlative — reviewer of Yeats. In a 1934 review of his *Collected Poems* for *The New Yorker*, Bogan commended his 'native gifts — the extraordinary ear underlying his technical brilliants, his heritage of blood in which run wit, bitter intelligence, and a fund of beautiful common speech'.[78] This emphasis on Yeats's 'native' genius runs through Bogan's reviews, as she increasingly portrays an ageing Yeats as an almost Messianic figure who has worked his magic over Irish literature — and also as a writer who has always had absolute belief in his poetic powers. As she puts it in an extended article for the *Atlantic Monthly* in 1938, entitled 'The greatest poet writing in English today':

> Yeats has advanced into age with his art strengthened by a long battle which has taken as its object a literature written by Irishmen fit to take its place among the noble literatures of the world. The spectacle of a poet's work invigorated by his lifelong struggle against the artistic inertia of his nation is one that would shed strong light into [sic] any era.[79]

Bogan's dismissal of the 'artistic inertia' of Ireland might be read against the context of her 1937 visit, when she had told Edmund Wilson that in Dublin 'The most moveless faces in the world confront you on all sides', so that 'Now I know where Yeats got his idea, his obsession, of the mask'; while her dissatisfaction and frustration with Dublin had led her to describe it as 'the city most displayed, dissected, hated, scorned, vilified, praised, wept over, distilled into literature, in modern time'.[80] Here Bogan seems to have more in common with the Joyce who she sees as harbouring 'love and hatred' for Ireland in *Finnegans Wake* than with the Yeats whom she praises for his noble quest to write national poetry.[81]

Nevertheless, in her reviews of Yeats Bogan continues to site her 'ageing' poet at the centre of a much-needed cultural revival in Ireland, praising the poetic passion that he extends to other poets. In a 1936 review of Yeats's edition of the *Oxford Book of Modern Verse*, discussing the 'young men' he has included in his collection, Bogan notes: 'His preface closes on a note of belief in the sincerity and intellectual passion of these young men. He does not assign the influence of his own sincerity and intellectual passion to them, although there is more Yeats in all of them than many of them would care to admit'.[82] This commentary on Yeats's apparent influence within 'all' of the poets included in the collection – which numbered among its living writers poets as diverse as Auden, Colum, Housman, Lawrence and MacNeice – tells us the extent to which Yeats had, by 1936, become something of a burden to them. Even nearly thirty years after Yeats's death, in 1966, we find Robert Lowell confronting the spectre of Yeats, and the burden of his influence: 'I gave a Yeats reading at Columbia', he wrote to Bishop, 'and my head rang with resonance'.[83] How to confront this 'resonance' is a returning question amongst Yeats's contemporaries and antecedents, and the writers who assess his legacy in the decades following his death.

This same question confronts Bogan in a posthumous review of Yeats for *The New Yorker*, written on the occasion of the publication of a new edition of his *Collected Poems* in 1951. Acknowledging the relative unpopularity of Yeats's later verse, Bogan contends: 'If the last poems often present the picture of a pride-ridden old man who clings to his crankiness with an almost insane zeal, they also present an old poet continuing to explore his complicated nature and his complicated times up to the last'; and when viewing his life as a whole, Bogan contends, we should celebrate him for 'knowing that without passion no art can live'.[84] Like Bogan's earlier praise of the 'sincerity and passion' that went into his edition of the *Oxford Book of Modern Verse*, she sees Yeats's legacy as one of determination and self-belief, despite its tendency in recent years to take some wrong turns.

What Bogan's reviews and Berryman's poem-letters share is a focus on Yeats's image as an old and ageing man – and here they also share similarities with Moore's 1918 and 1933 reviews of Yeats. Though they differ in their reasons for reading and reviewing Yeats – Berryman as the upstart poet (and critic) learning to make verse to emulate his great idol, Bogan searching for a sincerity and passion amongst the wrong turns of Yeats's old age – both see in the older poet a model for themselves, in Yeats's continued striving to write about, and write *for*. But of course Yeats has established this precedent, too, by continuing to assess his position as a poet throughout his life, and by portraying himself as an ageing poet from the elegiac opening lines of *Responsibilities* (1914), aged 49, through the 'sixty-year-old smiling public man' of 'Among School Children' (1927), to the excluded old and lecherous figure of 'Politics' (1939).[85] At the same time, of course, Yeats's age does give his poets and critics a slight advantage: as although he has passion and sincerity and longevity on his side, on their side they have youth (however relative), promise, and potential.

Yeats as mourned poet: Babette Deustch

Of Yeats's poetic legacy, Steven Matthews notes, 'His work shadows, and is mourned within, much major poetry written immediately after his death and subsequently'.[86] For the Jewish-American poet and critic Babette Deutsch (1895–1982), her sustained interest in the cultural legacy that Yeats inherited, and the poetic legacy that he passed on to others, culminates in her poem 'Lament for the Makers, 1964' (itself a spin on William Dunbar's late medieval poem 'Lament for the Makaris'). Yeats's work 'shadows' the poem as a constant presence, but this shadowing extends to a further allusion to Auden's elegy for Yeats, 'In Memory of W. B. Yeats', while Yeats's literal death is mourned in the poem as a catalyst for further mourning for the deaths of the other poets commemorated within it.

Deutsch's fascination with Irish art and culture, and her lifelong interest in the Yeats family, led her to regard Yeats as an inheritor of an artistic tradition that was essentially 'Irish': an attitude that provides an alternative route into Yeats from Moore's critical and moral assessment of the man and his art and from Berryman's devotion to, and imitation of, the older poet. Though Deutsch's attitude shares some similarities with Bogan's responses to Yeats's 'native genius' in her reviews of Yeats's work – where Bogan sees Yeats as almost the sole initiator of the Irish Revival, and draws inspiration from his passion for cultural reinstatement during a period of inertia – Deutsch emphasises Yeats's role as inheritor rather than progenitor. Her interest in Yeats and his family can be tracked and measured through her correspondence with the Irish poet and critic Thomas McGreevy, which was sustained over nearly twenty years from 1946 to 1965.

In Deutsch's first letter to McGreevy, she discusses the inclusion of McGreevy's poems in Yeats's *Oxford Book of Modern Verse* (1936), and celebrates the fact that 'The letters of John Butler Yeats have just been published over here. They are a great joy'.[87] In her next letter, she discusses the Yeats family once more. Having received from McGreevy his recently published book on Jack B. Yeats and another on Dublin's National Gallery,[88] Deutsch comments: 'I enjoyed the Yeats book partly for myself and not a little because I had recently finished reading a superb collection of letters by old Mr. Yeats and because W. B. Yeats is a poet I never tire of re-reading. ... As for your book on the Irish National Gallery, that was a revelation. I hadn't realized how many good things you have'.[89] Despite her slightly condescending appreciation of Dublin's art collection, Deutsch displays here a fondness for Irish culture, and a zest to learn more about it, on which McGreevy is keen to capitalise. Indeed, in his next letter he introduces Deutsch to the poems of Thomas Moore, and even considers the practicalities of accessing his work: 'you will find a dozen copies of Tom Moore if not more in the English literature part of the library. The Irish in New York will have seen to it that Moore is well represented there'.[90] But for Deutsch – who reveals in her next letter that she has been 'reviewing a fat book called 1000 Years of Irish Poetry, edited by Kathleen Hoagland', and determines to seek out Moore's work[91] – her attraction to Irish poetry is always linked to Yeats, whom she will 'never tire of re-reading'.

In February 1948, Deutsch – a self-confessed cynic regarding religion and mysticism[92] – announced to McGreevy that she was starting work on a chapter on Yeats:

> I am about the great business of trying to do a chapter on W. B. Yeats and had several questions to put to you, but felt shy about doing so. Altho [sic] I cannot accept his 'system' and am anything but sympathetic to his magical mumbo-jumbo, he remains the poet to whose work I return with the deepest satisfaction, largely, I think, because of the wisdom he learned from that grand old man, John Butler Yeats, whose letters I have been re-reading with fresh delight.[93]

The finished chapter, 'Vision of Reality', in Deutsch's book *Poetry In Our Time* (1952), reflects the sentiment of this letter by engaging more closely with the pleasure of reading Yeats, and the 'deep satisfaction' of his work, than with his 'magical mumbo-jumbo'. The chapter opens by rationalising Yeats's 'system' as a Blakeian response to modern life: 'William Butler Yeats was a religious man who lived in an age of reason like a wealthy exile', Deutsch argues, who 'early on made up a religion of his own out of the tradition that poets and painters and more systematic myth-makers had handed down from one generation to another'.[94] Deutsch's emphasis on the significance of inheritance from 'poets and painters' within Yeats's 'system' also reflects her conviction that Yeats's 'wisdom' is 'learned' from his father; but she is pursuing a kind of 'systematic myth-making' of her own.

In her chapter on Yeats, Deutsch tries to iron out the aesthetic experiments and spiritual evolutions of Yeats's career by seeing these changes as part of a sustained desire for 'superhuman nobility', which is linked to a quest for an Irish poetic identity:

> If, as he said in a lyric composed before the nineteenth century had entered on its last decade: 'words alone are certain good', it was because they could summon up the superb personages of legend and folklore created out of men's longing for a super-human nobility. The same thought dictated the admonition in a poem written a few months before his death:
>
> Irish poets, learn your trade,
> Sing whatever is well made ...
>
> His earliest lyrics, however, embroider Pre-Raphaelite flowers on the hem of Irish legendry in the palest colors.[95]

For Deutsch, then, Yeats is the pre-twentieth century Yeats – the late Romantic poet, searching for an identity amongst the 'legend and folklore' of Ireland, looking for something greater than himself. Thus the couplet borrowed from Yeats's late poem 'Under Ben Bulben' – with its echoes of Prospero's uncertain gift to his audience, and its sense of a mantle being passed on to the new poetic craftsmen (like the 'Grecian goldsmiths' of 'Sailing to Byzantium')[96] – becomes a statement of 'admonition'. For Deutsch, Yeats's warning to younger poets comes from a concern that they are moving away from an essentially 'Irish' view of the poet as one who 'summons up superb personages of legend and folklore'.

Yet in the context of 'Under Ben Bulben', Yeats's concern for younger poets seems as much aesthetic as it does nationalistic – the 'Irish' element related to a somewhat problematic fear of degeneration rather than to a desire to protect the nobility of 'legend and folklore':

> Irish poets, learn your trade,
> Sing whatever is well made,
> Scorn the sort now growing up
> All out of shape from toe to top,
> Their unremembering hearts and heads
> Base-born products of base beds.[97]

The key word here is 'unremembering'. Yeats leaves it unclear what is failing to be remembered – be this poetic 'trade' (the tools of the craft); the art of making formal poetry (rather than lines that are 'All out of shape'); or the recent troubled history of Ireland. But surely this is the point. The conclusion of Yeats's plea, that 'we in coming days may be / Still the indomitable Irishry',[98] seems to link together all of these concerns: but 'indomitable' tells us that it is the prowess of Irish poetry that Yeats ultimately wants to be upheld, rather than the 'legend and folklore' than first brought it about. The 'super-human' nobles of Deutsch's reading – represented by the great figures of Irish myth – have been replaced by the 'super-human' Irish poet: one who does not wish his legacy to degenerate into 'baseness'.

For Deutsch, Yeats is the Irish Pre-Raphaelite: an artist who decorates 'Irish legendry' with his flowers of verse. Such a romantic view of Yeats is far removed from the more problematic politics of his late poems.[99] Henry W. Wells, in a 1953 review of *Poetry In Our Time*, characterises Deutsch's style of criticism as personable and intimate, describing how she responds to those poets whose work she 'enjoys the most': 'Her approach is personal and intuitive. Hence her book resembles a novel in which the chief characters are the chief poets'.[100] This 'intuition' is apparent in her decisive reading of Yeats as a poet who constructed his own religion from an inherited tradition; but as we have seen, this reading comes as much from her personal antipathy towards Yeats's 'mumbo-jumbo' as from her desire to understand and appreciate Yeats's method. Wells sums up this paradox of intimacy with the poet and avoidance of the spiritual aspect of the poetry in

Deutsch's book. Though she is the 'friend, delegate and good angel of the major poet', thanks to a 'spiritual astigmatism' the book 'leaves the ideal for modern poetry suspended almost in a vacuum', so that 'it remains spiritually unresolved, if not actually chaotic'.[101] In the case of Yeats, Deutsch's blurred vision chooses to view Yeats's spiritualism as part of an attempt to make sense of an 'age of reason' and nothing more; to view his aesthetic as part of an ongoing desire to illustrate the 'folklore and legend' of Ireland, the nobility of which should not be forgotten; and to see his poetic appeal as derived from the inherited wisdom of his father.

Deutsch's readings of Yeats reflect a nostalgia for an Irish past that is revealed in her correspondence with McGreevy: a past filled with the kind of 'super-human nobility' that she envisages as rising out of the folklore and legend of Irish verse. In the same letter in which she first describes her chapter on Yeats, Deutsch writes of McGreevy's story of visiting Maud Gonne with a wistful lyricism that betrays her fascination with the figures of Irish 'nobility': 'It was strange and wonderful to hear you speak (the phrase I use indicates how lively my sense of it was!) of going to sit with Maud Gonne. I have never seen anyone as beautiful as the pictures I've seen of her show her to be, even the reproduction of the bronze head of her in old age'. Deutsch adds, commenting on Gonne's influence on Yeats's poetry, that 'some of the finest lyrics are hers'.[102] McGreevy's reply encourages the nostalgia trip, including in an anecdote about Gonne's past braveries during the Irish civil war a commentary on Gonne's own attitude to the past: 'at 82 she is best on the past and her eyes get starrier and starrier when she comes to the fun it used to be'.[103] For both poets, Yeats's legacy is tied up in the romance of such moments: he is a seen as a conduit to a troubled but glorious Irish past, as a mouthpiece for Irish cultural figures such as John Butler Yeats, and even as a poetic collaborator with the almost impossibly beautiful Maud Gonne. This sense is continued through their correspondence, as Deutsch takes continued fascination in Yeats's life story; for instance, in April 1949 she discusses a review that she has written for *The New Republic* on Richard Ellmann's new biography of Yeats (*The Man in the Masks*).[104]

These letters also see Deutsch taking delight, as a poet, in the apparent similarities that her work reveals with Yeats's poetry. In a letter of 1948, she tells McGreevy that John Crowe Ransom, on accepting a poem of hers 'for his quarterly (*Kenyon Review*) recently, said that lines made him think of Shakespeare and Yeats'.[105] Deutsch's poem 'Fountain and Unicorn' – consisting of six stanzas of six lines each, arranged into a loose iambic pentameter – was published in the *Kenyon Review* in the summer of 1948.[106] The poem, like Deutsch's commentary on Yeats in *Poetry in our Time*, seems preoccupied with issues of humanity and nobility. In a poem that collects together mythological pictures of a 'Tapestry [that] shows the fabulous unicorn' (l. 25) and 'a portico / Presided over by an angel' (ll. 19–20), the concluding stanza claims that:

> These images are so noble that they can call
> Into the mind a thought that's fugitive
> Yet noble, like themselves[107]

There are echoes, here, of Yeats's 'Circus Animals' Desertion' in the gathering of images, and in the contemplation of their nobility. We can hear in particular the opening lines of the last section of Yeats's poem, which ask: 'Those masterful images because complete / Grew in pure mind, but out of what began?'[108] Though Yeats's question, by doubting the origin of 'masterful' images that have sprung, apparently, from a 'pure mind', expresses a poetic self-distrust that is absent in Deutsch's later poem, we might see the latter as written in answer to Yeats's original. As if to assuage Yeats's doubt, Deutsch's poem notes that these sorts of 'images are so noble' that they are able to capture the glorious ephemerality of poetry itself.

Extending further the complex kinship between Deutsch, Yeats and Ireland, Deutsch's poem 'Lament for the Makers: 1964' seems to act as a culmination of her views on Yeats, in its combined elegy of Yeats – through Auden – with recently deceased poets MacNeice (d. 1963), Robert Frost (d. 1963), Kenneth Fearing (d. 1961), Robinson Jeffers (d. 1962), E. E. Cummings (d. 1962), William Carlos Williams (d. 1963) and Theodore Roethke (d. 1963). Meanwhile, Wallace Stevens (d. 1955) is mourned as one who 'from his ivory tower/ … invites us to look down with him at the dump',[109] thus confounding the connection between American modernism, Romantic poetry and the 'ivory tower' mentality of early Yeats. Complicating things even further is the British context of the poem, with its direct evocation of Auden's 1939 poem 'In Memory of W. B. Yeats'; its nod to Dylan Thomas's burial at Laugharne, Wales, in 1953; and its titular allusion to the fifteenth-century Scottish poet William Dunbar's 'Lament for the Makaris', which Deutsch references at the end of the poem (ll. 47–8). Deutsch provides another cultural mix by claiming of Williams that 'He was an American: his ancestors English, Dutch, French, even, as if known / A Jew' (ll. 33–4). This last qualification enables the Jewish-American Deutsch, with Williams as exemplar, to go beyond ethnic and religious lines and spin into her web of poetic and biographical allusions the Irish contexts of the poem as well.

The first two stanzas of 'Lament for the Makers: 1964' show most clearly Deutsch's imitation of Auden's elegy to Yeats:

> Those black shoes broken in for the burial
> At Drumcliff, MacNeice grew inured to: they were old
> When he wore them to the burial at Laugharne.
> Now he will not stoop again to pull on his shoes:
> He, too, is buried. And if a bird of gold
> Begins to sing? Snow falls where roses blow? Or a stale fern
> Seeds? Then these deaths are mocked apocryphal news.
>
> The deaths are mocked by the work. But the work is finished
> With the lives and the minds that shaped it. Punctual as bills,
> Though more like receipts, the books on Yeats arrive.
> But not one poem by the poet arrives. The masks
> His proud hands lifted gaily, the stubborn skills
> Are lost. His folly, his rage, his ecstasy survive
> In lines the young man envies, in a question the scholar asks. (ll. 1–14)

On first reading, echoes of 'In Memory of W. B. Yeats' seem to dominate. The first stanza concentrates on Yeats's burial at Drumcliff, Thomas's at Laugharne, and MacNeice's recent death ('He, too, is buried'), and worries that the deaths of such great men will be reimagined as 'mocked apocryphal news'. Similarly Auden's poem worries that the day of Yeats's death might merely be imagined as 'a day when one did something slightly unusual'.[110]

In the second stanza, Deutsch's echoes of Auden resonate still further. Here, too, is the separation of the artist and work through death – which generates Auden's concern that 'The words of a dead man' will be 'modified in the guts of the living' – and the purposelessness of Yeats's poetic passion ('His folly, his rage, his ecstasy'). But here, also, is the assertion of poetic survival, as summarised by Auden in section II of his poem:

> You were silly like us: your gift survived it all;
> The parish of rich women, physical decay,
> Yourself; mad Ireland hurt you into poetry.
> Now Ireland has her madness and her weather still,
> For poetry makes nothing happen: it survives
> In the valley of its saying where executives
> Would never want to tamper; it flows south
> From ranches of isolation and the busy griefs,
> Raw towns that we believe and die in; it survives,
> A way of happening, a mouth.[111]

Though Deutsch's idea of poetic survival – through reading poems sent by post, or in questions the scholar asks – is arguably more positive than Auden's (for whom poetry is merely 'A way of happening, a mouth'), both poets share the same fear of anonymity: of their work ending up on someone's doorstep 'like receipts', or existing merely in 'ranches of isolation', or in valleys where no one important would ever 'want to tamper'. For Deutsch, however, the 'survival' described is, appropriately, more personalised, more connected to the poet than the poem: 'His folly, his rage, his ecstasy survive'; whereas for Auden it is a depersonalised 'poetry', necessarily separated from the poet himself, that 'survives' by flowing from mouth to mouth, 'In the valley of its saying'. This rewriting of Auden's lines is, however, integral to Deutsch's method, which places the poet at the centre of the elegy – and combines poetic and personal allusions as if they are one and the same.

This combination of personal and poetic allusion extends beyond Auden in the two opening stanzas of 'Lament for the Makers', as Deutsch also includes references to the life and work of Yeats, MacNeice and Dylan Thomas. For instance, while biographically we see MacNeice breaking in his black shoes at Yeats's 1948 funeral at Drumcliff, and later at Thomas's funeral at Laugharne, the poetic resonances of the stanzas sound through Yeats, MacNeice and Thomas in turn. Within the sonnet-like frame of the two opening seven-line stanzas – at once an evocation of poetic form and a formal evocation of poets *as* poets – Deutsch includes references that might be to one or all of these three poets:

> Now he will not stoop again to pull on his shoes:
> He, too, is buried. And if a bird of gold
> Begins to sing? Snow falls where roses blow? Or a stale fern
> Seeds? Then these deaths are mocked apocryphal news.[112]

The first of these four lines echoes the mourning tones of Yeats's 'In Memory of Major Robert Gregory', as we hear tonal and rhythmic echoes of Yeats's prosaic but stirring line 'What made us dream that he could comb grey hair?' in the image of the deceased MacNeice, who 'will not stoop again to pull on his shoes'; while 'stoop' recalls Yeats's earlier poem 'A Cradle Song', with its imagery of 'angels ... stooping above your bed', who 'weary of trooping with the whimpering dead'.[113] In this context, then, it is natural that we might seek Yeatsian echoes in the subsequent lines, too: by hearing the 'gold enamelling' of Yeats's 'golden bough', created by 'Grecian goldsmiths' in 'Sailing to Byzantium';[114] by thinking of Yeats's constant use of snow and roses in his early symbolist poems from *Crossways* (1889) and *The Rose* (1893); or by recalling the multiple references to ferns – 'And makes the infant ferns unwrap' – in *The Wanderings of Oisin* (1889).[115]

But on closer inspection, certain of these lines contain more stable echoes of MacNeice's and Thomas's poetry. For while the rhetorical question 'Snow falls where roses blow?' recalls the combination of fertility and futility in MacNeice's concluding line 'There is more than glass between the snow and the huge roses' from his poem 'Snow',[116] the next – 'Or a stale fern / Seeds?' – evokes quite clearly Thomas's 1938 elegy 'After the Funeral (in memory of Ann Jones)',[117] with its memorable closing line 'And the strutting fern lay [sic] seeds on the black sill' (l. 40). In Thomas's poem the fern has previously represented death, enshrined as it is 'In a room with a stuffed fox and a stale fern' (l. 11); yet this fern can still 'lay seeds', almost in an act of mockery of the dead. Deutsch plays on this idea, so that in her poem the 'stale fern/ Seeds' as if in defiance of the death of Thomas, the original author of the metaphor. Even the ornithological references, so clearly gilded as to resemble similar metaphors in Yeats's 'Sailing to Byzantium', come to recall MacNeice's Byzantine challenge to Yeats in his last collection *The Burning Perch* (1963).[118] In a recent essay on 'MacNeice's Byzantium', Tom Walker contends that 'MacNeice's exploration of the Yeatsian terrain of Byzantium' in *The Burning Perch* can be seen as 'a means of challenging the use of history that underpins Yeats's symbolism'.[119] The 'terrain' occupied by Yeats in Deutsch's poem is necessarily re-evaluated by MacNeice's recent explorations.

Deutsch's conclusion of this stanza is two-fold, then: not only will the deaths of each poet become 'mocked apocryphal news' because people will eventually tire of the poets themselves, and the stories surrounding their demise, but the poems might also become part of this 'apocryphal news' – as other voices, and other poets, half remember their lines in new poems and (to borrow Auden's expression) new 'mouths'. Deutsch worries that if the poet dies, and the poems live on, not only will the poets be forgotten but their lines might also come to be reassessed – just as her own poem risks doing even in its attempts to remember.

Thus the concluding lines of 'Lament for the Makers: 1964' summarise that poetry, through its sheer ability to persist, might be closer to death than to life; its 'survival' a symbol of the process of continued grieving rather than of the endurance of life:

> Lament for the makers; it will never be over.
> Dante could not believe death had undone
> So many; since he said so, how many has death undone?
> How many will death take tomorrow, or this year, certainly?
> Dunbar made his lament over Chaucer and Henrysoun
> And Walter Kennedy. Now we must make our own.
> There is no end to grief. Nor no end to poetry.[120]

For Deutsch, it is the poet's duty to memorialise through elegy the poets who have gone before – 'Now we must make our own' – but the concluding line aligns the inevitability of death, and the grief that follows it, with the inevitability of poetry itself, leaving speaker and reader alike unsure of the exact legacy the poet leaves behind. This is far removed, arguably, from Yeats's own example; after all, in Deutsch's poem Yeats's 'proud hands' and 'stubborn skills' reveal a dogged determination that enables 'his folly, his rage, his ecstasy [to] survive'.[121] Auden's essay 'Yeats as an example' (1948), following the horrors of World War Two, questioned the legacy of Yeats's poetic conviction, and its link with 'the occult', asking 'How on earth, we wonder, could a man of Yeats's gifts take such nonsense seriously?'[122] Perhaps, then, the atheist Deutsch, writing in 1964 during an unsettled time in global politics – and following the recent death of several great poetic figures – doubts the same poetic conviction that enables her to write an elegy to other poets, through Yeats.

The poetic legacy that Deutsch asserts within the poem is curiously unstable, too, evoking a lineage that exceeds the confines of American, Irish and even British tradition; in fact, all that these poets have in common is that they are dead, white and male. Therefore Yeats functions in the poem as an example of poetic conviction, which continues a tradition of verse-making – as underlined by the elegy-making of Dunbar, Yeats ('In Memory of Major Robert Gregory'), Auden ('In Memory of W. B. Yeats') and Thomas ('After the Funeral (in memory of Ann Jones)'); yet this tradition seems increasingly unsustainable in an uncertain world. 'There is no end to grief. Nor no end to poetry', Deutsch asserts – but perhaps there is no purpose either, in a world where endings are the only certainties.

Critics have discussed in great detail Yeats's influence on twentieth-century American poetry, citing many and varied examples of Yeatsian allusion. Terence Diggory's discussion, for example, takes in Pound, Robert Frost, Stevens and Robinson Jeffers; and he even remarks that although Eliot denounced Yeats as a poetic influence, he did accept him as a dramatic 'ancestor'.[123] Diggory's critical precedent is Richard Ellmann's comparative Yeats study *Eminent Domain: Yeats Among Wilde, Joyce, Pound, Eliot and Auden* (1970). Meanwhile, assertions of Yeatsian echoes in Wallace Stevens's work can be found in Joseph Riddel's *The Clairvoyant Eye: The Poetry and Poetics of Wallace Stevens* (1963) and Frank Kermode's *Wallace Stevens* (1961). More recently, Steven Matthews has discussed Yeats's influence on mid and late twentieth-century American poets in his chapter 'Possession and dispossession: Yeats and American

Poetry' in *Yeats as Precursor: Readings in Irish, British and American Poetry* (2000);[124] and Edward Clarke's *The Later Affluence of W. B. Yeats and Wallace Stevens* (2012) has brought the two poets together as 'The last two Romantics', viewed as spiritual 'guides' to the twentieth century.[125]

But it is important to note the extent of Yeats's influence on American literature beyond the poetic tradition. Critics have identified the influence of Yeats's drama and theatrical endeavours on American theatre. Yeats's relationship with *Poetry* helped to inspire the 'Little Theatre' movement that began with the founding of Maurice Browne's Little Theatre in Chicago in 1911–12, but there are further resonances. For example, Tracy Mishkin has described the significance of the Abbey Theatre to the Harlem Renaissance, noting that 'the Abbey's representations of Irish life caught the imagination of those Americans interested in exploring the various facets of their own identity, including several people, black and white, who went on to participate in the Harlem Renaissance of the 1920s'.[126]

Meanwhile the influence of the Abbey company on Eugene O'Neill, who was first introduced to their plays during their American tour of 1911, has been widely noted. For example, Nicholas Grene has claimed that: '[i]t was the first visit of the Abbey company to New York in 1911 that helped to turn Eugene O'Neill into a playwright'.[127] As O'Neill put it himself, with reference to having been brought up by a father, James O'Neill, who starred for almost thirty years in a touring production of *The Count of Monte Cristo*: 'My early experience with the theatre through my father really made me revolt against it. As a boy I saw so much of the old, ranting, artificial, romantic stage stuff that I always had a sort of contempt for the theater. It was seeing the Irish players for the first time that gave me a glimpse of my opportunity'.[128] Much later in his career, in 1932, O'Neill expressed his pleasure at being invited to become an honorary member of 'the Irish Academy being organised by Shaw & Yeats & Robinson',[129] while in 1934 he cabled Yeats to announce that he was 'Only too delighted to have Abbey Theatre produce *Days Without End*'.[130] In the same year he wrote to his agent Richard Madden to say 'The Abbey is so much better than any company they could get together in London'.[131] This lasting fascination with, and admiration for, the Abbey was linked intrinsically to O'Neill's self-identification as an 'associate' Irish dramatist who 'treated Irish subjects' in his plays.[132]

A further area of critical interest is Yeats's influence on the Beat writers. In an essay on 'Blake, Ginsberg, madness, and the prophet as Shaman', Alicia Ostriker contends that 'The idea of a prophetic role clearly forms the core of Blake's influence on Ginsberg, and he is the only one of Blake's modern disciples who publicly assumes such a mantle or burden; doubtless Yeats would have if he could have'.[133] Of course Yeats was responsible for resurrecting the figure of Blake within twentieth-century poetry, through his 1893 edition of Blake's works with Edwin Ellis, *The Works of William Blake: Poetic, Symbolic, and Critical*, and his 1897 essay 'William Blake and the imagination'.[134] Extending the route drawn from Blake through Yeats to the Beats, and their emphasis on the connections between poetry and prophecy, James T. Jones notes that Kerouac's peculiar blend of spirituality, typified by a 'bohemianism' that 'involved a religious attitude toward life', finds a 'literary precedent' in Yeats's combination of 'native Protestantism with theosophical mysticism'.[135]

Ginsberg makes particular reference to Yeats; in his poem 'After Yeats' (1964) he combines lightly mocking allusions to Yeats's spiritualism ('Now incense fills the air') with a prosaic commentary on the affected nobility of such poems as 'Sailing to Byzantium', as he imagines the poet 'laughing at a mystic toy / statue painted gold, tea on a white table'.[136] Meanwhile, in a 1951 letter to Neal Cassady, Ginsberg describes his recurring dream of a stranger who encompasses elements of Shakespeare and Yeats: '[the man who] reappeared to me in a dream these last years is the same man who shrieked on the heath with King Lear, the Fool (this I gathered in memory a long while back) and also Old Tom the Lunatic of Late Yeats'[137] – the latter a figure in 'Tom the Lunatic', 'Tom at Cruachan' and 'Old Tom Again' from *The Winding Stair and Other Poems* (1933).[138]

Allusions to 'Late Yeats' can also be found in Kerouac's writings. Consider, for example, the last passages of *On The Road*, which seem to evoke Yeats's 'foul rag-and-bone shop of the heart' conclusion of one of his last poems, 'The Circus Animals' Desertion' (1939), through their preoccupation with brokenness and ageing:

> So in America when the sun goes down and I sit on the old broken-down river pier watching the long, long skies over New Jersey and sense all that raw land that rolls in one unbelievable huge bulge over to

the West Coast, and all that road going, all the people dreaming in the immensity of it … and nobody, nobody knows what's going to happen besides the forlorn rags of growing old, I think of Dean Moriarty, I even think of Old Dean Moriarty the father we never found, I think of Dean Moriarty.[139]

While in the conclusion of 'The Circus Animals' Desertion' Yeats assesses his own condition as an ageing poet, who must now 'lie down where all the ladders start' (l. 39), Kerouac's use of Yeatsian imagery extends to describe the American condition as his narrator, Sal Paradise, gazes from 'New Jersey' to the 'West Coast'. Here the ennui and despair underscored by the 'broken-down river pier' and the 'forlorn rags of growing old' are related to 'the father we never found', as if the inability to move beyond the present is somehow related to the lack of spiritual fathers. This 'father' is apparently Sal's free-spirited friend 'Dean Moriarty', but in the context of the passage – with its river setting, its thematic allusions to 'America', and its metaphorical style and cinematic perspective – this missing 'father' might also be Twain, or Whitman. Or it might even be Yeats, as the Irish counterpart to Whitman, and one who in Diggory's words 'created his nationality out of himself' – just as Kerouac tries, fails and tries again to do here.[140] By reading echoes of late Yeats into the writings of Kerouac and Ginsberg, we are confronted once again by the need to view Yeats as an aesthetic as well as a cultural influence, and as representative of an individual and a national voice.

It is perhaps most useful to see the trajectory of Yeats's influence on early and mid-twentieth-century American literature as starting with an intense and sometimes dogmatic poetic conviction – summed up by Longley's assertion that, for Irish writers, 'poetry matters'[141] – and ending 'where all the ladders start': at that moment where Yeats, despairing that 'my ladder's gone', hands on his 'masterful images'.

> Those masterful images because complete
> Grew in pure mind, but out of what began?
> A mound of refuse or the sweepings of a street,
> Old kettles, old bottles, and a broken can,
> Old iron, old bones, old rags, that raving slut

> Who keeps the till. Now that my ladder's gone,
> I must lie down where all the ladders start,
> In the foul rag-and-bone shop of the heart.[142]

But whereas, for Yeats, such despair might lead to an inevitable conclusion, the poet's legacy continues almost despite itself: so that for Kerouac, Yeats's 'foul rag-and-bone shop of the heart' informs and inspires a bittersweet moment of reverie; while for Berryman, the older Irish poet transfixes as an 'aged man' of 'bone & heat & rigid brow', whose raw passion inspires his 'burning' discipline.[143] The 'place where all ladders start', for disciples and readers of Yeats, then, is where his poetry ends and theirs begins – but it is also the place where they recollect (and re-collect) his 'masterful images' for themselves. The uncertain poetic gift offered here by Yeats, in which 'masterful images' are usurped by 'Old kettles, old bottles, and a broken can', and a 'pure mind' is sullied by a 'mound of refuse', is not wholly negative, however. In fact these lines show, through their triumph of poet over theme, that the desire for, and attainment of, a 'complete' image, grown of 'pure mind', might still be possible in an uncertain, broken world. This, then, is the ultimate legacy of Yeats's poetic conviction: his faith that poetry might still be built from the fragments. We might recall Moore's comment, in her 1933 review of Yeats, that 'there is no end to the beauties one might separate out from Mr Yeats' abundance'.[144] That we can still find 'beauties' in even his darkest poems is Yeats's enduring gift.

Notes

1 Edna Longley, 'Irish bards and American audiences', *Poetry and Posterity*. Northumberland: Bloodaxe Books, 2000, pp. 235–8 (238).
2 Terence Diggory, *Yeats and American Poetry: The Tradition of the Self*. Princeton: Princeton University Press, 1983, p. 7.
3 Philip Coleman, '"The politics of praise": John Berryman's engagement with W. B. Yeats', *Études Irlandaises*, 28.2 (Automne 2003), 11–27 (12, 16). Coleman expands significantly on this topic in his forthcoming monograph, *'The Scene of Disorder': John Berryman and The Public Sphere* (Dublin: UCD Press).

4 Michael Malouf, 'Duppy poetics: Yeats, memory, and place in Lorna Goodison's "Country, Sligoville"', in *Ireland and Transatlantic Poetics*, ed. Brian Caraher and Robert Mahony. Newark: University of Delaware Press, 2007, pp. 191–204 (191, 193, 203).
5 Sharon Olds, 'Easter, 1960', *The New Yorker*, 12.3 (February 2007), 158, ll. 29–37.
6 W. B. Yeats, refrain, 'Easter 1916', *The Variorum Edition of the Poems of W. B. Yeats*, ed. Peter Allt and Russell K. Alspach. New York: Macmillan, 1966, pp. 391–4.
7 In 'Easter 1916', Yeats notes that all is 'changed utterly' by the Easter Rising and subsequent execution of the rebels; see 'Easter 1916', l. 79.
8 Alex Petridis discusses the Fleet Foxes' use of Yeats's early poetry (and particularly 'The Lake Isle of Innisfree') in an article for *The Guardian*: 'The area in which rock music meets poetry is seldom a happy place, so it's with a mild sense of panic, five minutes into *Helplessness Blues*, that the listener realises they're in the presence of a song loosely based on the work of W. B. Yeats'. Petridis continues, 'The song stops dead, and the band's patented massed harmonies reiterate the point. "One day at Innisfree, one day that's mine", they sing, yearning for Yeats's pastoral utopia, where he announced he would build his own home, keep bees and "have some peace"'. Petridis concludes by wondering if the Fleet Foxes realised how much Yeats came to dislike the poem. See Alex Petridis, review of Fleet Foxes, *Helplessness Blues*, *The Guardian*, 21 April 2011: www.guardian.co.uk/music/2011/apr/21/fleet-foxes-helplessness-blues-review.
9 Diggory, *Yeats and American Poetry*, p. 22.
10 Ibid., pp. 7, 35.
11 Ibid., pp. 59–60. Pound made this comment on Yeats in his notes to 'Redondillas' (1911): see *Collected Early Poems of Ezra Pound*, ed. Michael John King (New York: New Directions, 1976), p. 313. The five Yeats poems in *Poetry* 1.3 (December 1912) were 'The Mountain Tomb' (p. 67), 'To a Child Dancing Upon the Shore' (p. 68), 'Fallen Majesty' (p. 68), 'Love and the Bird' (p. 69), and 'The Realists' (p. 70). The poems opened the issue.
12 James Longenbach, *Stone Cottage: Yeats, Pound and Modernism*. New York and Oxford: Oxford University Press, 1991, pp. 75–6.
13 Diggory, *Yeats and American Poetry*, p. 60; see also Pádraic Colum, 'Mr. Yeats's *Selected Poems*', *The Dial*, 71.4 (October 1921), 465.
14 Discussed in Diggory, *Yeats and American Poetry*, pp. 64–5. Vachel Lindsay made these comments in *The Art of the Moving Picture* (1915), and Corbin

Henderson made hers in an essay, 'Too far from Paris', published in *Poetry*, 4.3 (June 1914), pp. 107–11.
15 See Thomas L. Scott and Melvin J. Friedman (eds), *The Letters of Ezra Pound to Margaret Anderson: The Little Review Correspondence*. New York: New Directions, 1988, p. xvii.
16 Ezra Pound, *Literary Essays of Ezra Pound*, ed. T. S. Eliot. London: Faber and Faber, 1954, p. 287.
17 Pound to Margaret Anderson, 8 February 1917, *Little Review Correspondence*, pp. 15–16.
18 Pound to Anderson, 4 April 1917, *Little Review Correspondence*, pp. 24–5.
19 Pound summarises his ideas on 'imagisme' in his 1918 essay 'A retrospect', which aims to set straight the recent 'scribbling about a new fashion in poetry' by discussing in detail the aims of the imagists as set down by himself and H. D. in 1912–13. See Pound, 'A retrospect', in *Twentieth Century Literary Criticism: A Reader*, ed. David Lodge. London and New York: London, 1972, pp. 58–68. Pound makes several references to Yeats in this essay.
20 Robert Keating O'Neill, 'The Irish book in the United States', in *The Oxford History of the Irish Book, Volume V: The Irish Book in English, 1891–2000*, ed. Clare Hutton and Patrick Walsh. Oxford: Oxford University Press, 2011, pp. 413–39 (421).
21 Warwick Gould, 'W. B. Yeats on the road to St. Martin's Street, 1900 –1917', in *Macmillan: A Publishing Tradition*, ed. Elizabeth James (Basingstoke: Palgrave Macmillan, 2002), pp.192–217 (195).
22 See Chapter 2 for further discussion of the role Quinn played in bringing revivalist works to the USA.
23 Robin G. Schulze (ed.), *Becoming Marianne Moore: The Early Poems, 1907–1924*. Berkeley: University of California Press, 2002, p. 449. Marianne Moore was born in 1887, so would have turned 28 in 1915.
24 Charles Molesworth, *Marianne Moore: A Literary Life*. New York: Atheneum, 1990, pp. 98, 49.
25 Moore, 'To a Strategist', first published as 'To Disraeli on Conversation' in *Lantern*, 23 (1915), 60; this version reprinted from Moore's 1924 collection *Observations* in Grace Schulman (ed.), *The Poems of Marianne Moore*. London: Faber, 2003, p. 88, l. 12.
26 Moore, 'George Moore', *Others* I, 6 (December 1915), 105–6; this version reprinted from *Observations* (1924) in *The Poems of Marianne Moore*, p. 96, ll. 11–12.
27 Linda Leavell, *Marianne Moore and the Visual Arts*. Baton Rouge and London: Louisiana University Press, 1995, p. 72.

28 Moore, 'To a Prize Bird', first published in *The Egoist*, 2 (2 August 1915), 126; this version reprinted from *Observations* (1924) in *The Poems of Marianne Moore*, p. 90, ll. 4–6, 7, 9. For further discussion of this poem, and Moore's use of Shaw throughout her career, see Tara Stubbs, '"Writing was resilience. Resilience was an adventure". Marianne Moore, Bernard Shaw and the Art of Writing', *SHAW* 29 (Winter 2009), 66–78.
29 Schulze, *Becoming Marianne Moore*, p. 449.
30 *See* Moore, 'To Browning', *Egoist*, 2 (2 August 1915), 126, later published as 'Injudicious Gardening' in *Observations* (1924), reprinted in *The Poems of Marianne Moore*, p. 89.
31 Schulze, *Becoming Marianne Moore*, p. 358.
32 Mary Lago, *Imperfect Encounter – Letters of William Rothenstein and Rabindranath Tagore, 1911–1941*. Cambridge, Massachusetts: Harvard University Press, 1972, p. 44. Tagore would go on to win the Nobel Prize for Literature in 1913. Pound later regretted his earlier zeal regarding Tagore, however. In a letter to Margaret Anderson in 1917, he refers to an article he published in *The Egoist* 'some years ago', in which he deplored the fact 'that people made him [Tagore] into a sham messiah instead of treating him as a poet': Pound to Anderson, 25 May 1917, *Little Review Correspondence*, p. 58.
33 Moore, '"New" poetry since 1912', in *Anthology of Magazine Verse for 1926*, ed. William Stanley Braithwaite, reprinted in *The Complete Prose of Marianne Moore*, ed. Patricia Willis. London: Faber, 1987, pp. 120–4 (120–1). The title of Tagore's work, *Gitanjali*, is translated as 'song-offerings'; it was a collection of prose translations into English made by the author from the original Bengali. Yeats wrote the introduction. See Rabindranath Tagore, *Gitanjali/ Song-offerings*, with an introduction by W. B. Yeats. London: Macmillan, 1913, and especially pp.xvi–xvii., which echo Yeats's thoughts here.
34 R. F. Foster, *W. B. Yeats: A Life, Volume 1*. Oxford: Oxford University Press, 1998, p. 469; Foster refers to Lady Gregory's *Cuchulain of Muirthemne*, for which Yeats had written a preface (first published 1902).
35 Moore, 'To William Butler Yeats on Tagore' (whole poem), first published in the *Egoist*, 2 (1 May 1915), 77, reprinted in *The Poems of Marianne Moore*, p. 85.
36 Yeats, 'The Song of the Happy Shepherd', *Variorum Edition*, pp. 64–7; 'The Indian to His Love', *Variorum Edition*, pp. 77–8 ('enamelled sea': l. 5).
37 W. B. Yeats, *Ideas of Good and Evil* (London and Dublin, 1907), RML, Moore's private library, #MML D2.20; *The Winding Stair* (New York,

1929): '642 copies of this edition, 600 for sale, all signed by the author', #MML 1778; see also Molesworth, *Marianne Moore: A Literary Life*, p. 111.

38 Jeanne Heuving, *Omissions are not Accidents: Gender in the Art of Marianne Moore*. Detroit: Wayne State University Press, 1992, p. 66.
39 Letter dated 30 June 1912: see Lago, *Imperfect Encounter*, p. 18.
40 See Moore, 'Appellate Jurisdiction' and 'The Wizard in Words', reprinted in *The Poems of Marianne Moore*, p. 84.
41 Marianne Moore to John Warner Moore, 10 October 1915, *The Selected Letters of Marianne Moore*, ed. Bonnie Costello, Celeste Goodridge and Cristanne Miller. London: Faber, 1998, p. 101.
42 Elizabeth Bishop to Robert Lowell, 23 August 1950, *Words in Air: The Complete Correspondence between Elizabeth Bishop and Robert Lowell*, ed. Thomas Travisano and Saskia Hamilton. New York: Farrar, Straus, and Giroux, 2008, pp. 107–8 (107).
43 All reprinted in *The Variorum Edition* of Yeats's poems: 'The Rose of Peace', pp. 112–13; 'The Blessed', p. 166–8; 'The Lover Pleads with his Friend for Old Friends', pp. 172–3; 'Against Unworthy Praise', pp. 259–60; and 'To a Poet, who would have me Praise certain Bad Poets, Imitators of His and Mine', p. 262.
44 Yeats, 'The Lover Pleads with his Friend for Old Friends', ll. 1, 3.
45 Moore, 'Wild Swans', review of Yeats's *Wild Swans at Coole*, *Poetry*, 13 (October 1918), reprinted in *Complete Prose*, pp. 38–41 (38, 39–40).
46 Moore, 'Wild Swans', p. 39.
47 Patricia Willis, introduction to *Complete Prose*, p. v.
48 Moore, 'Wild Swans', p. 39.
49 Ibid., p. 40. The 'prose volume' to which Moore refers is Yeats's *Per Amica Silentia Lunae*, which was first published in 1918 and included 'Ego Dominus Tuus'; the poem was reprinted in *The Wild Swans at Coole*, which Moore reviews here.
50 Yeats, 'Ego Dominus Tuus', *Variorum Edition*, pp. 367–71, ll. 8, 10, 11–15.
51 Ibid., ll. 18–19, 33.
52 Moore, 'Wild Swans', p. 40. Moore refers to the rumoured 'miserliness' of English landscape painter J. W. M. Turner (1775–1851), whom Yeats does not reference in his poem.
53 A. Norman Jeffares, 'Yeats's Mask', *The Circus Animals: Essays on W. B. Yeats*. Stanford, California: Stanford University Press, 1970, pp. 3–15 (4).
54 Yeats, 'Anima Hominis' (1917), *Per Amica Silentia Lunae*, in *Mythologies*. London: Macmillan, 1959, pp. 325–42 (section V, p. 331).

55 Moore, 'Wild Swans', p. 40.
56 Moore's copy of Yeats's *Ideas of Good and Evil* (1907), back page.
57 Moore, Editor's 'Comment', *The Dial*, 81.3 (September 1926), 268.
58 Molesworth, *Marianne Moore: A Literary Life*, p. 49.
59 Marianne Moore, 'Words for Music Perhaps', first published in *Poetry*, 42 (April 1933), reprinted in *Complete Prose*, pp. 296, 294.
60 William Carlos Williams, 'Marianne Moore', *The Dial*, 78.5 (May 1925), 393–401 (395).
61 Berryman, 'One Answer to a Question: Changes' (1965), reprinted in *The Freedom of the Poet*. New York: Farrar, Straus and Giroux, 1976, p. 323.
62 John Berryman, from 'Dream Song 312', *The Dream Songs*. New York: Farrar, Straus and Giroux, 1969, p. 334.
63 Ibid., p. 334.
64 Coleman, '"The politics of praise"', p. 11.
65 Berryman to his mother (Martha Berryman, née Little), 11 November 1936, in *We Dream of Honour: John Berryman's Letters to his Mother*, ed. Richard Kelly. New York and London: W. W. Norton & Co., 1988, pp. 69–74 (69).
66 Berryman to his mother, 11 November 1936, *We Dream of Honour*, pp. 69–70.
67 Ibid., p. 74.
68 Enclosed in a letter from Berryman to his mother, 11 October 1936, *We Dream of Honour*, p. 57; compare with Yeats, 'Sailing to Byzantium' (and particularly 'An aged man is but a paltry thing', l. 9), *Variorum Edition*, pp. 407–8; 'The Fisherman' ('Imagining a man', l. 28), pp. 347–8; and 'Nineteen Hundred and Nineteen' ('Some moralist or mythological poet / Compares the solitary soul to a swan', ll. 59–60), pp. 428–33.
69 Yeats, 'The Circus Animals' Desertion' ('In the foul rag-and-bone shop of the heart', l. 40), *Variorum Edition*, pp. 629–30.
70 Berryman to his mother, 11 November 1936, *We Dream of Honour*, p. 71.
71 Yeats, 'In Memory of Major Robert Gregory', *Variorum Edition*, pp. 323–8, l. 88.
72 Harold Bloom, *The Anxiety of Influence: A Theory of Poetry*. First published 1973; New York and Oxford: Oxford University Press, 1997, p. 25.
73 Diggory, *Yeats and American Poetry*, p. 41.
74 Berryman to his mother, 14 February 1937, pp. 91, 90.
75 Ibid., p. 91.
76 Ibid., p. 91.

77 Bogan was born in 1897, so would have been in her late thirties when reviewing Yeats's work in the mid to late 1930s; Berryman, as discussed above, would have been in his early twenties during this period.
78 Louise Bogan, review of Yeats's *Collected Poems*, *The New Yorker*, 7 April 1934. Collected in *A Poet's Prose: Selected Writings of Louise Bogan*, ed. Mary Kinzie. Athens, Ohio: Swallow Press / Ohio University Press, 2005, pp. 200–1 (200).
79 Bogan, 'The greatest poet writing in English today', *Atlantic Monthly* (May 1938), reproduced in part in *A Poet's Prose*, pp. 202–13 (203).
80 See Bogan to Edmund Wilson, 21 April 1937, *A Poet's Prose*, pp. 150–1 (150), and Bogan to Morton D. Zabel, 14 April 1937, *A Poet's Prose*, pp. 147–8 (148).
81 See Bogan, 'Approaching Ur', review of *A Skeleton Key to Finnegans Wake* by Joseph Campbell and Henry Morton Robinson, first published in *The Nation* (19 August 1944), collected in *A Poet's Prose*, pp. 269–71 (271).
82 Bogan, review of the *Oxford Book of Modern Verse*, first published in *The New Yorker* (14 November 1936), collected in *A Poet's Prose*, pp. 201–2 (201). Edited by Yeats, the *Oxford Book of Modern Verse, 1892–1935* was published by Oxford University Press in 1936.
83 Lowell to Bishop, 25 February 1966, *Words in Air*, pp. 601–2 (601).
84 Bogan, review of the 1951 edition of Yeats's *Collected Poems*, first published in *The New Yorker* (20 October 1951), collected in *A Poet's Prose*, pp. 218–19 (218, 219).
85 See Yeats, 'Pardon, Old Fathers', opening lines to *Responsibilities*, *Variorum Edition*, pp. 269–70; 'Among School Children', pp. 443–6; and 'Politics', p. 631.
86 Steven Matthews, *Yeats as Precursor: Readings in Irish, British and American Poetry*. Basingstoke: Palgrave Macmillan, 2000. p. 1.
87 Babette Deutsch to Thomas M[a]cGreevy, 8 December 1946, Thomas MacGreevy Papers, Trinity College Dublin ['TCD'] MS 8120 (microform). John Butler Yeats (1839–1922), father of W. B. and Jack Yeats, was a renowned Irish artist; he settled in New York at the age of 69, and spent his final years there. Deutsch is most likely referring to the recent edition of letters, which had been first published by Faber in London in 1944: see *J. B. Yeats: Letters to his son W. B. Yeats and others, 1869–1922*, ed. Joseph Hone. New York: E. P. Dutton, 1946.
88 These books are McGreevy, *Jack B. Yeats: An Appreciation and Interpretation* (Dublin: Victor Waddington, 1945) and *Pictures in the Irish National Gallery* (Cork: The Mercer Press, 1945).

89 Deutsch to McGreevy, 9 February 1947, TCD MS 8120. McGreevy was to act as Director of the National Gallery of Ireland between 1950 and 1963.
90 McGreevy to Deutsch, 17 February 1947, Washington University Libraries, Missouri, Special Collections, MSS 034: Box 1, Folder 4.
91 Deutsch to McGreevy, 6 March 1947, TCD MS 8120. The book to which Deutsch refers is *1000 Years of Irish Poetry: The Gaelic and Anglo-Irish Poets from Pagan Times to the Present*, ed. Katherine Hoagland. New York: Grosset, 1947.
92 For example, in her first letter to McGreevy, Deutsch claims 'I have no more religion than John Butler Yeats', revealing her own reading of the older Yeats: this despite her correspondent McGreevy's strong Catholic faith. See Deutsch to McGreevy, 8 December 1946, TCD MS 8120.
93 Deutsch to McGreevy, 17 February 1948, TCD MS 8120.
94 Deutsch, *Poetry In Our Time*. New York: Henry Holt and Company, 1952, p. 254.
95 Ibid., p. 254: 'words alone are certain good' is taken from Yeats, 'The Song of the Happy Shepherd', *Variorum Edition*, pp. 64–7, l. 10.
96 'Irish poets, learn your trade, / Sing whatever is well made': Yeats, 'Under Ben Bulben', *Variorum Edition*, pp. 636–40, V, ll. 68–90; 'Grecian goldsmiths': 'Sailing to Byzantium', pp. 407–8, l. 27.
97 Yeats, 'Under Ben Bulben', ll. 68–73.
98 Ibid., ll. 82–3.
99 Donald J. Childs has related the problematic language of Yeats's late poems and plays to eugenicist theory: see Childs, *Modernism and Eugenics: Woolf, Eliot, Yeats and the Culture of Degeneration* (Cambridge: Cambridge University Press, 2001), and especially Chapter 7, 'The late eugenics of W. B. Yeats', pp. 149–69.
100 Wells, Henry W., review of *Poetry In Our Time* by Babette Deutsch, *American Literature*, 25.1 (March 1953), 113–17 (114). Deutsch's book covers a huge range of poets, its ambitious aim being to discuss 'the poetry written during the twentieth century wherever English (or American) is the literary language of the country': *Poetry in Our Time*, p. xi; see also 'Index of Poets' from p. 407.
101 Wells, review of *Poetry In Our Time*, pp. 116, 117.
102 Deutsch to McGreevy, 17 February 1948, TCD MS 8120.
103 McGreevy to Deutsch, 22 February 1948, Washington University Libraries, MSS 034: Box 1, Folder 5.
104 Deutsch to McGreevy, 19 April 1949, TCD MS 8120. Deutsch wrote a double review of Richard Ellmann's *Yeats: The Man in the Masks* and *New*

Irish Poets, ed. Devin A. Garrity: see *New Republic*, 120.12 (21 March 1949), 22.
105 Deutsch to McGreevy, 27 March 1948, TCD MS 8120.
106 See Deutsch, 'Fountain and Unicorn', *The Kenyon Review*, 10.3 (summer 1948), 39–40.
107 Deutsch, 'Fountain and Unicorn', ll. 31–3.
108 Yeats, 'The Circus Animals' Desertion', ll. 33–4.
109 'Lament for the Makers: 1964', *The Atlantic Monthly*, 214 (December 1964), 72–3, reprinted in *The Collected Poems of Babette Deutsch*. New York: Doubleday, 1969, pp. 5–6, ll. 22–3.
110 W. H. Auden, 'In Memory of W. B. Yeats', *Selected Poems*, ed. Edward Mendelson. London: Faber, 1979, pp. 80–3, ll. 28–9. This version was completed in February 1939; Yeats had died in January.
111 Auden, 'In Memory of W. B. Yeats', ll. 32–41.
112 Deutsch, 'Lament for the Makers: 1964', ll. 4–7.
113 Yeats, 'In Memory of Major Robert Gregory' (from *The Wild Swans at Coole*, 1919), *Variorum Edition*, pp. 323–8, l. 88; 'A Cradle Song' (from *The Rose*, 1890), p. 26, ll. 1, 2.
114 See Yeats, Sailing to Byzantium', ll. 27–8, 30. Deutsch also refers to 'Yeats's eagle' in line 35 of 'Lament for the Makers: 1964'.
115 See Yeats, *The Wanderings of Oisin*, *Variorum Edition*, pp. 1–63, l. 265 (p. 18).
116 See MacNeice, 'Snow' (January 1935), in *Selected Poems*, ed. Michael Longley. London: Faber, 1988, p. 23, l. 12.
117 Thomas wrote the poem as an elegy to his aunt; see Dylan Thomas, 'After the Funeral (in memory of Ann Jones)', in *Selected Poems*, ed. Walford Davies. Harmondsworth: Penguin, 2000, pp. 42–3.
118 See MacNeice, *The Burning Perch*. New York: Oxford University Press, 1963.
119 Tom Walker, 'MacNeice's Byzantium: The ghosts of Yeats and Eliot in *The Burning Perch*', *Review of English Studies* 62.257 (November 2011), 785–804 (785).
120 Deutsch, 'Lament for the Makers: 1964', ll. 42–8.
121 Ibid., ll. 12, 13.
122 See Auden, 'Yeats as an example', *Kenyon Review*, 10.2 (Spring 1948), 187–95 (188).
123 See Diggory, *Yeats and American Poetry*, p. 106.
124 See Matthews, *Yeats as Precursor*, pp. 146–84. Matthews's discussion of Yeatsian influence on American poetry extends to John Crowe Ransom, Allen Tate, Berryman, Robert Lowell, James Merrill, Adrienne Rich, Sylvia Plath and Jorie Graham, but in so doing takes the discussion in a

slightly different direction, by focusing on the questions and problems of influence beyond the modernist period (and beyond period labels).

125 Edward Clarke, *The Later Affluence of W. B. Yeats and Wallace Stevens*. Basingstoke: Palgrave, 2012, p. 1.
126 See Tracy Mishkin, *The Harlem and Irish Renaissances: Language, Identity and Representation*. Gainesville, Florida: University Press of Florida, 1998, p. 1; and the discussions in Chapter 2 of this book.
127 Nicholas Grene, 'The Abbey: National Theatre or Little Theatre', *Journal of Irish and Scottish Studies*, 1.1 (Autumn 2007), 211–20 (216).
128 Cited in Louis Sheaffer, *Eugene O'Neill: Son and Playwright* (London: Dent, 1969), p. 205.
129 Eugene O'Neill to Eugene O'Neill Jnr., 11 November 1932, *Selected Letters of Eugene O'Neill*, ed. Travis Bogard and Jackson J. Bryer. New Haven and London: Yale University Press, 1988, pp. 406–7 (407).
130 Wire from O'Neill to Yeats, 12 February 1934, *Selected Letters*, p. 430.
131 O'Neill to Richard Madden, 8 March 1934, *Selected Letters*, p. 431.
132 See O'Neill to O'Neill Jnr., 11 November 1932; O'Neill discusses his 'associate' membership of the Irish Academy and his 'treating' of Irish subjects in contrast to the playwright '[Lord] Dunsany' (Edward Plunkett): *Selected Letters*, p. 407.
133 Alicia Ostriker, 'Blake, Ginsberg, madness, and the prophet as Shaman', in *William Blake and the Moderns*, ed. Robert J. Bertholf and Annette S. Levitt. Albany: State University of New York Press, 1982, pp. 111–32 (113).
134 See Yeats and Edwin Ellis (eds), *The Works of William Blake: Poetic, Symbolic, and Critical*, in three volumes (London: Bernard Quaritch, 1893); and Yeats, 'William Blake and the imagination', reprinted in *The Collected Works of W. B. Yeats, Volume IV: Early Essays*, ed. George Bornstein and Richard J. Finneran (New York: Scribner, 2007), pp. 84–7.
135 James T. Jones, *A Map of Mexico City Blues: Jack Kerouac as Poet*. Carbondale: Southern Illinois University, 2010, p. 110.
136 Allen Ginsberg, 'After Yeats', dated 'New York, April 26, 1964', in *Collected Poems 1947–1997*. London: Penguin, 2009, p. 351, ll. 1, 7–8.
137 Barry Gifford (ed.), *As Ever: The Collected Correspondence of Allen Ginsberg and Neal Cassady*. Berkeley, California: Creative Arts Book Company, 1977, p. 93.
138 Yeats, 'Tom the Lunatic', 'Tom at Cruachan' and 'Old Tom Again', *Variorum Edition*, pp. 297–8, 298, 299.
139 See Yeats, 'The Circus Animals' Desertion' (1939), l. 40; and Jack Kerouac, *On The Road*. First published 1957; Harmondsworth: Penguin, 1991, p. 281.

140 Diggory, *Yeats and American Poetry*, p. 22.
141 Longley, 'Irish bards and American audiences', p. 258.
142 Yeats, 'The Circus Animals' Desertion', ll. 33–40.
143 See Berryman's poem to Yeats, enclosed in a letter from Berryman to his mother, 11 October 1936, *We Dream of Honour*, p. 57 (and discussions above).
144 Moore, 'Words for Music Perhaps', p. 294.

Conclusion
Cultural credibility in America's Ireland – and Ireland's America

> When Yeats wanted criticism to be 'as international as possible', he did not ask us to recruit a global fan-club for the national literature.

Edna Longley, writing in 2000, worries about the long-term consequences of the Irish Revival. Though spearheaded initially by Yeats's internationalism, the Revival has instead, Longley argues, become a by-word for a particular 'Irish' experience, which has been imposed on Ireland by its international fans. Despite the genuine aims of writers like Yeats to carve out a place for Irish culture on the international stage, in the century since the Revival 'a hybrid form of Hiberno-American blandness' has formed, as Longley puts it.[1] But were the beginnings of this 'blandness' already in evidence around the first half of the twentieth century? Can we see them, for example, in the unrelenting way in which Wallace Stevens viewed the Irish landscape as 'greener than it is', and thought of its people as pushing donkey carts through the rain?[2] This study has looked at various instances of interaction between America and Ireland during the modernist period, to assess the immediate and short-term consequences of a period in Irish history that was culturally and politically exciting and uncertain; but not all of these exchanges have been fruitful. Thus we need to ask how we might separate valuable cultural interaction from 'Hiberno-American blandness', or distinguish between fruitful cultural borrowings and cynical plundering, in order to consider the long-term legacy of American-Irish (and Irish-American) cultural exchange.

Fintan O'Toole, writing at the turn of the millennium, claims that the relatively new country of Ireland became an historical artefact before it had a chance to form its own identity, so that 'A country has become a heritage attraction long before the idea ought to have gained currency'.[3] Meanwhile Colin Graham argues, in a 2001 essay 'A glimpse of America', that Ireland in the late twentieth century has become 'a plenitude of images, replicating itself for continual consumption and at times achieving an over-satiation. It is here that the "Ireland" which is excessive topples into an Ireland of ceaseless reproduction and commodification'.[4] In this context MacNeice's sardonic comment in *Autumn Journal*, written on the cusp of World War Two, that Ireland is split from 'a more commercial culture', seems oddly prescient;[5] for what Ireland can and will exploit financially, MacNeice seems to say, is its apparent separation from the rest of the world.

What, then, are the lasting effects of Irish cultural influence upon American writing in relation to the increased commercialisation – and exportation – of Irish culture in the decades since MacNeice identified Ireland's growing cultural and political isolationism? Were those American modernists who engaged with Irish cultural and political issues in their writings partly to blame for turning Ireland into a 'heritage attraction'? We can certainly find evidence for this: in the idealisation of the 'Celt' within American modernist writing; in the romantic reactions to the Easter Rising expressed by critics like Bryant, Goldman and Mencken; or, indeed, in Moore's famous lines from 'Spenser's Ireland' – 'a place as kind as it is green / the greenest place I've never seen' – which take delight in a country whose unreality seems to be its most appealing quality.[6] Yet at the same time a rounded dismissal of these attitudes tells only one side of the story. Indeed, Diane Negra claims that 'the functionality of Irishness in American fantasies of political, familial, financial, and geographical innocence' is in fact derived from Irish writers themselves:[7] for 'associations of Irishness with antimaterialism and whimsy have existed at least since the publication of Yeats's *The Celtic Twilight*'. It is just that 'these associations are now ironically hyper-commercialized'.[8]

Another angle that needs to be considered is Ireland's lasting view of America, in terms of its own projected idealisation of the country to which a large proportion of its emigrants, since the 1800s, have travelled to seek a new way of life. As Mary McGlynn has pointed out, in a recent essay on 'New Irish New York', a 'dream of the United States as saving Ireland' is a common feature of contemporary Irish novels, in which New York becomes 'not an escape from the past so much as a direct line to it'; this view of course 'essentializes New York City, curiously and unexpectedly, as pure, authentic, and unchanging'.[9] This is the kind of language that American writers such as Stevens and Moore used in their descriptions of the Irish cultural landscape, with varying degrees of irony. Meanwhile, as Fran Brearton and Eamonn Hughes point out, 'In Ireland, America may be projected as the ideal, the aspiration, or as the elsewhere that validates a sometimes metaphysical sense of place – it offers a way of leaving, but also, significantly, a way of bringing it back home'.[10] Thus some of the satisfaction to be gleaned in one's view of America, from Ireland, is a comforting familiarity, and a possibility of new beginnings, without actually ever having to leave. Again we find echoes of American modernists' portrayals of Ireland – such as Stevens's transatlantic idealisations of Tarbert and the Cliffs of Moher as abstracted, 'metaphysical' locations rather than real places to visit.

The idea of America as a saviour for Ireland has been questioned, however, in some contemporary works. For example, the notion of New York as 'pure, authentic, and unchanging' is scrutinised in Colm Tóibín's 2009 novel *Brooklyn*, in which the comforting, familiar, but ultimately sterile Brooklyn where the Irish protagonist, Ellis Lacey, finds herself living and working proves to be as stultifying as home.[11] The point, for Tóibín, seems to be that for the Irish emigrant, the promise of a 'new world' in New York is as nostalgic as the idea that life there will be any different from that offered back home. A similar story is told through the private and public personas of Gar in Brian Friel's *Philadelphia Here I Come!* (1965).[12] Here the schizophrenic presentation of the central character adds to the sense of Ireland and America being two parts of the same world. Gar will neither move on from Ireland, nor leave behind the idea of emigrating to America, as he can never leave himself behind. Friel's inconclusive conclusion, where we are left unsure whether Gar will leave Ireland or not, tells us that this suspension between two places is merely delaying the inevitable: the realisation that, for Irish emigrants to America, Ireland and (Irish) America are essentially the same in their collusion in, and ultimate betrayal of, an unattainable ideal.

But if (Irish) America's nostalgia for Ireland has become interchangeable with Ireland's projected nostalgia for America, where then does that leave American-Irish critical studies? In *Autumn Journal*,

MacNeice argues of Ireland that 'There is no immunity on this island either',[13] yet McGlynn's commentary suggests that America itself has become the new 'Ireland' in this respect. Thus each country, and each culture, seems to be seeking solace, or even 'immunity', in the other – despite the underlying conviction that such immunity does not exist. Yet it is only through trying to untangle the roots of American-Irish (and Irish-American) cultural interaction – and through identifying the fruitful and the unfruitful products of this interaction – that any of the complex issues surrounding transatlantic American-Irish relations will begin to be addressed, or questions answered.

★

> I am aware that there are over-statements in this poem – e.g. in the passages dealing with Ireland. ... There are also inconsistencies. If I had been writing a didactic poem proper, it would have been my job to qualify or eliminate these over-statements and inconsistencies. But I was writing what I have called a Journal. In a journal or a personal letter a man writes what he feels at the moment; to attempt scientific truthfulness would be – paradoxically – dishonest.

In writing his prefatory 'Note' to *Autumn Journal*, a poem that functions in its author's words as a 'criticism of life' and in part as a criticism of Ireland, MacNeice unconsciously reveals himself to be at his most 'Irish'.[14] MacNeice's emphasis on being honest to 'what he feels at the moment' is seen through to the end of the passage, where he comments that 'poetry in my opinion must be honest before anything else, and I refuse to be "objective" or clear-cut at the cost of honesty'; but this throwing away of objectivity in the name of honesty rings with the same paradoxical assertion of truth-telling that resounds through Irish writers from Yeats to Friel. In MacNeice's claim that 'to attempt scientific truthfulness would be – paradoxically – dishonest' we hear echoes of Yeats's apparently ambiguous statement in 'The Second Coming' – 'The best lack all conviction, while the worst / Are full of passionate intensity'[15] – with its combined fear of faithlessness and insincerity. Meanwhile MacNeice's comment 'In a journal or a personal letter a man writes what he feels at the moment' anticipates the kinds of qualifications Friel used to excuse his tendency to take liberties with historical facts in his plays. Consider, for example, a *New York Times* review of Friel's play *Making History* (1989), a famously rewritten story of the life of Hugh O'Neill, Earl of Tyrone (1550–1616): 'The title of Brian Friel's "Making History" could be "Remaking History", for in it the playwright shows us how facts and opinions can be altered to suit the needs of their times'.[16] Thus what Irish writers from MacNeice to Friel seem to fear is not the loss of 'scientific truthfulness' or historical accuracy, but the untruth that comes with not writing of, and for, the moment of writing. This explains why, in *Autumn Journal*, MacNeice is so concerned with Ireland's 'self-deception' in its isolationist, protectionist pose, which denies the global moment:[17] because if Ireland is capable of deceiving itself, how can it perform on the international stage with any integrity?

In many ways, this book has been a study of integrity. It has questioned the 'mythologies of fraudulent innocence' that writers such as F. Scott Fitzgerald have clung to in relation to Ireland;[18] it has assessed the relationship between the ideal and the reality within American modernist writers' responses to the Celtic Revival; and it has shown how writers like Moore, Stevens and Steinbeck have idealised the Irish landscape for an American audience. It has also worried whether American writers' responses to Irish political issues were founded upon knowledge of the facts of these issues or instead upon romantic notions of poetic revolutionaries and martyred rebels. And it has become preoccupied with the idealisation of Yeats as a kind of poet-prophet within twentieth-century American writing.

But perhaps the problem is the search itself: this quest for integrity in relation to what MacNeice might term 'scientific truthfulness'. This is particularly relevant amidst the uncertainties and innovations of the modernist period. For what the Irish Revivalists did – and what they encouraged their American counterparts to do in turn – was to remake history: to borrow from past experiences, and half-realised mythologies, to create a new understanding of Irish culture that was as (possibly) inaccurate as it was (potentially) 'true'. MacNeice's self-confessed 'inconsistencies' in *Autumn Journal*, then, are excused by the same claim that informs Irish writers from Yeats to Friel: a claim to 'honesty' that is neither 'clear-cut' nor 'objective'. No wonder, then, that American writers turned to Ireland at this time, as Irish culture gave them permission to satisfy their own versions of the truth.

In *The Necessary Angel*, Stevens declares 'We have been a little insane about the truth. We have had an obsession', and offers up instead a paradigm whereby we locate 'authenticity' within our own imaginative strivings. Thus, under the pressure of modernity, 'reality changes from substance to subtlety' and we are confronted with 'a new reality, a modern reality', which is 'the momentous world of poetry'. Each American writer discussed in this study found in Irish culture a way to recalibrate their conceptions of reality, as part of this quest for an authenticity rooted in the imagination rather than in an impossible search for objective truth. 'Modern reality is a reality of decreation', Stevens claims.[19] For American modernist writers who turned to Irish culture, their enchantment (and disenchantment) with Ireland enabled them to decreate and then recreate their worlds anew.

Notes

1. Edna Longley, 'Irish bards and American audiences', *Poetry and Posterity*. Newcastle upon Tyne: Bloodaxe, 2000, pp. 237, 241.
2. See Wallace Stevens to Thomas McGreevy, 17 April 1953, Trinity College Dublin, MS 8123/29; and Wallace Stevens to Barbara Church, 7 September 1948, *Letters of Wallace Stevens*, ed. Holly Stevens. Berkeley and Los Angeles: University of California Press, 1996, p. 613. See also discussions in Chapter 3.
3. Fintan O'Toole, *Ex-isle of Erin: Images of a Global Ireland*. Dublin: New Ireland Books, 1997, p. 130.
4. Colin Graham, 'A glimpse of America', in *Last Before America: Irish and American Writing*, ed. Fran Brearton and Eamonn Hughes. Belfast: Blackstaff, 2001, pp. 159–77 (161).
5. Louis MacNeice, *Autumn Journal*, XVI, l. 68, in *Collected Poems*, ed. E. R. Dodds. London: Faber, 1966, pp. 101–53 (131); and see also extended discussions in the Introduction to this book.
6. For further discussions, see Chapter 2 (on 'American modernists and the Celtic Revival'), Chapter 4 (on 'Enchantment and disenchantment in political poetry') and Chapter 3 (on 'Rural Ireland, mythmaking and transatlantic translation'). See also Marianne Moore, 'Spenser's Ireland', *Complete Poems*, ed. Clive Driver. London: Faber, 1987, pp. 112–14 (112), ll. 3–4 (counting title as first line, as was Moore's practice).

7 Diane Negra, 'Irishness, innocence, and American identity politics before and after September 11', in *The Irish in Us: Irishness, Performativity, and Popular Culture*, ed. Negra. Durham and London: Duke University Press, 2006, pp. 354–71 (354).
8 Negra, introduction, *The Irish in Us*, pp. 1–19 (3).
9 Mary McGlynn, 'New Irish New York: contemporary Irish constructions of New York City', in *Ireland and Transatlantic Poetics*, ed. Brian Caraher and Robert Mahony. New Jersey: Rosemont, 2007, pp. 205–21 (218).
10 Brearton and Hughes, introduction, *Last Before America*, p. xi.
11 See Colm Tóibín, *Brooklyn*. London: Viking, 2009.
12 See Brian Friel, *Philadelphia, Here I Come!* First performed 1964; London: Faber, 1965.
13 MacNeice, *Autumn Journal*, XVI, l. 74.
14 MacNeice, 'Note' to *Autumn Journal*, *Collected Poems*, p. 101.
15 W. B. Yeats, 'The Second Coming', *The Variorum Edition of the Poems of W. B. Yeats*, ed. Peter Allt and Russell K. Alspach. New York: Macmillan, 1966, pp. 401–2, ll. 7–8.
16 Mel Gussow, 'Behind the legend of Hugh O'Neill', *New York Times*, 11 April 1991. Friel's play *Making History* has as its subject Hugh O'Neill, Earl of Tyron (1550–1616). See Friel, *Making History*. London: Faber, 1989.
17 See MacNeice, *Autumn Journal*, XVI, ll. 73–4: 'It is self-deception of course; / There is no immunity on this island either'.
18 John F. Callahan, *The Illusions of a Nation: Myth and History in the Novels of F. Scott Fitzgerald*. London and Chicago: University of Illinois Press, 1972, p. 3. See also discussions in Chapter 1.
19 Stevens, *The Necessary Angel: Essays on Reality and the Imagination*. First published 1951; London: Faber, 1984: 'The noble rider and the sound of words', pp. 3–36 (33); and 'The relation between poetry and painting', pp. 159–76 (174, 175).

Select bibliography

Allen, Michael, 'The parish and the dream: Heaney and America, 1969–1987', *The Southern Review*, 31.3 (Summer 1995), 726–38.
Anderson, Sherwood, *Winesburg Ohio: A Group of Tales of Ohio Small-Town Life*. First published 1919. Ed. Glen A. Love. Oxford: Oxford University Press, 1999.
Arnold, Matthew, *On the Study of Celtic Literature*. London: Smith, Elder & Co., 1867.
Auden, W. H., *Selected Poems*, ed. Edward Mendelson. London: Faber, 1979.
———, 'Yeats as an example', *Kenyon Review*, 10.2 (Spring 1948), 187–95.
Bannister, Henry S., *Donn Byrne: A Descriptive Bibliography 1912–1935*. New York and London: Garland, 1982.
Bates, Milton J. (ed.), *Sur Plusieurs Beaux Sujets: Wallace Stevens's Commonplace Book*. Stanford, California: Stanford University Press, 1989.
Beehler, Michael T., 'Kant and Stevens: The dynamics of the sublime and the dynamics of poetry', in Mary Arensberg (ed.), *The American Sublime*. Philadelphia: Penn State University Press, 1986, pp. 131–52.
Benedict, Ruth, *Patterns of Culture*. First published 1934. London: Routledge and Kegan Paul, 1961.
Benson, Jackson J., (ed.), *The Short Novels of John Steinbeck: Critical Essays with a Checklist to Steinbeck Criticism*. Durham and London: Duke University Press, 1990.
———, *The True Adventures of John Steinbeck, Writer*. London: Heinemann, 1984.
Berryman, John, *The Dream Songs*. New York: Farrar, Straus and Giroux, 1969.
———, *The Freedom of the Poet*. New York: Farrar, Straus and Giroux, 1976.
———, *We Dream of Honour: John Berryman's Letters to his Mother*. Ed. Richard Kelly. New York and London: W. W. Norton & Co., 1988.
Bishop, Elizabeth, 'A sentimental tribute', *Bishop: Poems, Prose, and Letters*. New York: Library of America, 2008, pp. 707–11.
———, *Complete Poems*. London: Chatto and Windus, 2004.

———, 'Efforts of affection: a memoir of Marianne Moore' (c. 1969). *Bishop: Poems, Prose, and Letters*. New York: Library of America, 2008, pp. 471–99.
Bloom, Harold, *The Anxiety of Influence: A Theory of Poetry*. First published 1973. New York and Oxford: Oxford University Press, 1997.
Bogan, Louise, *A Poet's Prose: Selected Writings of Louise Bogan*. Ed. Mary Kinzie. Athens, Ohio: Swallow Press / Ohio University Press, 2005.
Bogard, Travis, and Jackson R. Bryer (eds), *Selected Letters of Eugene O'Neill*. New Haven and London: Yale University Press, 1988.
Bornstein, George, *Material Modernism: The Politics of the Page*. Cambridge: Cambridge University Press, 2001.
Brazeau, Peter, 'The Irish connection: Wallace Stevens and Thomas McGreevy', *The Southern Review*, 17.3 (Summer 1981), 533–41.
Brearton, Fran, 'Heaney and the feminine', in Bernard O'Donoghue (ed.), *The Cambridge Companion to Seamus Heaney*. Cambridge: Cambridge University Press, 2008, pp. 72–91.
———, and Eamonn Hughes (eds), *Last Before America: Irish and American Writing*. Belfast: Blackstaff, 2001.
Brooks, Van Wyck, 'The literary life', in Howard E. Stearns (ed.), *Civilisation in the United States: An Enquiry by Thirty Americans*. London: Jonathan Cape, 1922, pp. 179–98.
Brown, Thomas, *Irish-American Nationalism 1870–1890*. New York: Lippincott, 1966.
Bruccoli, Matthew J. and Margaret M. Duggan (eds), *Correspondence of F. Scott Fitzgerald*. New York: Random House, 1980.
Buxton, Rachel, *Robert Frost and Northern Irish Poetry*. Oxford: Oxford University Press, 2004.
Byrne, Donn, *Blind Raftery and His Wife, Hilaria*. New York: Century, 1924.
———, *Ireland: The Rock Whence I Was Hewn*. Ed. T. P. O'Connor. London: Sampson Low, Marston and Co.,1929.
———, *Messer Marco Polo*. First published 1921. Charleston, South Carolina: Forgotten Books, 2008.
Byrne, James P., Philip Coleman, and Jason King (eds), *Ireland and the Americas: Culture, Politics, and History*. Santa Barbara: ABC-Clio, 2008.
Callahan, John F., *The Illusions of a Nation: Myth and History in the Novels of F. Scott Fitzgerald*. Urbana: University of Illinois Press, 1972.
Callan, Charles, *America and the Fight for Irish Freedom, 1866–1922*. New York: Devon Adair, 1957.
Cantrell, James P., *How Celtic Culture Invented Southern Literature*. Gretna, Louisiana: Pelican, 2006.
Caraher, Brian G. and Robert Mahony (eds), *Ireland and Transatlantic Poetics*. New Jersey: Rosemont, 2007.

Cargill, Oscar, *Intellectual America: Ideas on the March*. First published 1941. New York: Macmillan, 1959.
Carroll, F. M., *American Opinion and the Irish Question 1910–1923*. Dublin and New York: Gill and Macmillan and St. Martin's Press, 1978.
Casey, Daniel and Robert E. Rhodes (eds), *Irish-American Fiction: Essays in Criticism*. New York: AMS Press, 1979.
Childs, Donald J., *Modernism and Eugenics: Woolf, Eliot, Yeats and the Culture of Degeneration*. Cambridge: Cambridge University Press, 2001.
Clark, Dennis, *Irish Blood: Northern Ireland and the American Conscience*. New York: Kennikat, 1977.
Clarke, Edward, *The Later Affluence of W. B. Yeats and Wallace Stevens*. Basingstoke: Palgrave, 2012.
Coady, Michael, 'The sea-divided silence', *Poetry Ireland Review*, 46 (Summer 1995), 28–35.
Coleman, Philip, '"The politics of praise": John Berryman's engagement with W. B. Yeats', *Études Irlandaises*, 28.2 (Automne 2003), 11–27.
Colum, Pádraic and Mary Colum, *The Irish Rebellion of 1916 and its Martyrs: Erin's Tragic Easter*. Ed. Maurice Joy. New York: Devin-Adair Co., 1916.
Corkery, Daniel, *Synge and Anglo-Irish Literature*. Dublin and Cork: Cork University Press; and London and New York: Longmans, 1931.
Costello, Bonnie, Celeste Goodridge and Cristanne Miller (eds), *The Selected letters of Marianne Moore*. London: Faber, 1998.
Costello, Bonnie, *Marianne Moore: Imaginary Possessions*. Cambridge, Massachusetts and London: Harvard University Press, 1981.
———, 'The "feminine" language of Marianne Moore', in Harold Bloom (ed.), *Modern Critical Views: Marianne Moore*. New York and Philadelphia: Chelsea House, 1987, pp. 89–105.
Cunliffe, Barry, *The Ancient Celts*. Oxford and New York: Oxford University Press, 1997.
Deane, Seamus (ed.), *The Field Day Anthology of Irish Literature, Volume 3*. Derry: Field Day Publications, 1992.
DeMott, Robert J., *Steinbeck's Reading: A Catalogue of Books Owned and Borrowed*. New York and London: Garland Publishing, 1984.
Deutsch, Babette, 'Fountain and Unicorn', *Kenyon Review*, 10.3 (Summer 1948), 39–40.
———, 'Lament for the Makers: 1964', *The Atlantic Monthly*, 214 (December 1964), 72–3, reprinted in *The Collected Poems of Babette Deutsch* (New York: Doubleday, 1969), pp. 5–6.
———, *Poetry In Our Time*. New York: Henry Holt and Company, 1952.
Diggory, Terence, 'American poets' responses to Yeats's prose', *Yeats. An Annual of Critical and Textual Studies, 3*. Ed. George Bornstein

and Richard J. Finneran. Ithaca: Cornell University Press, 1985, pp. 34–55.

———, *Yeats and American Poetry: The Tradition of the Self*. Princeton: Princeton University Press, 1983.

Dimock, Wai Chee, *Through Other Continents: American Literature Across Deep Time*. Princeton and Oxford: Princeton University Press, 2006.

Dunaway, Wayland Fuller, *The Scotch-Irish of Colonial Pennsylvania*. London: Archon Books, 1962.

Dwyer, T. Ryle, *Irish Neutrality and the USA*. Dublin: Gill and Macmillan, 1977.

Ebest, Ron, 'Donn Byrne: Bard of Armagh', in Charles Fanning (ed.), *New Perspectives on the Irish Diaspora*. Carbondale and Edwardsville: Southern Illinois University Press, 2000, pp. 266–80.

———, *Private Histories: The Writing of Irish Americans, 1900–1935*. Notre Dame, Indiana: University of Notre Dame Press, 2005.

Edgeworth, Maria, *Castle Rackrent*. First published 1800. Ed. George Watson. Oxford: Oxford University Press, 1999.

———, *The Absentee*. First published 1812. Ed. W. J. McCormack and Kim Walker. Oxford: Oxford University Press, 2001.

Eeckhart, Bart and Edward Ragg (eds), *Wallace Stevens Across the Atlantic*. Basingstoke: Palgrave Macmillan, 2008.

Egan, Mary Joan, 'Thomas McGreevy and Wallace Stevens: a correspondence', *Wallace Stevens Journal*, 18.2 (Fall 1994), 123–45.

Eglinton, John (W. K. Magee), 'Dublin letter', *The Dial*, 75.2 (August 1923), 179–83.

———, 'Dublin letter', *The Dial*, 76.1 (January 1924), 53–7.

Eliot, T. S., *Selected Essays*. First published 1932. London: Faber, 1969.

———, *The Sacred Wood: Essays on Poetry and Criticism*. London: Faber, 1997.

———, 'The three provincialities'. First published 1922. *Essays in Criticism*, 1.1 (January 1951), 38–41.

Fallon, Brian, *An Age of Innocence: Irish Culture 1930–1960*. Dublin: Gill and Macmillan, 1998.

Fanning, Charles (ed.), *New Perspectives on the Irish Diaspora*. Carbondale and Edwardsville: Southern Illinois University Press, 2000.

———, *The Irish Voice in America: Irish-American Fiction from the 1760s to the 1980s*. Lexington, Kentucky: University Press of Kentucky, 1990.

Fench, Thomas (ed.), *Conversations with John Steinbeck*. Jackson and London: University Press of Mississippi, 1988.

Fitzgerald, F. Scott, *Tender is the Night*. First published 1934. Ed. Arnold Goldman. London: Penguin, 2000.

———, *The Beautiful and Damned*. First published 1922. Ed. Alan Margolies. Oxford: Oxford University Press, 2009.
———, *The Great Gatsby*. First published 1926. London: Penguin, 2000.
———, *The Last Tycoon*. First published 1941. Ed. Edmund Wilson. London: Penguin, 2001.
———, *This Side of Paradise*. First published 1920. London: Penguin, 2000.
Fogarty, William, 'Wallace Stevens, in America, thinks of himself as Tom MacGreevy', *Wallace Stevens Journal*, 35.1 (Spring 2011), 56–78.
Foster, R. F., *W. B. Yeats: A Life. Volume I: The Apprentice Mage, 1865–1914*. Oxford: Oxford University Press, 1998.
———, *W. B. Yeats: A Life. Volume II: The Arch-poet, 1915–1939*. Oxford: Oxford University Press, 2003.
Friel, Brian, *Making History*. London: Faber, 1989.
———, *Philadelphia, Here I Come!* London: Faber, 1965.
Garratt, R. F., *Modern Irish Poetry: Tradition and Continuity from Yeats to Heaney*. Berkeley: University of California Press, 1986.
Gelb, Arthur and Barbara Gelb, *O'Neill*. London: Jonathan Cape, 1962.
Genet, Jacqueline (ed.), *Rural Ireland, Real Ireland?* Gerrards Cross: Colin Smythe, 1996.
Gerstle, Gary, *American Crucible: Race and Nation in the Twentieth Century*. Princeton and Oxford: Princeton University Press, 2001.
Gifford, Barry (ed.), *As Ever: The Collected Correspondence of Allen Ginsberg and Neal Cassady*. Berkeley, California: Creative Arts Book Company, 1977.
Giles, Paul, *American Catholic Arts and Fictions: Culture, Ideology, Aesthetics*. Cambridge: Cambridge University Press, 1992.
———, 'From decadent aesthetics to political fetishism: the "oracle effect" of Robert Frost's poetry', *American Literary History*, 12.4 (Winter 2000), 713–44.
———, *Virtual Americas: Transnational Fictions and the Transatlantic Imaginary*. Durham: Duke University Press, 2002.
Ginsberg, Allen, *Collected Poems 1947–1997*. London: Penguin, 2009.
Goldman, Emma, *The Social Significance of [the] Modern Drama*. First published 1914. New York: Applause Books, 1987.
Gould, Warwick, 'W B. Yeats on the road to St. Martin's Street, 1900–1917', in Elizabeth James (ed.), *Macmillan: A Publishing Tradition*. Basingstoke: Palgrave Macmillan, 2002, pp. 192–217.
Grant, Madison, *The Passing of the Great Race*. First published 1916. London: G. Bell and Sons, Ltd., 1921.
Green, Fiona, '"Your trouble is their trouble": Marianne Moore, Maria Edgeworth and Ireland', *Symbiosis: A Journal of Anglo-American Literary Relations*, 1.2 (October 1997), 173–85.

Gregory, Horace and Marya Zaturenska, *A History of American Poetry, 1900–1940*. First published 1942. New York: Gordian Press, 1969.
Grene, Nicholas, 'The Abbey: National Theatre or Little Theatre', *Journal of Irish and Scottish Studies*, 1.1 (Autumn 2007), 211–20.
Hackett, Francis, 'A muzzle made in Ireland', *Dublin Magazine* (October to December 1936), 8–17.
———, *Ireland: A Study in Nationalism*. New York: B. W. Huebsch, 1920.
Harper, Margaret Mills, *Wisdom of Two: The Spiritual and Literary Collaboration of George and W. B. Yeats*. Oxford: Oxford University Press, 2006.
Harrington, John P., 'Transatlantic transactions: Irish players and American reviewers', in Brian G. Caraher and Robert Mahony (eds), *Ireland and Transatlantic Poetics*. Newark: University of Delaware Press, 2007, pp. 168–78.
———, *The Irish Play on the New York Stage, 1874–1966*. Lexington, Kentucky: University Press of Kentucky, 1997.
Heaney, Seamus, *Preoccupations: Selected Prose 1968–1978*. London: Faber, 1980.
Hendriksen, Jack, *This Side of Paradise as a Bildungsroman*. New York: Peter Lang, 1993.
Henn, T. R. (ed.), *Riders to the Sea* and *In the Shadow of the Glen* by J. M. Synge. London: Methuen, 1961.
Heuving, Jeanne, *Omissions are not Accidents: Gender in the Art of Marianne Moore*. Detroit: Wayne State University Press, 1992.
Hirst, Désirée, 'The sequel to "The Irish Renaissance"', *Canadian Journal of Irish Studies*, 13.1 (June 1987), 17–42.
Hoagland, Katherine (ed.), *1000 Years of Irish Poetry: The Gaelic and Anglo-Irish Poets from Pagan Times to the Present*. New York: Grosset, 1947.
Hone, Joseph (ed.), *J. B. Yeats: Letters to his son W. B. Yeats and others, 1869–1922*. New York: E. P. Dutton, 1946.
Howard, Ben, *The Pressed Melodeon: Essays on Modern Irish Writing*. Brownsville, Oregon: Story Line Press, 1996.
Hutton, Clare and Patrick Walsh (eds), *The Oxford History of the Irish Book, Volume V: The Irish Book In English, 1891–2000*. Oxford: Oxford University Press, 2011.
Ignatiev, Noel, *How the Irish Became White*. New York and London: Routledge, 1995.
Jacobson, Matthew Frye, *Whiteness of a Different Colour: European Immigrants and the Alchemy of Race*. Cambridge, Massachusetts and London: Harvard University Press, 1998.
Jarrell, Randall, 'Verse chronicle', *Nation*, 167 (17 July 1948), 80–1.

Jay, Paul, 'The myth of "America" and the politics of location: modernist border studies, and the literature of the Americas', *Arizona Quarterly* 54.2 (1998), 165–92.

Jeffares, A. Norman, *The Circus Animals: Essays on W. B. Yeats*. Stanford, California: Stanford University Press, 1970.

Jenkins, Lee, 'Thomas McGreevy and the pressure of reality', *Wallace Stevens Journal*, 18.2 (Fall 1994), 157–69.

———, *Wallace Stevens: Rage for Order*. Brighton and Portland: Sussex Academic Press, 2000.

Johnson, James Weldon (ed.), *The Book of American Negro Poetry*. New York: Hartcourt, Brace & Co., 1922.

Johnston, Maria, '"This endless land": Louis MacNeice and the USA', *Irish University Review*, 38.2 (Autumn/Winter 2008), 243–62.

Jones, James T., *A Map of Mexico City Blues: Jack Kerouac as Poet*. Carbondale: Southern Illinois University Press, 2010.

Jones, Maldwyn A., 'The Scotch-Irish of British America', in Bernard Bailyn and Philip D. Morgan (eds), *Strangers within the Realm: Cultural Margins of the First British Empire*. Chapel Hill and London: University of North Carolina Press, 1991, pp. 284–313.

Joyce, James, *A Portrait of the Artist as a Young Man*, with an introduction and notes by Seamus Deane. Harmondsworth: Penguin, 1992.

Kelly, Joseph, *Our Joyce: From Outcast to Icon*. Austin, Texas: University of Texas Press, 1998.

Kennedy, Billy, *The Scotch-Irish in Pennsylvania and Kentucky*. Belfast: Causeway Press, 1998.

Kerouac, Jack, *On The Road*. First published 1957. Harmondsworth: Penguin, 1991.

Kilroy, James, *The Playboy Riots*. Dublin: Dolmen Press, 1971.

Knight, Marian A. and James, Mertice M., *The Book Review Digest: Reviews of 1921 Books*. New York: H. W. Wilson Company, 1922.

Lago, Mary, *Imperfect Encounter – Letters of William Rothenstein and Rabindranath Tagore, 1911–1941*. Cambridge, Massachusetts: Harvard University Press, 1972.

Leavell, Linda, *Marianne Moore and the Visual Arts*. Baton Rouge and London: Louisiana State University Press, 1995.

Lewis, R. W. B., *The American Adam: Innocence, Tragedy and Tradition in the Nineteenth Century*. Chicago: University of Chicago Press, 1955.

Longenbach, James, *Stone Cottage: Yeats, Pound and Modernism*. New York and Oxford: Oxford University Press, 1991.

Longley, Edna, *Poetry and Posterity*. Newcastle upon Tyne: Bloodaxe, 2000.

MacNeice, Louis, *Collected Poems*. Ed. E. R. Dodds. London: Faber, 1966.

———, *Selected Poems*. Ed. Michael Longley. London: Faber, 1988.
———, *The Burning Perch*. New York: Oxford University Press, 1963.
Malins, Edward, 'Yeats and the Easter Rising', *Dolmen Press Yeats Centenary Papers*, ed. Liam Miller. First published 1965. Dublin: Dolmen Press, 1968, I, pp. 1–28.
Malouf, Michael, 'Duppy poetics: Yeats, memory, and place in Lorna Goodison's "Country, Sligoville"', in Brian Caraher and Robert Mahony (eds), *Ireland and Transatlantic Poetics*. Newark: University of Delaware Press, 2007, pp. 191–204.
Martin, Taffy, *Marianne Moore: Subversive Modernist*. Austin, Texas: University of Texas Press, 1986.
Matthews, Steven, *Yeats as Precursor: Readings in Irish, British and American Poetry*. Basingstoke: Palgrave Macmillan, 2000.
Matthiessen, F. O., *American Renaissance: Art and Expression in the Age of Emerson and Whitman*. First published 1941. Oxford and London: Oxford University Press, 1968.
McCaffrey, Lawrence, *Textures of Irish America*. Syracuse: Syracuse University Press, 1992.
M[a]cGreevy, Thomas, *Jack B. Yeats: An Appreciation and An Interpretation*. Dublin: Victor Waddington, 1945.
———, *Pictures in the Irish National Gallery*. Cork: The Mercer Press, 1945.
———, *Poems*. London: Heinemann, 1934.
———, 'Three historical paintings by Jack B. Yeats', *The Capuchin Annual 1942* (Dublin 1942), 238–51.
McGlynn, Mary, 'New Irish New York: Contemporary Irish constructions of New York City', in Brian Caraher and Robert Mahony (eds), *Ireland and Transatlantic Poetics*. New Jersey: Rosemont, 2007, pp. 205–21.
McKay, Claude, 'How black sees green and red' (1921), in Wayne Cooper (ed.), *The Passion of Claude McKay*. New York: Schocken, 1973, pp. 57–62.
Miller, Kerby A., '"Scotch-Irish" myths and Irish identities in eighteenth- and nineteenth-century America', in Charles Fanning (ed.), *New Perspectives on the Irish Diaspora*. Carbondale and Edwardsville: Southern Illinois University Press, 2000, pp. 75–92.
Mishkin, Tracy, *The Harlem and Irish Renaissances: Language, Identity and Representation*. Gainesville, Florida: University Press of Florida, 1998.
Mizener, Arthur, *Scott Fitzgerald and His World*. London: Thames and Hudson, 1972.
Molesworth, Charles, *Marianne Moore: A Literary Life*. New York: Atheneum, 1990.

Moore, Marianne, *Becoming Marianne Moore: The Early Poems, 1907–1924*. Ed. Robin G. Schulze. Berkeley: University of California Press, 2002.

———, 'Comment', *The Dial*, 81.3 (September 1926), 268.

———, 'Comment', *The Dial*, 84.1 (March 1928), 269–70.

———, *Complete Poems*. First published 1967. Ed. Clive Driver. London: Faber, 1984.

———, *The Absentee: A Comedy in Four Acts. Based on Maria Edgeworth's Novel of the Same Name*. New York: House of Books, 1962.

———, *The Complete Prose of Marianne Moore*. Ed. Patricia Willis. London: Faber, 1987.

———, *The Poems of Marianne Moore*. Ed. Grace Schulman. London: Faber, 2003.

Montague, John, 'Global regionalism: interview with John Montague', *Literary Review*, 22.2 (Winter 1979), 153–74.

Negra, Diane (ed.), *The Irish in Us: Irishness, Performativity, and Popular Culture*. Durham and London: Duke University Press, 2006.

Nolte, William H. (ed.), *H. L. Mencken's Smart Set Criticism*. Ithaca, New York: Cornell University Press, 1968.

O'Brien, Michael J., *A Hidden Phase of American History*. New York: Dodd, Mead & Co., 1919.

O'Connor, Frank, *The Lonely Voice: A Study of the Short Story*. London: Macmillan, 1963.

O'Connor, Laura, *Haunted English – the Celtic Fringe, the British Empire, and De-Anglicization*. Baltimore: Johns Hopkins University Press, 2006.

———, 'Flamboyant reticence: an Irish incognita', in Linda Leavell, Cristanne Miller, and Robin G. Schulze (eds), *Critics and Poets on Marianne Moore: 'A Right Good Salvo of Barks'*. Lewisburg: Bucknell University Press, 2005, pp. 165–83.

Ó'Drisceoil, Donal, '"The best banned in the land": Censorship and Irish writing since 1950', *The Yearbook of English Studies*, 35 (2005), 146–60.

Olds, Sharon, 'Easter, 1960', *The New Yorker* 12.3 (February 2007), 158.

O'Neill, Eugene, *Complete Plays 1932–1943*. New York: Library of America, 1988.

O'Neill, Robert Keating, 'The Irish book in the United States', in Clare Hutton and Patrick Walsh (eds), *The Oxford History of the Irish Book, Volume V: The Irish Book in English, 1891–2000*. Oxford: Oxford University Press, 2011, pp. 413–39.

Ostriker, Alicia, 'Blake, Ginsberg, madness, and the prophet as Shaman', in Robert J. Bertholf and Annette S. Levitt (eds), *William Blake and the Moderns*. Albany: State University of New York Press, 1982, pp. 111–32.

O'Toole, Fintan, *Ex-Isle of Erin: Images of a Global Ireland*. Dublin: New Ireland Books, 1997.
Parini, Jay, *John Steinbeck: A Biography*. London: Heinemann, 1994.
Pound, Ezra, 'A retrospect' (1918), in David Lodge (ed.), *Twentieth Century Literary Criticism: A Reader*. London and New York: London, 1972, pp. 58–68.
———, *Collected Early Poems of Ezra Pound*. Ed. Michael John King. New York: New Directions, 1976.
———, '*Dubliners* and Mr. James Joyce', *The Egoist*, 1, 14 (15 July 1914), 267.
———, *Literary Essays of Ezra Pound*. Ed. T. S. Eliot. London: Faber and Faber, 1954.
Railsback, Brian and Michael J. Meyer (eds), *A John Steinbeck Encyclopaedia*. Westport: Greenwood Press, 2006.
Richardson, Joan, *Wallace Stevens: The Later Years, 1923–55*. New York: Beech Tree, 1988.
Ridge, Lola, *Red Flag*. New York: The Viking Press, 1927.
———, *The Ghetto and Other Poems*. New York: B. W. Huebsch, 1918.
Ross, Edward A., *The Old World in the New: The Significance of Past and Present Immigration to the American People*. New York: The Century Co., 1914.
Scott, Thomas L. and Melvin J. Friedman (eds), *The Letters of Ezra Pound to Margaret Anderson: The Little Review Correspondence*. New York: New Directions, 1988.
Schreibman, Susan (ed.), *Collected Poems of Thomas MacGreevy: An Annotated Edition*. Dublin and Washington, D. C.: Anna Livia Press and Catholic University of America Press, 1991.
——— (ed.), *The Thomas MacGreevy Archive*: www.macgreevy.org.
Shannon, Willam Vincent, *The American Irish: A Political and Social Portrait*. New York: Macmillan, 1966.
Shaughnessy, Edward L., *Down the Nights and Down the Days: Eugene O'Neill's Catholic Sensibility*. Notre Dame, Indiana: University of Notre Dame Press, 2000.
Sheaffer, Louis, *Eugene O'Neill: Son and Playwright*. London: Dent, 1969.
Shillinglaw, Susan and Jackson J. Benson (eds), *Of Men and Their Making: The Selected Non-fiction of John Steinbeck*. London: Allen Lane / Penguin, 2002.
Shoemaker, Mary Craig, *Five Typical Scotch-Irish Families of the Cumberland Valley*. Pennsylvania: self-published, 1922.
Spenser, Edmund, *A View of the Present State of Ireland*. First published c. 1598. Ed. W. L. Renwick. Oxford: Clarendon Press, 1970.
Stamy, Cynthia, *Marianne Moore and China: Orientalism and a Writing of America*. Oxford: Oxford University Press, 1999.

Steinbeck, Elaine and Robert Wallesten (eds), *Steinbeck: A Life in Letters*. Harmondsworth: Penguin, 2001.

Steinbeck, John, *Burning Bright: A Play in Story Form*. First published 1951. *Travels with Charley and Later Novels, 1947–1962*. New York: Library of America, 2007, pp. 229–96.

———, 'Critics, critics, burning bright', *Saturday Review of Literature* (11 November 1950), 20–1.

———, *Cup of Gold – A Life of Henry Morgan, Buccaneer, With Occasional Reference to History*. New York: Robert M. McBride and Company, 1929.

———, *East of Eden*. First published 1952. London: Pan, 1963.

———, *Journal of a Novel: The East of Eden Letters*. First published posthumously in 1969. Harmondsworth: Penguin, 2001.

———, *The Pastures of Heaven*. First published 1932. London: Penguin, 2001.

———, *To a God Unknown*. First published 1935. Heinemann: London, 1970.

Stevens, Holly (ed.), *The Letters of Wallace Stevens*. Berkeley and Los Angeles: University of California Press, 1996.

Stevens, Wallace, *Collected Poems*. London: Faber, 2006.

———, *The Necessary Angel: Essays on Reality and the Imagination*. First published 1951. London: Faber, 1984.

Stubbs, Tara, 'Irish by descent? Marianne Moore's American-Irish inheritance', *IJAS online*, June 2009: www.ijasonline.com/TARASTUBBS.html.

———, 'New readings of Marianne Moore's "Spenser's Ireland"', *Peer English: A Journal of New Critical Thinking*, 2 (December 2007), 32–44.

———, 'One title, three works? Marianne Moore, Maria Edgeworth and *The Absentee*', *Romantic Ireland from Tone to Gonne: Fresh Perspectives on Nineteenth-Century Ireland, Volume 1: Literature*. Ed. Paddy Lyons, Willy Maley and John Miller. Cambridge: Cambridge Scholars Publishing, 2013, pp. 12–19.

———, '"So kind you are, to bring me this gift": Thomas MacGreevy, American modernists, and the "gift" of Irishness', *The Life and Work of Thomas MacGreevy: A Critical Reappraisal*, ed. Susan Schreibman. New York and London: Continuum, 2013, pp. 227–41.

———, 'W. B. Yeats and the Ghost Club', *Irish Writing London, Volume 1: Revival to Emergency*, ed. Tom Herron. New York and London: Bloomsbury, 2013, pp. 21–33.

———, '"Writing was resilience. Resilience was an adventure". Marianne Moore, Bernard Shaw and the Art of Writing', *SHAW* 29 (Winter 2009), 66–78.

Synge, J. M., *The Aran Islands*, with drawings by Jack B. Yeats. First published 1907. London: Serif, 2008.

———, *The Collected Works, Volume II: Prose*. Ed. A. Price. London: Oxford University Press, 1966.
———, *The Collected Works, Volume III: Plays, Book I*. Ed. Ann Saddlemyer. Gerrards Cross: Colin Smythe, 1982.
———, *The Collected Works, Volume IV: Plays, Book II*. Ed. Ann Saddlemyer. Gerrards Cross: Colin Smythe, 1982.
———, *Travelling Ireland Essays, 1898–1908*. Ed. Nicholas Grene. Dublin: Lilliputt Press, 2009.
Tagore, Rabindranath, *Gitanjali/ Song-offerings*, with an introduction by W. B. Yeats. London: Macmillan, 1913.
Tedlock, E. W. and C. V. Wicker (eds), *Steinbeck and his Critics: A Record of Twenty-Five Years*. Albuquerque: University of New Mexico Press, 1957.
Thomas, Dylan, *Selected Poems*. Ed. Walford Davies. Harmondsworth: Penguin, 2000.
Tobin, Daniel, *Awake in America: On Irish American Poetry*. Notre Dame, Indiana: University of Notre Dame Press, 2011.
———, 'Irish-American poetry and the question of tradition', *New Hibernia Review*, 3.4 (Winter 1999), 143–54.
Toíbín, Colm, *Brooklyn*. London: Viking, 2009.
Travisano, Thomas and Saskia Hamilton (eds), *Words in Air: The Complete Correspondence Between Elizabeth Bishop and Robert Lowell*. New York: Farrar, Straus and Giroux, 2008.
Turnbull, Andrew (ed.), *Letters of F. Scott Fitzgerald*. Harmondsworth: Penguin, 1968.
Vendler, Helen, *Seamus Heaney*. London: HarperCollins, 1998.
Walker, Tom, 'MacNeice's Byzantium: The ghosts of Yeats and Eliot in *The Burning Perch*', *Review of English Studies* 62.257 (November 2011), 785–804.
Wall, Eamonn, *From the Sin-é Café to the Black Hills: Notes on the New Irish*. Madison, Wisconsin and London: University of Wisconsin Press, 1999.
Ward, Alan J., *Ireland and Anglo-American Relations, 1899–1921*. London: LSE / Weidenfeld and Nicolson, 1969.
Ward, Patrick, *Exile, Emigration and Irish Writing*. Dublin and Portland, Oregon: Irish Academic Press, 2002.
Warner, W. Lloyd and Leo Srole, *The Social Systems of American Ethnic Groups* (Yankee City Series, Vol. III). New Haven: Yale University Press, 1945.
Watson, Nicola J. *The Literary Tourist: Readers and Places in Romantic and Victorian Britain*. Basingstoke: Palgrave Macmillan, 2006.
Wells, Henry W., '*Poetry In Our Time* by Babette Deutsch', *American Literature*, 25.1 (March 1953), 113–17.

Wenthrop, Witherbee Jnr., *Donn Byrne: A Bibliography*. New York: New York Public Library, 1949.
West, James L. III, *The Making of This Side of Paradise*. Philadelphia: University of Pennsylvania Press, 1983.
Whitman, Walt, *Complete Prose Works*. Philadelphia: David McKay, 1892.
———, *Leaves of Grass*. Philadelphia: David McKay, 1891–2.
Williams, Daniel G., 'Introduction: Celticism and the Black Atlantic', *Comparative American Studies*, 8.2 (June 2010), 81–7.
Williams, William Carlos, 'Marianne Moore', *The Dial*, 78.5 (May 1925), 393–401.
Wills, Clair, *That Neutral Island: A Cultural History of Ireland During the Second World War*. London: Faber, 2007.
———, 'The aesthetics of Irish neutrality during the Second World War', *Boundary 2*, 31.1 (Spring 2004), 119–45.
Wilson, Edmund, 'F. Scott Fitzgerald', *Bookman*, 55 (March 1922), 20–5; collected in *The Shores of Light: A Literary Chronicle of the Twenties and Thirties*. London: W. H. Allen, 1952, pp. 27–35.
Wu, Duncan (ed.), *Romanticism: An Anthology*. Oxford: Blackwell, 1998.
Yeats, W. B., *Autobiographies*. London: Macmillan, 1966.
———, *Ideas of Good and Evil*. Dublin: Maunsel & Co., Ltd., 1905.
———, *Mythologies*. London: Macmillan, 1959.
———, *The Winding Stair*. New York: Fountain Press, 1929.
———, *The Variorum Edition of the Poems of W. B. Yeats*. Ed. Peter Allt and Russell K. Alspach. New York: Macmillan, 1966.
Zingman, Barbara, *The Dial: An Author Index*. New York: Whitston, 1975.

Index

Abbey company 78, 168, 170, 197
Abbey Theatre 65, 168
Æ (George Russell) vii–ix, xiii, 5, 66, 169
Anderson, Margaret 168
Anderson, Sherwood
  Winesburg, Ohio 103
Anglo-Irish Treaty (1921) 141, 156
Arnold, Matthew 4–5, 64, 73
  On the Study of Celtic Literature 4–5
Auden, W. H. 136, 186, 191–3, 196
  'In Memory of W. B. Yeats' 136, 186, 191–3
  'Yeats as an example' 196

Bede, The Venerable ix
Benedict, Ruth, *Patterns of Culture* 22
Berryman, John 165, 180–3, 200
  'Dream Song 312' 180
Bishop, Elizabeth 47, 105–6, 149, 174
  'Efforts of affection: a memoir of Marianne Moore' 106, 149
  'Over 2000 Illustrations and a Complete Concordance' 105
  'Questions of Travel' 105–6
  'The Map' 106
Blake, William 198
Bogan, Louise 9, 72–3, 92, 126–8, 158, 184–6

'The greatest poet writing in English today' (on W. B. Yeats) 184
Bookman, The 28, 104
Boyd, Ernest
  Ireland's Literary Renaissance 142
Brooks, Van Wyck
  'The literary life' 2
Brown, Maurice 168, 197
Bryant, Louise 142
Burns, Robert 73
Byrne, Donn 40–1, 78–83, 85
  Blind Raftery 79
  Changeling 79
  Ireland: The Rock Whence I Was Hewn 80–3, 85
  Messer Marco Polo 40, 80
  Stories Without Women 80

Cabell, James Branch 80
Campbell, Joseph 68–70
Celtic Twilight (definition) 64
Censorship of Publications Act (1929) 6–7, 37
civil war, American 74
civil war, Irish 141
Clan na Gael 138–9
Colum, Pádraic viii, 68–70, 83, 120, 138, 153–5, 168
  The Big Tree of Bunlahy 120
  The Irish Rebellion of 1916 and its Martyrs 138

Connolly, James 139
Corkery, Daniel 103
Cox, Eleanor 138, 139
Cuala (formerly Dun Emer) Press 5, 66, 121, 169

Deutsch, Babette 121, 186–96
  'Fountain and Unicorn' 191
  'Lament for the Makers, 1964' 186, 191–6
  Poetry In Our Time 187–90
de Valera, Éamon 1, 7, 150, 156
Dial, The vii–viii, 69–70, 104, 108, 122, 179
DuBois, W. E. B. 65
Dunbar, William 186, 192
Dun Emer Press *see* Cuala Press
Dunn, Joseph
  The Need and Use of Celtic Philology 69

Easter Rising 135–6, 137–9, 140, 142, 143, 146–8, 156
Edgeworth, Maria 103, 107
  The Absentee 107
Eglinton, John (W. K. Magee) viii, 8
Egoist, The 46, 91–2, 172
Eliot, T.S. xiv, 3, 92, 196
  'The three provincialities' 3, 92

Faulkner, William 65, 71
Fay, Father Sigourney 24–5
Fitzgerald, F. Scott ix, 4, 12, 17–19, 21, 22–36
  Tender is the Night 21, 32–3, 35–6
  The Beautiful and Damned 23, 30–2
  The Great Gatsby 18–19
  The Last Tycoon 33–5
  This Side of Paradise ix, 4, 23, 25–8, 36

Fleet Foxes 166
Freeman's Journal 77
Friel, Brian 213–15
  Making History 215
  Philadelphia Here I Come! 213
Friends of Irish Freedom (FOIF) 138–9
Furioso 149

Ginsberg, Allen 198
  'After Yeats' 198
Goldman, Emma 142
Gonne, Maud 109, 190
Goodison, Lorna
  'Country, Sligoville' 165
Grant, Madison
  The Passing of the Great Race 18–21, 23, 71
Gregory, Horace 140
Gregory, Lady Augusta 66, 78, 172

Hackett, Francis 6, 139
  Ireland: A Study in Nationalism 139
Harlem Renaissance 65, 197
Harper's 104
Heaney, Seamus xiii–xiv, 120, 136–7
  'Belfast' 120
  'The Flight Path' 136
Henderson, Alice Corbin 168
Hepburn, Katharine 54
Hogg, James 73
Home Rule 32, 139
Howard, Ben xi, 8, 23
Huston, John 38
Huxley, Aldous 64
Hyde, Douglas 66, 79

Immigration Act (1924) 22

Irish Statesman, The vii
Irish Times 77–8
Irish War of Independence 85

Johnson, James Weldon
    The Book of American Negro Poetry 65
Joyce, James vii–viii, 25–8, 92, 127, 184
    A Portrait of the Artist as a Young Man 25–8
    Dubliners 92, 127
    Finnegans Wake 184
Judge magazine 40

Kerouac, Jack 198–200
    On The Road 198–9
Kilmer, Joyce 80

Leslie, Shane 23–4, 25
Lindsay, Vachel 168
Literary Digest, The 139, 146
Lowell, Amy 80
Lowell, Robert 174, 185

McCarthy, Cormac
    No Country for Old Men 166
M[a]cGreevy, Thomas ix, 83–91, 109, 110, 114, 121–4, 186–7
    'Homage to Hieronymus Bosch' 85
    'Three historical paintings by Jack B. Yeats' 122–3
Macmillan Company of New York 169–70
MacNeice, Louis 1–7, 17, 64, 150, 157, 193–5, 212, 213–15
    Autumn Journal 1–7, 17, 64, 157, 213–15
    'Neutrality' 150
    'Snow' 194
    The Burning Perch 195
Magee, W. K. *see* Eglinton, John
Malory, Thomas 73
Matthiessen, F. O.
    American Renaissance 10
Mencken, H. L. 142
Mitchell, Margaret 65, 71
    Gone With The Wind 71
Monroe, Harriet 167
Montague, John xii
Moore, George viii, 171
    Hail and Farewell viii
Moore, Marianne vii–ix, xiv, 2, 6, 7–8, 12, 17–18, 21, 45–50, 67–70, 72–3, 80–3, 102–3, 106–8, 110, 122, 128–9, 143–57, 170–80, 200
    'Black Earth' 46
    'George Moore' 171
    'In Distrust of Merits' 149
    '"New" poetry since 1912' 172
    'New York' 145
    'Poetry' xiv
    'Pym' 21
    'Sojourn in the Whale' ix, 143–8, 156–7
    'Spenser's Ireland' viii–ix, 6, 7–8, 21, 68, 80–3, 102, 108, 128, 148–55
    The Absentee 107–8
    'To a Prize Bird' 171–2
    'To a Strategist' 171
    'To William Butler Yeats on Tagore' 170, 172–5
    'Wild Swans' (review of W. B. Yeats) 175–8
    'Words for Music Perhaps' (review of W. B. Yeats) 179
Moore, Sturge 174
Moore, Thomas 187
Mosher, Thomas Bird 66, 169

O'Casey, Sean
   The Plough and the Stars vii–viii
O'Connor, Flannery 65
O'Connor, Frank 104
   The Lonely Voice 104
O'Connor, T. P. 80–1
O'Doherty, Brian 49
O'Faoláin, Seán 104
   'The Bomb-Shop' 104
O'Flaherty, Liam 104
O'Hara, John 18, 29–30
Olds, Sharon
   'Easter, 1960' 165–6
O'Neill, Eugene 18, 50–4, 197
   A Touch of the Poet 50, 52–3
   Days Without End 197
   Long Day's Journey into Night 52–4

Pearse, Pádraic 135, 138, 140
'Playboy Riots', the 76–8
Poetry 167–8, 170, 175, 197
Pound, Ezra 5, 12, 46, 91–3, 167–9
Powys, Llewellyn 70
Proclamation of the Irish Republic 138

Quinn, John 66, 169–70

Raftery, Anthony 79
Renan, Ernst 4–5, 64
   'La poésie des races Celtiques' 4–5
Ridge, Lola ix, 139–42, 143, 156
   'Incompatibility' 141
   The Ghetto and Other Poems 156
   'Tidings (Easter, 1916)' ix, 140–1, 156
Robinson, Lennox 108
Ross, Edward A.
   The Old World in the New 18–20, 40, 70–1
Rossi, Mario
   Pilgrimage in the West 67, 83–4
Russell, George *see* Æ

Seldes, Gilbert viii
Shaw, George Bernard 29, 42, 171–2
Shelley, P. B.
   'The Mask of Anarchy' 141
Sinn Fein 31, 77
Spenser, Edmund 81, 149–50, 155
   A View of the Present State of Ireland 81, 149, 155
Steinbeck, John ix, 2, 4, 6, 17, 18, 36–45, 73–5, 75–6, 80, 103, 125–6
   Burning Bright 36, 41–3
   Cup of Gold 36, 41, 80
   East of Eden ix, 4, 36, 38–9, 43–5, 125
   'E pluribus unum' 39–40
   'I go back to Ireland' 6, 45, 125–6
   Journal of a Novel 43–5
   'Paradox and dream' 2, 74
   The Pastures of Heaven 103
   'The Play-novelette' 42
   To a God Unknown 4
Stephens, James 3, 70
   Etched in Moonlight 70
Stevens, Wallace ix, 3, 67, 83–91, 109, 110–20, 121–4, 128, 191, 196–7, 213, 216
   'Notes Towards a Supreme Fiction' 119–20
   'Of Modern Poetry' 116–17
   'Our Stars Come From Ireland' 6, 84–91, 111, 113–14, 120

'The American Sublime' 118–19
'The Irish Cliffs of Moher' 6, 110, 113–16, 119, 122
The Necessary Angel 88, 122, 216
'The relations between poetry and painting' 122
Stoddard, Lothrop
 The Rising Tide of Color Against White-World Supremacy 18
Sweeney, John L. ('Jack') 47, 110, 114
Synge, J. M. 5, 8, 41–3, 65, 66, 76–8, 170
 Riders to the Sea 42–3
 The Playboy of the Western World 8, 76–8, 170

Tagore, Rabindranath 168, 172–5
 Gitanjali 172
Thomas, Dylan 193–5
 'After the Funeral (in memory of Ann Jones)' 194
Tóibín, Colm, *Brooklyn* 213

Warner, W. Lloyd and Leo Strole
 The Social Systems of American Ethnic Groups 20
Washington Post, The 138
Whitman, Walt 112–13, 164, 199
 'Old Ireland' 112–13
Wilde, Oscar 64
Williams, William Carlos 179, 191–2
 'Marianne Moore' 179
Wilson, Edmund 289, 126–7
 'F. Scott Fitzgerald' 29
World War One 17, 25, 27, 136
World War Two 149, 212

Yeats, Elizabeth 5, 66
Yeats, Jack B. 89, 120–4

Yeats, John Butler 121, 187
Yeats, William Butler 5, 7, 9, 66–8, 76, 78, 87, 104–5, 117, 135–6, 141, 158, 164–200, 212, 214, 216
 'A Cradle Song' 194
 'Among School Children' 105, 186
 A Vision 76, 174
 'Away' 76
 Collected Poems (1951) 185
 Dramatis Personae 76
 'Easter 1916' 135–6, 141, 158, 165–6
 'Ego Dominus Tuus' 177–8
 Fairy and Folk Tales of the Irish Peasantry 76
 Ideas of Good and Evil 173, 179
 'In Memory of Major Robert Gregory' 182, 194
 'Nineteen Hundred and Nineteen' 117, 181
 'On Being Asked for a War Poem' 7, 136, 158
 'On the Celtic element in literature' 5
 Oxford Book of Modern Verse 184–5, 187
 Per Amica Silentia Lunae 178
 'Politics' 186
 'Sailing to Byzantium' 181, 188–9, 194, 195
 The Celtic Twilight 76, 212
 'The Circus Animals' Desertion' 182, 191, 198–200
 'The Fisherman' 181
 'The Lake Isle of Innisfree' 165, 166
 The Land of Heart's Desire 169
 'The Lover Pleads with his Friend for Old Friends' 175

'The Municipal Gallery Revisited' 105
'The Second Coming' 87, 181, 214
The Wanderings of Oisin 194

The Winding Stair 173
'Under Ben Bulben' 188

Zabel, Morton 126